THE NEW THINKER'S LIBRARY
General Editor: RAYMOND WILLIAMS

BROADCASTING AND
THE COMMUNITY

BROADCASTING AND THE COMMUNITY

BY

J. SCUPHAM

LONDON
C. A. WATTS & CO. LTD.
1967

First published 1967

©

J. Scupham

1967

PRINTED IN GREAT BRITAIN IN THE CITY OF OXFORD AT THE ALDEN PRESS

36/618

PREFACE

THIS little book deals with questions that have been deeply considered and looked at from many points of view during the past forty years. Circumstances may alter, but the insights of the great pioneers of broadcasting, the findings of the major committees of inquiry, and the reflections of the men and women who have developed the art of broadcasting to serve its wide range of special purposes are of perennial value, and wholly relevant to our own problems. In the hope that some readers will turn to them as rich sources of information and ideas I have quoted freely from the writings of my predecessors and contemporaries in the service of the BBC as well as from official reports, and should like to record my debt of gratitude to all those whose writings I have pillaged to grace my own text.

I should, in particular, like to pay tribute to the outstanding contribution to the sociology of broadcasting made by the late Dr. Joseph Trenaman, first Granada Research Fellow in Communication at the University of Leeds, with whom I used to discuss the central themes of this book. It is good to know that an edited version of his Doctor's Thesis will be published this year and will stand as a monument to his work.

I also wish to thank my son, John Peter Scupham, most warmly for all the help he has given me as a "common reader" in shaping the following chapters.

I have drawn in part on articles that have appeared in
EBU Review and *The Advancement of Science*, and am grateful
to the editors of these publications for allowing me to make
use of them.

J. S.

CONTENTS

I

BROADCASTING AT HOME AND ABROAD: PROBLEMS AND PROSPECTS

I

ON 1st January, 1927, after four years of existence as the British Broadcasting Company, the BBC entered on a new lease of life as the British Broadcasting Corporation. In its new form it was destined to provide a model for public service broadcasting systems throughout the world. The Managing Director of the Company, J. C. W. Reith, welcomed the change whole-heartedly. As he said in his speech to the retiring Directors and the newly appointed Governors, he and his colleagues in the task of broadcasting had from the first tried "to give a conscious social purpose to the exploitation of this medium". The aim of the present book is to consider what conscious social purposes for broadcasting are valid and acceptable forty years later in a changed and rapidly changing society.

It can of course be argued that broadcasting need have no social purpose. The logic of that argument leads to a wholly commercial system with the minimum of regulation, and Great Britain has never accepted the play of the market as the main determinant of what shall be broadcast. The Corporation, which is still the principal national instrument of broadcasting, was conceived as "a trustee for the national interest", and even when its monopoly was broken by the introduction of commercial television the new operation was placed under the control of a second public body with social responsibilities. Successive committees of inquiry and successive governments have indicated in broad terms the purposes that broadcasting can best serve. They have agreed that these may be listed as information, education and entertainment, which should be thought of as overlapping categories. The Beveridge Committee of 1949 maintained that the highest social purpose of broadcasting is in the last resort one of education, and the Pilkington Committee of 1960 that "almost all broadcasting should have an educative effect".

Whether views as absolute as these are accepted or not, it is the thesis of this book that the contribution which broadcasting can make to education, both formally and informally, is of great and growing importance in relation to our present hopes for society and our present educational situation. We look forward to a progressive economy resting on consent and making few inroads on individual liberty. It is idle to believe that we can reach that goal without a deliberate effort towards a better informed democracy. We need to achieve an easier and more equal social intercourse between man and man. We can do so only by making all men free, to the measure of their capacities, of the same enjoyments and of a common universe of discourse. We are moving towards a greater equality of opportunity, both as a measure of social justice, and as an economic necessity if we are to make the best use of our reserves of talent and ability. With all these ends in view we have embarked on a programme of expansion that will strain our resources to the limit.

We have set before our schools and universities two heavy and unprecedented tasks. They have to maintain teaching standards in spite of the pressure of numbers, and at the same time to preserve the continuity of a culture in an age of social mobility. They need to use all the teaching resources that can be made available to them, but they need even more the support of a community that shares their values and is willing to reinforce their work in every way that lies open to it. In the long run we shall have an educated populace. For the next twenty-five years we must face the problems of a society in which most mature men and women had left school before they reached the age of fifteen. At this juncture broadcasting can render two services of signal importance to the nation.

On the one hand it can give its support to the national system of education. On the other hand it can help through the great body of general programmes to close some of the great gaps that still exist between leaders and led, experts and plain men, the home and the school, the educated and those who missed the opportunity of education.

There is no automatic guarantee that the unique powers of broadcasting will be so used, and no Olympian tribunal determining how they shall be used in the light of pure reason and with no regard for anything but the long-term public interest. Society is unlikely to come to much harm because of an unduly limited range of light entertainment. It may run into grave difficulties because we do not understand one another well enough. The pressures of the electronics industry, of the allied retail trade, of the commercial broadcasting lobby, and of show business are constant, assiduous, and well organized. They are all exerted in the same direction; they can only too easily lay claim to a degree of popular support which may intimidate a government; and they can only be countered by an equally energetic assertion of informed and responsible opinion. The national capacity to make a constructive use of broadcasting in the years ahead will depend on the wise allocation of scarce resources now. It is therefore important that the relationship between methods of control and the fulfilment of social purposes should be clearly understood.

Our problems can be isolated and discussed in purely national terms. They are, nevertheless, no more than local variants of problems that every country in the world is facing. The difficulties that they have encountered may throw some light on our own situation. In any event, the revolution in communications is a world-wide development in which we are deeply involved, of astonishing technical complexity and far-reaching social consequences.

II

On any day during the coming winter the television set will have been turned on by eight o'clock in ten million British homes, and half of the population will be exposed to television on one channel or another. Nearly half of the sets will stay on for the rest of the evening. Nearly half of the viewers will have had no say in the family choice of programme.

The average time now spent by British people in watching television varies from winter to summer, but is round about two hours a day. A further hour goes in listening to radio. No single activity has ever claimed so large a share of people's leisure time as broadcasting does now.

The average figures mask some significant differences between groups. Children between twelve and fourteen are by far the heaviest consumers of television, and average sixteen hours of evening viewing each week. It is often said that young people like to go out in the evening and are therefore relatively uninterested in television. Those between fifteen and nineteen nevertheless view for twelve hours a week; one in ten of them is an addict whose weekly viewing amounts to thirty hours or more. The group as a whole compensates for its comparative neglect of television by a devotion to "pop" music on the ubiquitous transistor radio.

Professional people spend least time on broadcasting, un-skilled workers spend most, but the thirteen million holders of combined radio and television licences, the twenty-five million people who view something or other in the course of any one day, and the like number who listen to something on the radio constitute a broadly representative cross-section of the British public. Broadcasting has established a new social habit which cuts right across the boundaries of sex, of age, and of social class.

Where radio and television have been fully developed side by side the new habit follows a world-wide pattern. By eight o'clock the Japanese family, too, has settled down for its evening viewing. Perhaps because he has a choice of seven television programmes instead of our three, ranging from Kabuki theatre and modern-language teaching at one end of the scale to family serials and wrestling in the Japanese mode at the other the average citizen of Tokyo has cut down his radio listening to half an hour a day and expanded his viewing to two and three-quarter hours. His adolescent son views for half an hour less.

Every country in the world now has at least one radio service. The brisk competitive salesmanship of the great industrial nations and the desire everywhere to be in the van of progress are ensuring that every country will soon have television. Nigeria, which is not a rich country, already has regional as well as national services in both media. According to the latest census there are 490 million radio sets in operation throughout the world, and 162 million television receivers. Their distribution follows the broad pattern of the distribu-tion of the world's wealth. In the United States there are more radio sets than people, and a television receiver for every three of the population. In Africa north of the Union there is still only one radio set for every fifty people, though the number is doubling every year. Japan has sixteen million television receivers. Communist China has thirty thousand. As in most of the developing countries that have started television services the number of private receivers is small, but the government is making a steadily increasing provision for communal viewing.

As the network of telecommunications within each country develops, so does the practice of broadcasting from one country to another. The effective range of a single television transmitter does not exceed fifty miles. Away from the frontiers the inhabitants of one country can see television from another only through the agency of their own national broadcasting organization, which can receive a programme for rebroadcasting by cable, by microwave transmission, or by satellite. The countries of Western Europe share their "live" television programmes through the Eurovision network, which can link up on occasion with Intervision, the union of the broadcasting organizations of the East European countries. There is already a limited scope for intercontinental transmissions by satellite. A combination of the various technical means now available enabled 400 million people in four continents to watch the final game of football in the World Cup series of 1966—some fifty million more than had watched the state funeral of Sir Winston Churchill in the year before. During the coming decade the development of satellites will give altogether new dimensions to this kind of interchange.

The satellites that have so far been used by this country for broadcasting purposes—Telstar and Early Bird—belong to two different categories. The movements of Telstar, orbiting a few hundred miles up, have not been synchronized with the earth's revolution. It is therefore visible from any one point and useful for communication with another for brief periods only. Early Bird, however, maintains a constant position in relation to the earth's surface, and is capable of providing a continuous coverage of the same Transatlantic area just as if it was the top of an immensely high transmitter mast. A group of three such "synchronous" satellites disposed in equatorial orbit at their proper height of 37,700 kilometres could make the same television programme available for simultaneous transmission throughout the habitable world. A single synchronous satellite can overcome those difficulties of programme distribution by cable or microwave that are still insuperable in the less-developed regions, and Japan now has in hand a project designed to serve the whole of South-East Asia. The time is still distant, however, when broadcasting from satellites directly to the home will be both practicable and economically possible. The weak signals from the solar batteries of a satellite of the Telstar type call for aerials so sensitive and amplification so great that they are outside the range of any conceivable domestic apparatus, and stronger signals must wait for the development of new and portable sources of power—perhaps ultimately in the form of small atomic generators. So long as their effective range is limited by the use that national broadcasting organizations choose to make of them satellites can neither be used for propaganda nor serve as a major means of cultural penetration.

Radio suffers from no such limitations. Since the longer waves that it uses bounce back from the ionosphere to follow the curvature of the earth the range of a high-powered transmitter can be reckoned in thousands of miles. It is that fact which has made it possible for all of the great powers and an increasing number of the small ones to broadcast freely to their neighbours, their friends, and most persistently of all to their enemies. The owner of a radio receiver has a real liberty of choice, whether his political masters approve or not. As the quality of his apparatus, his geographical situation, and his linguistic capacities may allow he can supplement the deliverances of his home transmitters by listening to West Germany broadcasting in Kinyarwanda, Cuba in Guarani, London in impeccable Kuoyu, Peking in equally admirable English, or Moscow in any one of the fifty-three languages that Russia now uses for her external services, and transmits from a chain of stations stretching for five thousand miles from the Baltic to the Sea of Japan.

When Sir William Haley was Director General of the BBC he once said that broadcasting was still in the Caxton stage. Five hundred years after the invention of printing there are still 720 million illiterates in the world. Since the supply of teachers has failed to keep pace with the birth-rate the number is still increasing. The printed word has only remotely and indirectly touched the lives of the villagers in the great subsistence economies of Africa and Asia, and for those of them who have painfully mastered an unfamiliar skill there can for many years be little enough to read. As a medium for the diffusion of news, radio has everywhere overtaken the Press. In the underdeveloped regions it is, as a UNESCO conference declared in 1962, "the most powerful single medium for mass education and information".

The countries of Western Europe have achieved universal literacy. No country has yet succeeded in fostering a universal habit of reading that goes much beyond the popular news-paper, the manual of instructions, and the football coupon. In Britain some sixty per cent of the population had left school by the age of fourteen. Compulsory education of so short a duration against the traditional background of working-class life stood little chance of achieving a mass enlistment in the ranks of the common reader.

Dr. Johnson once observed that people do not willingly read if they can have anything else to amuse them. Distractions have grown more numerous since his time for all of us. Gardening, "do-it-yourself" activities, and motoring claim an increasing share of the available time of working-class men. Five years ago Ferdynand Zweig found that among a sample of factory workers consisting mainly of semi-skilled and skilled men there were a few serious students, a group of addicts of "westerns" and detective stories, another group of men who read only about their hobbies, a quarter of the total number who were miscellaneous readers, and forty per cent who never touched a book at all. "In this group", he records, "are heard comments such as 'Not for many years'; 'Not since I got TV'; 'TV has killed my reading'." Television, however, was "obligatory in nearly every working class household".[1]

For the educated middle classes, the "book-oriented", in Marshall McLuhan's phrase, television, like radio, is a complement to the printed word. For the great bulk of the population television is now the chief mode of access to a knowledge of the world outside the confines of their own experience; to an enjoyment of the arts; to an acquaintance with the full range of human personality; and to contact with ways of speaking and thinking other than those of their own social group.

The more serious programmes have not the mass appeal of crime stories or of light comedy, with their audiences on each channel ten million strong. They nevertheless reach millions of men and women whose reading is of a far less wide-ranging, imaginative, and intellectually demanding kind. Eight and a half million people watch the BBC news magazine, *Panorama*, and as many the Independent Television series, *World in Action*. A Shakespeare play on either channel may have an audience of four million. A million and a half saw the historic meeting between the Archbishop of Canterbury and Pope John. The audiences for all these stretch far beyond the circle of the privileged and the cultivated.

[1] F. ZWEIG, *The Worker in an Affluent Society*, 1961, pp. 100–3.

The range of the new media is world wide. The social habit to which they have given rise is pervasive; for many people, obsessive. Its long-term effects are incalculable. Its short-term effects are argued on as yet insufficient evidence between the social scientists and the "moralizing literati".[1] The sociologists plead for a more rigorous definition of terms like "mass" and "minority", "culture" and "seriousness", proclaim that we know nothing yet, and ask for time and all the resources called for by long-term research. The moralists insist that value judgements lie outside the range of the sciences, and that society must make its provisional judgement now.

There has never been any dearth of interesting speculation. A good many years ago Canon Demant hazarded the conjecture that too much exposure to broadcast programmes might make for "an inner mental flitter with fewer central discriminatory principles" and thereby "tend to undermine the continuity of a man's inner life which he requires for a truly human and responsible existence".[2] More recently Mr. Marshall McLuhan has been assuring us that broadcasting is urging us towards total social involvement and "a general cosmic consciousness". It is not easy to discern what programme of research could validate the views of either of them. They both bear witness to a growing perception of the vast possibilities of the new media; but neither of them offers any firm basis for the kinds of practical decision that must everywhere be taken.

Such firm evidence as there is about the social effects of broadcasting gives little cause for complacency. The family clustered round the television set are staying at home and together more than they used to do. The extent to which the

[1] See J. D. HALLORAN, The Effects of Mass Communication, 1964.
[2] V. A. DEMANT, "The Unintentional Influences of the Wireless", BBC Quarterly, October, 1948.

creation of new common interests is offset by a decline in sociability is hard to estimate. There may be more to talk about; there is certainly less time for talking. The time that is now spent on television is taken largely from listening to radio, from cinema-going, from social drinking, and from casual and desultory rather than from purposive reading, but there is evidence that more active pursuits suffer too. The only major investigation undertaken in this country[1] of the effect of television on the interests of adult viewers showed that the acquisition of a receiver was generally followed by a sharp decline in enthusiasm for other activities, and in acts of social initiative, followed by a slow period of recovery of some five years' length. In so far as we are still in George Orwell's words "a nation of flower-lovers, but also a nation of stamp-collectors, pigeon fanciers, amateur carpenters, coupon snippers, darts players, crossword puzzle fans", it seems that television has done little yet to widen or deepen our active minority interests.

As for the children, Dr. Hilde Himmelweit has followed up her classic study of *Television and the Child* with evidence to show that there has been a steady narrowing of taste since the introduction of a second channel as children have become conditioned and attuned to the monotonously competitive fare of the rival providers.[2]

The concern for children's welfare, however, goes far beyond questions of taste. Dr. Eysenck, from a behaviourist point of view, and Baroness Wootton, as a magistrate and sociologist, are only two among those who in this country have stated a prima facie case against those beneficiaries of the mass media who have underestimated the influence of television so as to minimize their own responsibilities. In this country the Television Research Committee appointed

---

[1] By W. A. Belson; *see* bibliography. [2] H. HIMMELWEIT, "Television Revisited", *New Society*, No. 5, 1st November, 1962.

by the Home Secretary in 1963 to study the development of
social attitudes and moral attitudes in young people under
the impact of television has established a Centre for Mass
Communication Research at Leicester University which will
concentrate at first on studies in that field. In the United
States there has issued from a Senate inquiry into juvenile
delinquency and a conference held by the Department of
Health, Education, and Welfare a Joint Committee for
Research on Television and Children.

In Japan the great public service broadcasting organization,
Nippon Hoso Kyokai, has taken drastic interim action, and
has imposed an absolute ban on the showing of offensive
weapons and acts of violence, from whatever source the
programmes may come. It is not only in Japan that the
international traffic in television is arousing a new sense of
concern among the controllers of the medium.

In 1962 Sir Hugh Greene, the Director General of the
BBC, spoke to an American audience about his reactions to
a feature film which the BBC had recently compiled showing
Television in the World. "The main impression", he said,
"was of the way in which television is being misused—of the
way, it would not be too harsh to say, in which broadcasters
are betraying their responsibilities".[1] More recently Mr.
Kenneth Adam, the Director of BBC Television, has returned
from a tour round the world with the sombre reflection:
"One is bound to ask oneself sometimes whether television
has not come too soon".[2]

There is no need to go round the world before reflecting
on what is happening here at home in Britain. Satellite
communication is one of the most astonishing triumphs of
the age. It could serve as the vehicle of a world news service

[1] SIR HUGH GREENE, *The Broadcaster's Responsibility*, 1962, p. 9.
[2] KENNETH ADAM, "Commonwealth Broadcasting from Singapore to
Antigua", *The Listener*, 23rd June, 1966.

of incomparable speed and scope. It has indeed brought to
our homes the strangeness, the heightened awareness of men's
courage in the exploration of a mysterious universe of the
American space-flights; and the historic plea for world peace
of Pope Paul on his visit to the headquarters of the United
Nations. The Press comment on the inaugural use of Early
Bird told the other side of the satellite story with a gloomy
unanimity. As *The Economist* put it: "What the first transmissions have drearily shown, as usual, is that what the broadcasting authorities think it proper to transmit are Italian
bands, Russian dancers, Scotland Yard rogues, untopical
interviews and tired newsclips, all of which could be better,
and much more cheaply committed to film and transported
by jet plane, or for that matter by paddle-steamer." The
Sunday Times thought that perhaps sedan-chairs would serve.

What we do with broadcasting is a matter of our own
deliberate decision. Broadcasting is peculiarly amenable to
social control.

All over the world the debate goes on about the purposes
that might best be served and the methods of social control
that would prove most effective. For those who wish to
know how it stands in Britain the best source is still the
two great official Reports, with their massive supplementary
volumes of evidence which have directed the post-war
course of British broadcasting and recorded the hopes and
fears of responsible public opinion. To turn their pages is to
stir the dust of old battles, but the campaign that they chronicle
is not yet ended.

Since 1945 there have been two full-scale official inquiries
into the conduct of the radio and television services of the
United Kingdom. In 1949 there appeared the Report of a
Committee under the chairmanship of Sir William Beveridge.
The majority of its members had no doubt that the BBC
should retain its monopoly and that broadcasting should

continue to be organized as a public service. In all the memo-
randa from those bodies and individuals which it classified
as "disinterested outsiders"—the Churches, the major organizations representing education, the political parties with the
exception of the Conservatives—the only support for the
introduction of commercial television had come from three
sources: the Listeners' Association (a body concerned to
prove that the BBC was under Communist control), a three-
man Liberal Research Committee; and the Port of Plymouth
Junior Chamber of Commerce. The Labour Party had urged
the Committee in a strongly argued memorandum "not to
depart from the principle of the public corporation which
has served the public so well". Lord Reith, who had shaped the
whole course of British broadcasting throughout its formative
years, had given his uncompromising testimony. "It was the
brute force of the monopoly that enabled the BBC to become
what it did; and to do what it did;" he wrote, "that made it
possible for a policy of moral responsibility to be followed".[1]
A single member of the Committee itself, Selwyn Lloyd,
who had not then reached the front rank of politicians, had
felt obliged to dissent. His minority report dwelt on the
dangers of monopoly and the virtues of commercial competition, commended the American example, and recommended
that new services competitive with those of the BBC and
financed from advertising revenue should be established both
nationally and locally.

In 1954 as the result of an intensive campaign by a highly
efficient commercial lobby (the story of whose triumph has
been fully told by an American scholar)[2] the Conservative
Government passed a Television Act which made just such a

[1] *Report of the Broadcasting Committee, 1949*, Cmnd 8117, Appendix H,
p. 363, HMSO, 1951.
[2] *See* H. H. WILSON, *Pressure Group: The Campaign for Commercial Television*, 1961.

service possible. It did not commend itself to the whole of the party leadership, but Sir Winston Churchill who was then Prime Minister had no reason to love the BBC monopoly. Throughout the years when he had been a lonely warning voice he had been excluded by its orthodoxies from the microphone. As Lord Reith, still an unrepentant monopolist put it six years later: "The Conservatives quickly pushed the wretched maggot of commercialism into the body politic of broadcasting; and that was that".[1]

The Television Act of 1954 established a new public body, the Independent Television Authority, charged with the task of introducing and regulating a commercial television service. After a slow start the new enterprise achieved a financial success so notable that one of its pillars, Mr. Roy Thomson, was able to inform a Canadian audience that having a commercial television contract in Britain was like having a licence to print one's own bank notes. In the areas where BBC Television and Independent Television were both available ITV secured and retains a majority of the viewing audience, and a very substantial majority of working-class viewers.

Six years later the time had come for a national stocktaking of the two competitive services; a stocktaking made imperative in any event by the fact that the Independent Television Authority had been established only for a ten-year term, and that the current Charter of the BBC would fall to be renewed at the same time. There was, furthermore, the urgent question of possible new television channels and their disposal.

This second inquiry was undertaken by a Committee under the chairmanship of Sir Harry Pilkington, which issued its Report in 1960. Like its predecessor the Committee had to take into consideration the submissions of a wide range of public bodies. There were none this time from either the

---

[1] LORD REITH, "The Future of British Broadcasting", *Manchester Guardian*, 29th December, 1960.

Trade Union Congress or the Labour Party. It found that there was a general and justified satisfaction with the radio services of the BBC, but that the progress of television had aroused widespread "disquiet and dissatisfaction". These, it believed, must be attributed primarily to the spirit in which the television Programme Companies created under the terms of the 1954 Act had approached their task, and to a failure by the Independent Television Authority to enforce standards. The Committee therefore recommended that the powers of the Authority should be greatly strengthened and that there should be no extension of commercial services until a re-constituted and reorganized system of independent television had "proved its capacity to realize the purposes of broad-casting". The Pilkington Committee has been criticized for coming to these conclusions. On the evidence before it no other conclusions were possible. The Churches and other public bodies that gave evidence were, like the National Union of Townswomen's Guilds "overwhelmingly against the extension of Commercial channels on both sound and vision", and the Association of Education Committees spoke for the whole range of educational interests when it declared that the television programmes which had become customary in the evening were in "complete and insulting contrast to the values implicit in a good school".

The Pilkington Report was followed by the grant of an additional television channel to the BBC. In accordance with its recommendations the government also proceeded in 1964 to the passage of a new Television Act.

In 1965 the Independent Television Authority celebrated the tenth anniversary of commercial television in Britain. The Prime Minister, Mr. Harold Wilson, spoke at its Guild-hall banquet. He thought it would be wrong to say that no anxieties remained. He nevertheless believed that since the powers of the Authority had been strengthened those anxieties had sharply diminished. In any event, he said, "Independent Television has become part of our national anatomy. More than that it has become part of our social system and part of our national way of life."

There is a sense, for Mr. T. S. Eliot, in which a way of life can be equated with a culture, a culture with a religion, and a religion therefore with "the characteristic activities and interests of a people". In that sense *Coronation Street* has taken its place with *The Archers*—and the Third Programme of the BBC—alongside "Derby Day, Henley Regatta, Cowes, the twelfth of August, a cup final, the dog races, the pin table, the dart board, Wensleydale cheese, boiled cabbage cut into sections, beetroot in vinegar, nineteenth-century Gothic churches and the music of Elgar".[1]

It is against this background that the country has still to make up its mind about a wide range of unresolved problems. The decisions that must be made in the next few years will not be irrevocable. Since they will involve the allocation to specific groups of people for specific purposes of wavelengths that cannot be duplicated and a large subsequent capital expenditure it is unlikely that they will in fact be revoked.

The government has within its gift the use of a fourth television channel in the same waveband as BBC2 and capable of being received by the same apparatus. The BBC2 network of transmitters has been so planned that a new service could use the same masts and achieve the same coverage after a time-lag of some two to three years, at a capital cost of some £35 million. There was a time when it seemed certain that this channel would be allotted to the Independent Television Authority for use by commercial companies. The White Paper of December 1966[2] has, however, left the position open for the

---

[1] T. S. ELIOT, *Notes Towards a Definition of Culture*, 1948, p. 31.
[2] *Broadcasting*, Cmnd 3169.

next three years. The fourth channel can then be energized—
or reserved—for educational purposes.

There is room for one or more new national radio networks
in the Very High Frequency band. A network of some sixty
VHF stations, each with a six- to twelve-mile radius, could
cover most of the population. Since the transmitters could
equally readily operate as separate units or be linked together
and transmit the same programme such a network might
serve both the national purposes of a University of the Air
and the needs of local communities. Since the cheap transistor
radio set is not a VHF receiver it could not meet the demand for
a continuous stream of light music. A medium-wave transmission network for this purpose is, however, to be provided
at the expense of the medium-wave coverage of the BBC
Light Programme.

There is little scope in Britain for the development of local
television by means of "open-air" transmissions. The necessary frequencies are not available. There is, however, an
unlimited scope for the development of wired "closed-circuit"
television systems, either for private subscribers or for educational institutions. Within the next decade the country could
if it wished ensure that every large urban local education
authority and every university had control of such a system,
that they were in communication with each other by means
of an electronic grid—a national network of communication
cables—and that they were working in close partnership with
the national broadcasting organizations.

The country will in any event see an experiment in colour
television now that it has been decided that Britain shall
use the West German PAC system rather than the SECAM
system which Russia and the Eastern European countries have
adopted as the result of a vigorous campaign by its French
sponsors.

Whether any of the extensions of our system that are

now possible represent value for money depends on their cost in relation to the uses that we propose to make of them. The use that we are able to make of them will depend on the patterns of organization that we adopt.

II

SYSTEMS AND PURPOSES

I

EVERY national system of broadcasting is an expression of the will of the sovereign state, and embodies a national assertion of values, either explicitly or in its unspoken assumptions. A totalitarian state may assume complete control of the Press; a democratic state may leave it in unfettered liberty. They must both alike ensure that there is an orderly allocation of the available wavelengths to appropriate purposes. Frequencies are in short supply. They are shared out by international agreement, and the number that goes to any one country is limited, especially in Europe with its close-packed populations and multiplicity of national states. The claims of telegraphic and telephonic communication, of navigational signals, and of the armed forces must all be satisfied. "Pirates" are a national and international nuisance. A network of telecommunications is no more capable of indefinite expansion than a network of roads or railways. Like them it represents a heavy capital investment and is a part of the economic substructure of a country. Like them it can only emerge as a coherent and efficient whole as the result of foresight and careful planning.

There are three broad patterns of relationship between governments and broadcasting organizations. The government may run a service itself; it may license one or more commercial companies to do so, or it may establish one or more public bodies with specific tasks and obligations. The three approaches have clear exemplars in the USSR, in the USA, and in Sweden. The United Kingdom must serve now as the type of a mixed system.

In Russia broadcasting is under the immediate control of the State Committee for Broadcasting and Television, which is attached to the Council of Ministers. In any totalitarian state the mass media are a direct part of the machinery of government. In quiet times the broadcasting organization is bureaucratic. In troubled times it is convulsed. The day after Kruschev's fall the editors of *Pravda* and *Izvestia* and the chief of the broadcasting service (with whom the Director General of the BBC had just built up a cordial working relationship) were dismissed and replaced.

From the earliest days the Communist leaders have seen the importance of broadcasting as an instrument for moulding opinion, and as likely to function best for them in the absence of competition. There was a time when they were as deeply concerned to exclude foreign broadcasts as they still are to exclude foreign newspapers. At the height of the Stalin era there was an attempt to cut off the whole of Eastern Europe from the West by a jamming of signals which called for the use of two thousand transmitters in the USSR alone and must have cost as much as the transmission of all our own overseas services. At the same time there was a heavy emphasis on the development of wired radio services rather than the use of individual receivers. Since the thaw the process of jamming (which never achieved any complete technical success) has been abandoned. There has been a striking rise in the number of radio and television receivers; nevertheless, a third of the radio sets are still wired sets.

Radio and television can serve the purposes of governments only if people use them. As the Nazis knew, a service that wishes to be heard must provide programmes that people will wish to hear. Their own intensive war-time propaganda was carried into every home by the entertainment programmes.

Russia appears to be a little more austere. In radio half the time is given to music, with news in the second place, and "socio-political" broadcasting in the third. It is a fine distinction. In television films and drama provide the staple fare, music has a much more prominent place than in our own television service, there is more news, and more socio-political broadcasting.

In the satellite countries broadcasting follows much the same organizational pattern, but with significant national variations. I can speak with confidence only of their educational programmes. In Yugoslavia the television programmes for schools have the lively technical inventiveness, the gaiety, and the stimulating quality that good programmes for good primary schools should have everywhere. In Poland school radio and school television have the broad humanity, the concern for the rights of the emotions and imagination that Polish films display. The characteristic virtues of both countries are too often missing in the products of the more rigid system, which appears to prefer a heavy didacticism and a monotonous celebration of Russian achievement. On one of the two Soviet television channels a "People's University" offers courses in Science, Technology, Arts, and English. Programmes for schools have been developed regionally as well as centrally. They are not likely to improve much while it remains the official doctrine that there is no need to study their impact on children, since instruction conceived on sound Marxist-Leninist lines cannot fail.

In China broadcasting is controlled by the governmental Broadcasting Administration. Its distinguishing features are the full-scale development of group listening and viewing, and an emphasis on adult education. Every commune is equipped with a radio set and there are already 25,000 viewing centres. Almost all of the television receivers in use are installed in public places and workers' clubs, and the government is said to have plans for the development of colour transmissions designed for large-screen commercial viewing. Peking has its Radio University, with Sunday courses for workers, peasants, teachers, and the armed forces, supported by correspondence tuition; and its Television University with 23,000 enrolled students following courses in mathematics and the sciences. It is far from easy to discover just what lies behind these baldly stated facts.[1]

Not all of the authoritarian states are Communist. All of them must control public opinion. Some are whole-hearted and single-minded. Some suffer from the embarrassments of a situation in which the trumpet must give forth an uncertain sound. The Turkish broadcasting organization is expressly dedicated to the aims and ideas of the Kemalist revolution that broke the political power of Islam, and to the maintenance of a secular state. It operates in an overwhelmingly Moslem country and cannot altogether ignore the demand for religious programmes. It therefore places their conduct not in the potentially dangerous hands of believers, but in those of "responsible secular-minded men".

The control of broadcasting is vital in any authoritarian régime. A government service is the natural instrument of the one-party state, however enlightened that state may be. In the absence of any effective political democracy the status of a public corporation can offer little more than the shadow of independence, as some of the last expatriate Directors of Broadcasting of the independent African states discovered. A close integration of broadcasting with the machinery of government may well contribute more to the fulfilment of specific social aims than a nominal independence, even in a democracy. Israel is a country that has received a million

---

[1] See U N E S C O, *World Communications*, 1965, for brief statements about the status and activities of broadcasting organizations throughout the world.

immigrants drawn from seventy ethnic groups since 1945.
For many years she has used radio as one way of giving them
the freedom of a new language and a new culture. There have
been radio courses in basic Hebrew for groups gathered
together in synagogues and programmes for the latest wave
of illiterates designed to bring them abreast of their children
without losing their dignity.

Now Israel has decided that television for the present shall
have one function only. It shall help the schools. It can clearly
do so most effectively under the wing of the Department of
Education.

II

In the United States no recent administration has even called
for a comprehensive survey of broadcasting in all its ramifications. It has grown up piecemeal within the matrix of a
free-enterprise economy in a society with an overriding
presumption in favour of commercial competition. There
was a brief period in the 1920s when things might have been
otherwise. At the first American Radio Conference in 1922,
Herbert Hoover, the Secretary of the Department of Commerce, said that it was "inconceivable that we should allow
so great an opportunity for service ... to be lost in advertising
chatter".[1] Alone among his contemporaries David Sarnoff,
the general manager of the Radio Corporation of America,
a company formed to market receiving sets for the great
electrical manufacturers, had a vision of the future possibilities as far-reaching as that of his contemporary, John Reith.
"Broadcasting", he wrote in 1922, formulating for the first
time the classic trinity of broadcasting purposes, "represents

[1] Quoted by C. SIEPMANN, *Radio, Television and Society*, 1950, p. 10.

a job of entertaining, informing and educating the nation, and should therefore be distinctly regarded as a public service." He dreamed of an endowed organization which would remove broadcasting from "the atmosphere of a commercial institution",[1] and when the National Broadcasting Company, the first of the great networks, was established as an offshoot of his own company, it adhered for a time to a non-profit-making policy. The pressures of the American economy and the American ethos were too strong. Sponsored broadcasting had already begun, and its rewards proved irresistible. In 1961 General Sarnoff, chairman of an RCA now grown to a gigantic combine, announced that its broadcasting subsidiary, the NBC, had "achieved an all-time high in profitability".[2]

The earliest phase of broadcasting in the United States afforded the first and last national experience of wholly unregulated competition on the air. It resulted in a chaos of clashing signals from which the industry itself begged to be delivered. A series of makeshift enactments led in 1927 to the establishment of a Federal Radio Commission, which in turn gave way in 1934 to a Federal Communications Commission, charged as it still is with the duty of regulating all forms of telecommunication, and of licensing broadcasting organizations. It must ensure that they are politically neutral and free from foreign control, and that broadcasting conforms to "the public interest, convenience, or necessity". It has no more specific powers than this in relation to programmes.

Armed with inadequate powers, understaffed, subject to pressures exercised directly or through Congress on behalf of big business, and not exempt from the tendency of controlling commissions to adopt the values of those whom they control, the FCC has never been able to shape the destinies of

[1] Quoted by Asa Briggs, *The Birth of Broadcasting*, vol. I, 1961, p. 63.
[2] Quoted by H. J. Skornia, *Television and Society*, 1965, p. 110.

C

American broadcasting. Whenever any suggestion has been made that its powers should be strengthened the broadcasting industry has always been ready to mobilize public opinion in defence of "freedom" and against the threat of Federal interference and government censorship. In the unfettered pursuit of their own internal logic commercial radio and commercial television have successively run the same melancholy course.

The United States has 3,500-odd radio stations and 665 commercial television stations, each with some degree of independence. The tendency of big business to grow bigger has, however, led to the emergence of three coast-to-coast broadcasting networks, each operating in both media, and each with its chain of affiliated stations under contract to take some specified proportion of its programmes, together with the allied advertising material, from the parent service. In this way the advertisers obtain national coverage, and the affiliates obtain programmes that they could not individually afford.

The three great networks—the American Broadcasting Company, the National Broadcasting Company, and the Columbia Broadcasting System—dominate the industry. They are in turn dominated by some twenty or thirty great business corporations which between them account for the bulk of the advertisement revenue. The advertiser is charged a fixed sum for "air time". Since the American commercial system, unlike our own, allows direct sponsorship and the association of the advertiser's name with a particular programme, the major entertainment programmes have come to be produced by outside agencies belonging to the worlds of advertising or show business, and working directly for the sponsors. The great soap firm of Procter and Gamble spends a hundred million dollars a year on television advertising and controls all its own "shows". "Soap opera" has become a household word for the type of serial story that it favours.[1] So far has the process gone that General Sarnoff has been quoted as saying: "We're in the same position as a plumber laying a pipe. We're not responsible for what goes through the pipe."[2] Advertisers have been known to sponsor almost every kind of programme, including the broadcasting of the great party conventions. The range grows steadily narrower, and the burden of "public service" broadcasting has to be carried by the unsponsored "sustaining" programmes provided by the networks at their own cost, bringing in no revenue, taking up time that might be sold, and carried reluctantly if at all by the affiliates.

Both the networks and the individual stations are fiercely competitive. In New York there are seven regular television channels and fifty radio stations to choose from. Each station depends for its survival on its "ratings", that is on its estimated audience sizes. The emphasis lies on a high average figure. One "sustaining" programme, or one programme of entertainment that fails can let the average down. One outstanding success can bring it sharply up. Through its production of the interminable entertainment *Peyton Place* (which has now reached Britain) ABC has overtaken the lead which the other two networks held. There has been a sharp rise on the stock exchange in the value of its shares.[3]

There was a time in the heyday of radio when the networks were willing to devote enough funds to their sustaining programmes to build up services of news and documentary programmes as good as any in the world. The names of Clifford Uttley, of Raymond Gram Swing, and of Ed Murrow

---

[1] On "soap opera" *see* JAMES THURBER, *The Beast in Me and Other Animals*, 1949.

[2] Quoted by H. J. SKORNIA, op. cit., p. 54.

[3] In an address to the Radio and Television News Directors' Association Convention, 1958, reprinted fully in SKORNIA, op. cit.

stood for authority, respect for the subject matter, and a splendid professional competence as communicators. Sometimes these programmes found a sponsor. Sometimes they were carried without one. Ed Murrow has himself described how, long before the full impact of television had made itself felt, the intensification of competition had reduced the news services to a morass of five-minute reports interspersed with "singing commercials".[1] In television the same pressure of competition has led to ever more lavish expenditure, but only on programmes that seem certain of success. The need to prepare them in colour drives expenditure to fantastic heights. In the eyes of those who dispose of it the profit margin no longer leaves room for unprofitable public service, or for risks. The resignation this year of Mr. Fred Friendly, the President of the News Division of CBS, in protest against the decision of a new superior to replace the Senate hearings on Vietnam with a fifth showing of *I Love Lucy* has emphasized the precarious position of such public service programmes as remain.

The apparent range of choice has become wholly illusory. As Mr. Newton Minow, the cultured lawyer whom President Kennedy appointed as Chairman of the FCC (and who soon found his powers inadequate) has put it, there is only "a procession of games shows, violence, audience participation shows, comedies about totally unbelievable families, blood and thunder, mayhem, violence, sadism, murder, western good men, western bad men, private eyes, violence and cartoons". The whole of American commercial television no longer provides a single regular weekly space for drama.

Slowly and painfully, through the enthusiasm of scattered groups and institutions, a nation with as lively an interest in the arts, as vigorous a habit of debate, as great a concern

[1] In an address to the Radio and Television News Directors' Association Convention, 1958, reprinted fully in SKORNIA, op cit.

for education as any in the world is struggling to call into existence a new system of broadcasting that will redress the balance of the old.

There are now rather over one hundred ETV—educational television—stations in operation throughout the United States. They are financed by subscriptions, by local education authorities, by universities, by the great Foundations, and sometimes by Federal grants. Some of them concern themselves in the daytime with ITV—instructional television—programmes for schools, and with college credit courses for universities. What we call cultural broadcasting the Americans call educational; what we call educational they call instructional. The main task of the ETV stations is to provide for the communities that they serve those programmes of news, of information, of debate, of music, and of drama that are taken for granted as part of the normal duties of the great public service broadcasting organizations of more fortunate countries. "Broadly speaking, in England you must take avoiding action to escape culture by television; in the United States you must desire it and take positive action to find it."[1] You will be fortunate if you can.

Handicapped both by lack of present funds and by uncertainties for the future the ETV stations are feeling their way now to forms of co-operation and to regional networking arrangements that will allow them to offer their audiences a higher standard of programme than they can individually afford. Most of them are affiliated to National Educational Television (NET), which is backed by the Ford Foundation, and distributes syndicated programmes made under contract or bought abroad—often from the BBC. The Carnegie Corporation, with the blessing of President Johnson, has now set-up a strong committee, presided over by Dr. James

---

[1] H. OLDMAN, *Educational Television: Impressions Following a Visit to the United States*, 1964.

Killian, Chairman of the Massachusetts Institute of Technology, to conduct a study of non-commercial television and recommend lines of development and financial possibilities.

The boldest plan before the committee comes from the Ford Foundation, and has already been submitted to the Federal Communications Commission. It envisages the creation of a "Broadcasters' Non-Profit Satellite Service", to be administered by a new public corporation, which would send up and maintain four communications satellites, one for each time-zone in the country. Each satellite would be capable of transmitting eleven programmes. Six channels in each zone would be reserved for commercial use, and five for ETV and instructional television. The Foundation estimates that the saving to the networks in transmission costs that could be achieved by a changeover from their present system of distribution to the local stations by means of cable and microwave transmissions would be of the order of forty-five million dollars a year. It suggests that thirty million dollars a year of this total might go to educational and cultural television.

If an equivalent amount could be made available annually from Federal or other sources the United States could establish a nation-wide system of public service broadcasting. If it is indeed achieved it will be of immense educational value, but, as a cultural service, will still have the limitations of what the Americans themselves call an egghead channel, or, more pungently still, an intellectual ghetto. It will serve admirably those who already know what they want. The great majority of viewers will still be watching *The Untouchables* and *I Love Lucy*, and on the channels of their choice will have nothing else to watch.

In the meanwhile the running cost of the hundred or so ETV stations is of the order of twenty million dollars a year; that of the 650 commercial TV stations is well over one thousand million. Almost any ETV station would be happy to run for a year, and most of them for two, on the cost of a single "pilot" programme launching a new serial in colour for one of the great commercial networks.

III

Until 1954 the British Broadcasting Corporation held an absolute monopoly of all broadcasting in Britain. The Television Act of that year created a new public body, the Independent Television Authority, charged with the task of providing a public service of television "for disseminating information, education and entertainment" as an alternative to that of the BBC. The Authority was empowered to build and operate transmitters and to select and appoint Programme Companies which would plan and produce programmes, pay a rental for their franchise and the use of transmitting facilities, and derive their own revenue from the acceptance of advertisements. Sponsorship of the American type was forbidden. The Authority was required to control the amount of advertising and to prescribe standards that must be observed. Its control of the programmes themselves was limited to the broad duty (which it had no effective means of fulfilling) of seeing that they maintained "a proper balance in their subject matter and a high general standard of quality".

In a letter to Sir Harry Pilkington at the time of his inquiry Sir Kenneth Clark, the first Chairman of the Authority, called this "a feeble clause". "If America be an indication," he wrote, "then I think more control will be necessary to prevent a Gadarene descent." It was provided by the Television Act of 1964, which gave to the Authority a new and commanding position; provided that no item should be broadcast unless it formed "part of a programme drawn up in consultation with the Authority and approved by the Authority in advance", enjoined the Authority "to secure a wide showing for programmes of merit", and empowered it to control networking operations.

Armed with these powers the ITA presides over a Programme Policy Committee representing the fourteen Programme Companies which now operate, each in its own area or areas. Under its present Chairman, Lord Hill, it has used them vigorously, and with a new sense of purpose and direction.

It has issued an edict that the proportion of crime stories broadcast between eight and nine in the evening must be cut down, and has encouraged the networking of serious programmes. It has published an admirable Code governing the display of violence. Its new Advertising Code is definite, comprehensive, and properly restrictive, with a special stringency in its medical provisions. It gathers together under the general rubric that advertisements must be "legal, clean, honest and truthful" a range of clear, categorical, and carefully exemplified rulings, ranging from an absolute prohibition of subliminal advertising[1] to a caution against deliberate deception (illustrated by a ban on the use of sheet glass to give an illusory brilliance to floors in advertisements for floor polish). Its concern for children extends to the prohibition of any emotional blackmail exercised through an appeal to their group loyalties or an exploitation of their social insecurities. In 1965 the Authority showed its determination that the rules should be obeyed by viewing in advance some 7,500 advertisement scripts (in addition to a great many other scripts) and rejecting one-fifth of them.[2] The United Kingdom now has a well-regulated commercial system;

---

[1] i.e. advertising conveyed by signals below the threshold of conscious awareness.

[2] See the Annual Report and Accounts of the ITA for 1964–65. The codes are given fully in ITA, 1965, *A Guide to Independent Television*, 1965.

perhaps the best regulated in the world. If the flow of programmes should continue to be narrow in range it will be
because of tendencies that cannot be eliminated from any
broadcasting system which exists to make a profit from
advertising.

The case against financing broadcasting from advertisement revenue rests on a variety of grounds that are wholly
distinct in kind. It has its economic aspect. In 1965 General
Sarnoff succinctly stated the position as the American world
of business sees it to the Federal Communications Commission.
"It is elementary economics", he said, "that advertising produces increased sales which in turn make possible increased
production, lower costs, and lower prices to the consumer."
It is the doctrine of an expanding economy. So long as the
present prosperity lasts it is unlikely to face any serious
challenge in America.

In this country Lord Thomson of Fleet has recently argued
in the same way that mass-production and mass-communica-
tion techniques have together made possible our present
affluence. He has vigorously and justly taken to task those
apostles of the Spartan virtues who have never themselves
known poverty. He has not succeeded in proving that he has
the remedy for our own economic discontents.

In 1965 £590 million was spent on all forms of advertising
in the United Kingdom, amounting to 1·9 per cent of the
Gross National Product and 2·6 per cent of our total consumer expenditure. Television advertising accounted for
£107 million. Its share of the total continues to rise which
suggests that its selling power commends itself to those who
have goods to sell. The significance of these figures in our
present economic situation is a matter for the economists.
The layman can only note that the Television Act of 1954
deliberately evoked a new and powerful stimulus to consumption at a time when the government was urging people

to spend less in the interests of an overstrained economy; and that it is still overstrained. The time may not yet have come for taking too seriously the recent complaint of the Chairman of the Advertising Association Executive that the resources of the BBC represent a national asset whose earning power is neglected.[1]

There are indeed moralists who appear to deplore prosperity. There are others who accept it as a good, but who do not believe that it has to be achieved at the cost of a constant barrage of appeals to "acquisitiveness, snobbery, fear, uncritical conformity",[2] or through a constant and simple equation of the good life with consumption. There are few more enlightening pages in the Pilkington Report than those in which the Committee records its reasons for disagreeing with the Director General of the Independent Television Authority, Sir Robert Fraser, who saw the image of a way of life portrayed by the television advertisers as a pleasing one, "and expressed himself unable to follow the argument that the nature of the appeal of some advertisements was socially or individually damaging". The Committee found itself equally unable to accept the plea of the advertisers that their representations had no power to mould attitudes. "Since they sell goods by holding up certain attitudes as admirable", they noted, "it seems obvious that they are at the same time and to some degree 'selling' the attitudes also."

The moral argument against advertising still comes, as it came then, from another but allied source. It is the protest of those who passionately resent what Miss Marghanita Laski

[1] H. G. LAZELL at the Annual Conference of the Advertising Association, May 1965, as reported in *The Times*, 6th May, 1966. The figures here quoted are from the same report.

[2] *Report of the Committee on Broadcasting, 1960* (The Pilkington Report). Cmnd 1753. H M S O, p. 77 *et seq.*

has characterized as an invasion of the temple by the market place: the wanton and deliberate exploitation of fine feeling and fine impulse for the purposes of salesmanship. It was as an echo to that protest that the ITA, before the Government banned all TV advertisements of cigarettes, included in its Code of Advertising a flatly worded prohibition of "advertisements that strikingly present romantic situations and young people in love in such a way as to seem to link the pleasures of such situations with the pleasures of smoking". Its particularity and its confinement to a single dangerous commodity bear witness to the impossibility of holding in restraint over the whole broad field a commercially useful technique and a pervasive attitude.

All these are arguments of wide and general scope. If many television advertisements debase the currency of emotion and of speech, so can other forms of advertisement. Television is nevertheless likely to have by far the greatest effect because of its penetration of the home, its dramatic quality, and its special appeal to children. It has given the force of its own modes of expression to older approaches, and not least to the technique of mindless and insistent iteration coupled with factitious enthusiasm which has already infected the announcements of programmes, so that a coming performance of *Macbeth* can be sold like a breakfast food. An encouragement to act on wholly irrational persuasions runs counter to the whole tenor of education. It has reached its final term, short of the acceptance of subliminal advertising, in the American "irritation commercial"—the advertisement that sets out to outrage the viewer, that is forgotten, but that leaves with him the imprint of a brand name, and without his knowing influences his next purchase of soap or of cigarettes.

The ITA at present allows the Programme Companies to accept six minutes of advertising an hour averaged over the day's programmes. They may be placed not only between programmes but at "natural breaks" within them, though not within school programmes, religious programmes, news bulletins, or broadcasts involving the Royal Family. The exclusions bear witness to the obvious truth that an interruption by advertisements is incompatible in mood or incidence, or both, with serious and intent listening. The fact that the exclusions are so few is the symptom of a far deeper malaise.

The Television Act of 1964, like its predecessor in 1954, forbade sponsorship of the American type, and made it clear that advertisers must have no share in programme production, or say in programme decisions. It was hoped that this provision would offer some protection against the abuses of the American system. Looking back it is difficult to believe that the banning of sponsorship has had any very significant influence on the character of the programmes. So large a slice of "peak" time is indeed taken up by American films originally produced for sponsors and broadcast here "on their merits" that the Authority has recently imposed limits on their use. Sponsorship or no sponsorship, there is no escape, within a broadcasting system which exists to make money through advertising and has no statutory ceiling to its profits, from the tyranny of the "ratings".

The size of audiences can be estimated in a variety of ways, and sometimes with confusingly different results. The leading "rating firm" in the United States, the A. C. Nielsen Company, and the leading firm here, TAM (which stands for Television Audience Measurement), use electrical devices installed in a sample number of homes which show when the set is turned on. They do not show whether anyone is viewing, and indeed an equally ingenious American invention, the dynascope, which photographs the area in front of the set at intervals when it is turned on has with some frequency shown empty rooms, children playing and people asleep, fighting or making love. In this country there are now "Tammeters" in some 2,400 homes, disposed as far as possible in accordance with the geographical and social distribution of the population, though willingness to accept such devices may introduce some element of bias.

The BBC adopts a wholly different approach, through interviews with a similarly balanced sample of people, designed to discover through a simple standardized series of questions what programmes they have actually heard or seen in the previous twenty-four hours. At present a different sample of 2,250 people is questioned each day.

Since the two methods measure different things, and since the number of people viewing is far from being a straightforward and unvarying multiple of the number of sets turned on, it is not surprising that the resultant figures show wide differences. A more significant difference lies in the fact that the two sets of figures are prepared for two very different types of organization, and that the pressures they exert need not operate in the same direction. The analyses of audience by education and by social grouping and the "appreciation indices" with which the BBC Audience Research Department supplements its daily barometer of listening and viewing can have an important influence on programme planning.[1]

The first interest of a commercial company must be in the gross total figures. Its concern is to earn the greatest possible advertising revenue for the longest possible period of the day. Television is an expensive medium and the cost of advertising is inevitably high. At the time of the Pilkington Report a characteristic price was £750 for a fifteen-second spot during peak evening hours (though less than half as much after 10.35 p.m.).

---

[1] On the whole question of audience measurement *see* R. J. SILVEY, *The Measurement of Audiences* (BBC Lunch-time Lectures, 1966) and in *BBC Handbook*, 1966.

A company can only attract the great national advertisers, who alone can afford to pay, by maintaining for the whole of the time the largest possible audience, and thereby, as a Vice-President of NBC once put it, making the all-set audience available to advertisers to sell their goods.[1]

The programmes must therefore aim at a breadth of appeal that cuts across all distinctions of sex, of age, of social class, and of educational background. They must appeal to those interests that men have, or can be persuaded to have, in common. Since a succession of royal weddings and world heavyweight boxing championships cannot be contrived there grows up an industry devoted single-mindedly to the popularization of existing but as yet unregarded "occasions" and the mass-production of synthetic new ones. Their general character will inevitably be determined by the marginal audience at the bottom of the educational scale, which out-numbers by far the marginal audience at the top of the educational scale. They must be designed to bring in that sector of the population which is not yet "in the market" for anything but the sensational and the undemanding.

The argument that profitability is the only measure of success is, on its own ground, inexpugnable. It commends itself entirely on its own merits to a large part of the business community. The proprietors of the great mass media are not always content to leave it at that. With an eye to the renewal of a franchise or the allocation of a new channel they sometimes like to provide a rationale for their profits in social terms. Mr. Frank Stanton, the President of the Columbia Broadcasting System, is one of the more articulate spokesmen for their interest. He has always held that there is "no satis-factory alternative to letting the people set the standards of

[1] PILKINGTON, op. cit., vol. II, p. 821.

programming by the simple act of accepting or rejecting what is offered".[1] The ratings are the instrument of cultural democracy.

Providing people with what they want may indeed be a form of "public service" properly rewarded by profits. As it is here stated the argument nevertheless rests on a threefold fallacy. It assumes that "the people" are an undifferentiated group; that they are offered the opportunity of a considered and effective choice among the whole range of possible alternatives; and that there is no reciprocal relationship between supply and demand.

The audience that watches Z Cars or the World Cup Final is an audience of individuals, each with interests that he shares with some smaller group. No commercial system can afford to think of its clientele as an aggregate of minorities. The audiences for the BBC Third Network and Third Programme range from 50,000 to 100,000 for any particular programme. Its clientele consists of more than a million men and women who find in it from time to time a reflection of their own interests whether in chamber music or in chess, in jazz or in learning Russian. As Lord Reith once said of the BBC: "With us, 'minorities' are very important sections of the community, and a 'limited appeal' may still involve many hundreds of thousands". A programme of very limited appeal indeed may furthermore serve purposes that in the long run benefit the whole community. Once a month the BBC offers a television programme of uncompromising professional refreshment to medical practitioners. It is prepared in consultation with the Association for the Study of Medical Education and reaches more than half the doctors in the service area of the second BBC channel.

No commercial television programme has much chance of

[1] H. J. SKORNIA, op. cit., p. 316.

reaching the air during peak evening hours unless its audience is likely to amount to at least five million.

The ratings do not and cannot measure demand. They measure the response to what is offered, confused by channel loyalties, by viewing habits, by inertia, by the timing of programmes and by their juxtaposition. There is a great section of the viewing public for which rejection and switching over to the other channel is the only mode of choice.

The audience for symphony concerts and for "satire" stands where it does not because people wanted them, but because the BBC provided them. Lord Reith's blunt dictum, "Few people know what they want and fewer still what they need",[1] has been condemned as an arrogance. In relation to broadcasting it is a simple statement of facts familiar to every broadcasting man who has ever conducted a wide canvass of opinion in the search for new ideas and constructive suggestions. The programme-makers and the advertisers of ITV are alike engaged in the business of creating or stimulating those kinds of "demand" which they can most readily satisfy, whether it is for a cheap new sensation or a cheap new detergent. Even if it could be assumed that there was a stable pattern of "demand" no conceivable machinery of audience research could yield a true image of its complexities, and even if those complexities were fully known there would be no similarity between the position of the broadcasting organizations in relation to the public and that of the Press. The output of broadcasting is not, like the number of journals, capable of indefinite expansion. To satisfy one demand is to forego the satisfaction of another. The planning of programmes is always an act of editorial judgement, and every inclusion or exclusion is an assertion of relative values. In ITV audience size is the final criterion of choice during peak hours.

[1] J. C. W. REITH, *Broadcast Over Britain*, 1924, p. 34.

Broadcasting controlled by governments reflects the vices of the governments that it serves; and has a sad variety of shortcomings. The vices of commercial television are inherent and universal, and operate in the same way from Australia to Zambia. They may be tempered by the personal policy of a director with a touch of missionary zeal serving a board with an adequate profit margin; a precarious situation. They may fluctuate in their intensity with the approach or the recession of a commission of inquiry. Experience has shown that they can only be held in bounds with any certainty by a controlling authority armed with adequate powers and determined to use them.

The major commercial companies of Great Britain have all produced excellent programmes, and the network has carried them. Three companies, Rediffusion, Associated TeleVision, and Granada T.V. between them provide a service of school television programmes almost as extensive as that of the BBC, and informed by the same sense of standards. A number of the smaller companies produce programmes for the local schools. The companies have been as enterprising as the Corporation in striking out in new directions for adult education through courses planned in partnership with educational bodies and linked with correspondence tuition or group discussion. Their religious programmes are varied and inventive, and they share an admirable news service provided by an independent company, Independent Television News Ltd. These activities, valuable as they are, must always be marginal to the central concern of any profit-making broadcasting organization, which must be the maintenance of a mass audience during peak viewing hours. Programmes with no mass appeal must be placed at times that advertisers know to be inconvenient for most people. As competition intensifies, they run the risk of being squeezed out altogether.

Commercial broadcasting cannot afford to invest in the

D

future; shareholders take short views. The music policy of the BBC is paying its highest social dividend after some forty years. Commercial broadcasting cannot take risks; the serial is the safest bet of all. It must not shock or alienate any large section of opinion; advertisers are cautious people. It must in the long run be comfortable, even in its daring. The range of its social criticism is limited in the last resort by the nature of its backing. The first Head of School Broadcasting to serve a commercial company found, perhaps not surprisingly, that his liberty of action certainly did not extend to the provision of a series of programmes, endorsed by his advisory body and moving within a field familiar to many schools, with the aim of cultivating a rational attitude to advertisements and some power of discriminating between them. The BBC has since then provided just such a series.

Broadcasting financed from advertisement revenue need not be commercial broadcasting. The Canadian Broadcasting Corporation accepts advertisements in competition with its commercial rivals, and the last major report on its activities offers a variant on a familiar formula. The purposes of broadcasting, it holds, are "to inform, to enlighten, to entertain, and to sell goods". The Governors of the BBC have been asked in the past, and will no doubt be asked again and more insistently, if they are willing to accept advertisement revenue in respect of any part of their output. No government likes to raise the licence fee. They have always held resolutely that their sole concern must be the public interest, and that any dependence on advertisements introduces other criteria. It may be argued that a continuous programme of "pop" music would suffer little aesthetic harm from the introduction of a modest number of "singing commercials". The Governors must prize even that liberty of judgement which distinguishes between one kind of "pop" and another on purely artistic grounds rather than in terms of audience size. Advertisement revenue is a temptation that a public body which prizes its independence does well to resist. It may, nevertheless, be the necessary instrument of a poor but resolute government, like that of Pakistan, determined to use television for social ends, and to match advertisement fees to the programmes it needs rather than programmes to the need for advertisements. It may furnish the only form of increased revenue for broadcasting that appears to be politically possible to the government of the day. Radiotelevisione Italiana derives eighty per cent of its income from licence revenue, the rest from advertisements. Holland, after a Cabinet crisis, has introduced advertisements into its television service.

So long as the broadcasting organization derives only a fixed proportion of its income from that source and is not allowed to increase the amount, its own temptations are lessened; those of the government remain, and the chances of an increased licence revenue to meet rising costs and discharge new responsibilities diminish.

IV

The BBC was started as a commercial company in 1922 by a consortium of makers of radio sets. In 1926, in accordance with the recommendations of a Committee of Inquiry and the wishes of its Managing Director it became the prototype public corporation: the first body not directly responsible to Parliament to be entrusted with the conduct of a nation-wide service, and therefore the ancestor in some sort of the coal, electricity and transport boards, and of the recently reconstituted Post Office.

It operates under the terms of a Royal Charter, reviewed from time to time, and granted, as its preface states, in view of the great value of the broadcasting services as means of disseminating information, education, and entertainment. The present Charter runs from 1963 to 1976. It provides for the appointment by the government of the day (but for a specified term of years) of a Chairman and eight other Governors, including those National Governors who preside over Councils charged with the duty of controlling the policy and content of programmes provided primarily for Scotland, Wales, and Northern Ireland. It is their duty to ensure that full regard is paid to "the distinctive culture, language, interests and tastes" of each of those countries.

Legally the Governors are the Corporation. They control its budget, and their sanction is required for all major items of expenditure. They appoint the Director General, and the five Directors—of Sound Broadcasting, of Television, of the External Services, of Engineering and of Administration—who together constitute the Director General's Board of Management. They are ultimately responsible for everything that goes on the air, and the present Chairman, Lord Norman-brook, has reminded the public that their responsibility must sometimes be directly exercised in relation to individual programmes. "I should like to refer briefly", he said, "to the action which I took as Chairman, in October last, when I decided not to renew an invitation made to Mr. Ian Smith, then Prime Minister of Rhodesia, to appear in the programme *Twenty-four Hours*. I am not here concerned to argue whether that decision was right or wrong. I am concerned only with my right to make it. . . . No producer enjoys an absolute and unlimited right of editorial control. Though he is allowed a considerable latitude, he is subject to directions from above; and on matters of the highest importance these directions may come to him from the highest level within the Corporation."[1]

[1] LORD NORMANBROOK, *The Functions of the BBC's Governors*, B B C Lunchtime Lectures, 1965, p. 11.

The Royal Charter prescribes the constitutional form which the BBC as a body corporate must take, and states its purposes in general terms. It does not empower the Corporation to undertake any specific broadcasting operations. The nature and the limits of these are determined by a Licence and Agreement, negotiated between the Governors and the Postmaster General acting on behalf of the government of the day, and valid for the same period as the Charter. The Licence and Agreement imposes on the BBC only a very limited number of restrictions and obligations. It forbids the BBC to accept advertising or sponsored programmes without the specific consent of the Postmaster General. It reserves for the government the right to veto any programme or any category of programmes, though this right has never been exercised. It requires the BBC to broadcast announcements if required to do so by any Minister, and to offer to any Minister, "in whose opinion an emergency has arisen or continues", such further broadcasting facilities as he may require. It was under this rubric that the Prime Minister, Mr. Harold Wilson, spoke to the country during the economic crisis of 1966. In all these instances the Corporation retains the right to inform the public that it is acting on government orders.

In the current Charter it is further required, for the first time, that "the Corporation shall broadcast an impartial account day by day prepared by professional reporters of the proceedings in both houses of the United Kingdom Parliament". Otherwise the BBC is left with a free hand to shape its own programme commitments.

The Charter and the Licence and Agreement[1] give to the Corporation a degree of independence and freedom from day-by-day political interference that is of immense value. It is fully buffered against attempts to influence the nature of

[1] The Charter and the Licence and Agreement are given fully in *BBC Handbook*, 1966.

its programme planning through Parliament, and the loaded question in the House is always met by the Postmaster General with the bland reminder that programme policy lies wholly within the province of the Governors. Within the limits set by the government in the two basic documents, the Corporation can shape its own financial course. It enjoys a continuity and stability which cannot exist where the top posts are held as in Russia (and in France) at the will of the government of the day. It has a reasonable freedom of manœuvre even in the field of party politics.

The party political broadcasts of an election campaign are arranged by the parties themselves, and their allocation is decided at a meeting between the party whips and the BBC in a ratio related to the number of votes cast for each party at the last election. The BBC is not formally compelled to make any fixed quota of time available. In normal times it chooses speakers at its own discretion from the ranks of party politicians to broadcast on political or other topics (watching the overall "balance" of speakers so carefully that a school service which has used an M.P. of one party to talk about his travels may find itself searching for an M.P. of another to talk about birds so that neither party gains undue publicity). It retains a full formal liberty to deal as it wishes with matters of current political controversy. The perils of the path which it must tread were thrown into sharp relief by the tension that arose between Mr. Harold Wilson and the BBC during the election campaign of 1966, by the suggestion that the Corporation had shown bias, and by the rumours that the Labour Government, when it took office, had plans for a new machinery of control and a political "watch dog" over the BBC.

It has in times of stress that freedom of action which arises from the existence of an effective parliamentary democracy, a two-party system, and a long national tradition of free speech. It survived its first major test during the very first year of its existence. During the General Strike of 1926 one party in the Cabinet was in favour of commandeering its resources. The BBC retained the liberty to provide a service of news rather than of propaganda throughout the emergency (though it was not, as Reith wished, allowed to invite a Labour spokesman to address the nation as well as Ministers). In the last resort it owed its immunity from direct control to the fact that although Reith thought it was "not a time for dope" he was "for the Government in the crisis".

At the time of the Suez invasion of 1956 the BBC insisted on its right to keep the world informed not only of the government view, but of the debate of a deeply divided nation, and to provide a platform for the Leader of the Opposition. At such times it can count on the sympathy of a watchful opposition party, and has a limited power to appeal to the national sentiment. No government can relax altogether its hold on such a powerful organ of political opinion. The BBC would clearly not be allowed to stress a minority view at a time of crisis against the united views of the major political parties. It operates within the limits of tolerance of successive governments, which must have a wary regard for public opinion, but cannot hope to be an *imperium in imperio*.

The Postmaster General not only retains the right of veto and direction on such occasions. He also has less publicly apparent but very real methods of persuasion and compulsion in peaceful times.

The BBC is in a sense financed from licence revenue, but the allocation of funds for its operations is related only by convention to the licence fee. The present Licence and Agreement provides that "the Postmaster General shall pay to the Corporation (out of moneys provided by Parliament during the period ending on the 31st March, 1965) a sum equal to the whole of the net licence revenue, and thereafter . . . a sum or sums equal to the whole of the net licence revenue or to such percentage or percentages thereof as the Treasury may from time to time determine". The BBC can broadly speaking make what use it likes of the available air time; but the Postmaster General has absolute power to specify the maximum and minimum permitted hours of broadcasting in each service and the hours of the day when broadcasts may be given. He may, moreover, "allow for programmes or items of specified kinds being left out of account in determining the maximum". Programmes for schools have always been exempted, and after the publication of the Pilkington Report a like provision was made for programmes of adult education, defined as programmes "arranged in series and planned in consultation with appropriate educational bodies so as to contribute to the progressive mastery or understanding of some skill or body of knowledge". Any persuasions that the government of the day may wish to exercise are therefore backed by sufficient sanctions; and a government has both formal and informal ways of making its wishes known to the Governors. In the last resort it can introduce new legislation.

Beneath the Board of Governors extend the ramifications of a huge and intricate structure. The BBC is responsible for three great programme services: Sound Broadcasting with three channels, Television with two, and the External Services. It has six major regional centres. The staff numbers more than 20,000, half of them on the engineering side, and there is a complex network of advisory councils and committees. Like the British Constitution as Bagehot saw it the BBC has its formal and visible aspects, and its dignified parts. It has, too, its internal balance of powers, its unwritten laws, and its uncodified conventions.

The Governors are the Corporation. They must therefore have a large say in the financial and administrative conduct of the broadcasting operation. The BBC exists, however, to produce programmes, and it is much more difficult for them to exercise real power in that field.

The Board must concern itself with programmes that may have large political implications, and with those that deal with matters of the gravest public concern. It took its own decision that *The War Game* (a film dealing in fictional form with the consequences of nuclear war) should not be shown. The more general process of "editorial control by retrospective review" which Lord Normanbrook holds to be the best method of giving direction to the programmes was never within my own experience mediated downwards in any effective way.

The BBC machine concentrates great powers in the hands of the Director General—as Lord Reith always held that it should. For any Director General the ideal Chairman must be a wise elder statesman whose views on major questions coincide by a fortunate dispensation of Providence with his own, but whose name carries enormous weight under a defensive letter to *The Times*.

Lord Simon, who was Chairman from 1947 to 1952, has recorded the vicissitudes of his own unsuccessful struggle with Sir William Haley, a Director General whom he liked and admired, to assert a more positive and constructive role for his office.[1] He was the only Chairman for the past twenty years who has tried to familiarize himself with the work of the programme departments through direct and familiar acquaintance with their Heads, and with the producers who shape the output from day to day.

From their point of view the effective source of direction is first of all the Head of Department, then the Director of the Service to which they belong, and ultimately the "D.G."

[1] LORD SIMON OF WYTHENSHAWE, *The BBC from Within*, 1953, pp. 49-72.

rather than any of the remote and shadowy figures who succeed one another without perceptibly deflecting programme policy from the course on which it has been set.

A new Director General brings a new ethos; perhaps a revolution in policy and approach. The three under whom I served could hardly have differed more. The first, Sir William Haley, was a distinguished newspaper editor, largely self-taught, and widely read in the tough Victorian tradition. He was more at home, his critics in the Talks Division sometimes said, with John Stuart Mill and FitzJames Stephen than with Marx and Freud and their successors, but perhaps all the stronger for his immunity from intellectual fashion; a moralist, and a resolute believer in purposive broadcasting.

Next came a distinguished soldier, Sir Ian Jacob, whose career had stretched from Sandhurst to the service of the Imperial War Cabinet; an able administrator, who found administration compatible with great warmth and friendliness. Primarily interested in the "public affairs" output he was not by training or habit of thought a sociologist, and was, from my limited point of view, a slow convert to a belief in the significance of the Corporation's educational work, but then its firm supporter.

In 1950 the present Director General, Sir Hugh Greene, was appointed. He was the first to reach the post after a long career in broadcasting, spent mainly in News and the External Services; deeply committed to the orthodoxies of the progressive left, but first and foremost an able tactician, placed by circumstances in a more difficult position than any of his predecessors. No immortal Chairman could possibly have found equally congenial the views of each of his three successive chief executive officers.

The BBC owes its strength and its qualities to its status as a public corporation, and to the men and women who have served it because they believed in public service broadcasting. As a complex working machinery it now has the defects (as well as some of the advantages) that go with sheer size. It achieves only a very imperfect co-ordination of its programme plans; its administration is too highly centralized, and its relationship with the outside world is neither as close nor as sensitive as it might be.

A decentralized system of programme planning and production rightly gives a large liberty to Departmental Heads, and through them a wide area of creative freedom to individual producers. There is not and never has been a bureaucratic and restrictive approach to the Corporation's central task. It would be impossible and undesirable to achieve a degree of co-ordination between Departments or Services sufficient to ensure that there were neither overlaps nor coincidences of theme and approach in the day-by-day output. The task of shaping the future schedules is shared between the specialist producing departments and the chief planners, each of whom controls and is primarily concerned with his own "channel". The jigsaw puzzle is so complex that it is not surprising when no clear pattern emerges. If the size and unity of the BBC are to be more than an administrative convenience offering the economies of shared facilities there should, nevertheless, be a broad consonance of purpose throughout the whole organization, and, in appropriate fields, a close and effective liaison. Departmental separatisms develop, and are allowed to stand in the way.

One of the strengths of the Corporation lies in its control of both radio and television. Their headquarters are five miles apart; they are worlds apart, and there has so far been a very imperfect co-ordination between them. There are fields of discourse like science in which the BBC should watch the coverage and comprehensiveness of what it offers through both media in terms of subject matter and of the different levels of audience to be addressed. For years it resisted the suggestions of the great outside scientific bodies that it should take steps to do so, and it was only at the direct instance of the Pilkington Committee that it finally appointed an advisory body and created an internal machinery for co-ordination.

Programme planning is decentralized. The administrative system is highly centralized, and often too rigid and inflexible to meet specialized departmental needs. A far more serious implication of the present size of the BBC, and its system of centralized control, arises from the fact that every department must constantly be bidding against every other to the Board of Management for its share of the available air time, the available money, and the available professional resources. Even if the management could always adjudicate between these bids entirely on their intrinsic merits and in academic calm it would still be presented with the task of measuring incommensurables in terms of hours on the air; of weighing the claims of religion against those of show-jumping in the financial balances.

In practice the bidding is inevitably complicated by the power-politics of a great organization, by individual pertinacities and persuasions, by the personal views of the Directors concerned, and by the tactical considerations uppermost in their minds at the moment.

A number of outsiders, not all of them disinterested, have argued that competition afforded a stimulus to the BBC that has been reflected in livelier and more vigorous programmes. To those inside whose concern was broadcasting with a social purpose its results were wholly disastrous. They were made worse by the fact that successive governments, each with an eye on the electoral consequences of raising the licence fee, have kept the Corporation short of the money which it patently needs to run the services that those same governments have sanctioned.

The BBC has thus been placed in a wholly unenviable position. It has refused to be forced into the position of the Australian Broadcasting Commission, which now commands only twenty per cent of the listeners and twelve per cent of the viewers, and concentrates heavily on news, farming, music, education, and those other kinds of "public service" programmes which its commercial rivals do not provide. It has rightly judged that its opportunities to serve the community depend on the maintenance of a wide and comprehensive range of popular programmes, appealing to every class.

It has, furthermore, been very conscious of the danger that a fall in its share of the audience might well lead to a political campaign against the increase, or even the maintenance, of its licence revenue. There has been, and still is, a danger point somewhere on the daily chart which the BBC knows as the Audience Research Barometer of Viewing, which on last year's averages showed the BBC share of the television audience as forty-six per cent, the Independent Television share as fifty-four per cent. As a troublesome further complication the BBC has witnessed a steady inflation of its costs as its rich competitors bid against it for staff, and in the show-business market.

Perhaps inevitably the emphasis shifted from the strategy of social purpose to the tactics of survival. Perhaps inevitably the balance of power within the BBC, always in delicate equilibrium between light entertainment and the more purposive kinds of broadcasting, shifted towards that section of middle management most anxious to fight the rival on his own grounds and achieve mass audiences at any price. If the yardstick is crude enough there is indeed a sense in which religion is a "minority" and show-jumping a "majority" interest.

An organization of the size of the BBC has its own sheer weight and momentum. For those working within it, survival can easily come to seem an end in itself rather than a means towards the well-being of the community. In a free society the state establishes monopolies and creates special agencies only to serve purposes that would not otherwise be achieved, and that it believes to be valuable. The more the output of a public corporation resembles that of its rivals, the less justification there is for its continued existence. After six years' experience of competition in this country, the Roman Catholic Body in England and Wales could justly say in its evidence to the Pilkington Committee: "It is our opinion that the competition between the BBC and the ITA has been of a destructive rather than a creative character, for each has seemed to be driven excessively, though possibly to varying degrees, by the desire to secure large audiences and each has shown the kind of programme which is calculated to attract the largest audience. This destructive competition has proved not to be competition at all in that there is more of duplication than variety."

It is sometimes said that rivalry with the admirable service provided for the Programme Companies by their joint organ, Independent Television News, did at least lead to a new vigour and liveliness in the BBC presentation by television of the news. It can as readily be argued that the BBC was already emerging from its difficulties into a new conception of what the television medium could achieve.

The story of educational broadcasting does, however, afford an ironic footnote. There was a long-standing agreement between the BBC and the School Broadcasting Council which is its official link with the world of education that a service of television programmes for schools would be launched as soon as possible. When competition came the Corporation (faced with a ruthless commercial competitor) was for a long time very unwilling to contemplate any entry into this new field. The School Broadcasting Council attempted to enlist the support of Lord Eccles, the Minister of Education at the time. He professed obscure doubts about the value and propriety of any use of television in schools, and stipulated that any experiment must be both limited and revocable. The Corporation agreed to make a very modest start, insisting on its part that the programmes must be filmed since no studio facilities could be made available. The School Broadcasting Council entered into an agreement with the local education authorities that they would provide by a specified date the number of receivers which the Minister had sanctioned. Preparations to make a start on that day were carefully made. Three months before it arrived one of the Programme Companies announced that it proposed to anticipate that date with a school service of its own. It has since then claimed the sturdier pioneer virtues. The Corporation fortunately found that it had facilities to match theirs. Two years later the Company decided to double its service. So, at very short notice, did the BBC. Until the appearance of the Pilkington Report it was Independent Television and not the BBC that set the pace in the educational field.

It is not easy for a great metropolitan organization to establish a close relationship with the whole national community. Its senior officers move in the worlds of politics, of the arts, of learning, and of business at a level remote from that of the great mass of listeners and viewers and rank-and-file contributors. The burden of shaping the programmes which will in Britain reach thirteen million infinitely various homes rests with the producers, each with his limited range of social and professional outside contacts. London is vast. The work of a television producer is arduous and absorbing. He has far less time for meeting people than a talks producer used to have in the heyday of sound broadcasting. Television Centre—any national television centre—is a whole self-contained world of like-minded people. There is a perennial temptation to produce for them, and not for the unknowable millions, provided only that the ratings stay high enough. The belief that "good television" is an entity, self-subsistent, capable of assessment only by one's colleagues, and divorced from purpose takes root and grows. The atmosphere is a hothouse atmosphere.

In Cardiff, Edinburgh, or Belfast, in Bristol, Birmingham, or Manchester a fresher air from outside blows through the studios. There is a living bond between broadcasting and the regional community and a sense of participation in a communal activity which the scale of the national operation forbids (and which the present English regions are too large and artificial to foster to the full). Only those national activities which have a clear and specific purpose for a clearly definable group can achieve a relationship with their audiences that goes much deeper than a scrutiny of the Audience Research reports. Their formal instruments of co-operation are Advisory Councils and Committees.

Apart from the National Broadcasting Councils of Scotland, Wales, and Northern Ireland only one of them, the General Advisory Council, is a statutory body for which provision is made in the Charter. It has the function "of advising the Corporation on all matters which may be of concern to the Corporation",[1] but no officers of its own, and no mandatory powers. From its earliest days the BBC has had "no intention of making the Council a really active agency", and has preferred to think of it as "ambassadorial"—an agency for representing the views of the Corporation to the influential world outside. It was always "rather too much like the House of Lords even for some of its members", and one of the ablest of them, Sir Ernest Barker, pressed that it should have a smaller and less distinguished member-

---

[1] BBC Charter.

ship, more in touch with the general body of consumers.[1] Nearly sixty strong it can have no common mind. Its discussions on any controversial topic reflect every conceivable shade of opinion for the Corporation to select from. It has not yet been reorganized as the Pilkington Committee suggested, so as to be "capable of taking a sharply focused, critical view of the BBC's policies and services".[2] It possesses, and has in its time exercised, the persuasive force of near-mutiny, but little more.

The Beveridge Report strongly recommended that the BBC should be required to establish a Public Representation Service which would bring opinion from outside to bear on the work of the Corporation. It was not sufficient in the view of the Beveridge Committee to "trust to the mutual criticism of those within the Corporation" or "to trust to discussions by Advisory Committees without making certain that they have all the material they need to be useful". Lord Reith has continued to hold, as he held then, that "listener research is a waste of time and money and a real menace", but that "public relations should be taken far more seriously, inwards as much as outwards".[3] It is through a few small and specialized committees that the BBC has so far gone furthest in that direction.

These derive their strength from being compact, homogeneous, and single-minded.

The Central Religious Advisory Committee (which also serves the ITA) speaks with the full weight of the "mainstream" Churches. It has no coercive powers, but within the time allotted by the Corporation to the activities of his Department the Head of Religious Broadcasting would make any major new departure without being sure of its support.

[1] ASA BRIGGS, op. cit., vol. II, pp. 469–72, Clause 8.
[2] *Pilkington Report*, p. 134.
[3] LORD REITH, "The Future of British Broadcasting", *Manchester Guardian*.

E

The Agricultural Advisory Committee, shrewd, well-informed, well-led, and small enough to be on cordial terms with an able specialist staff deeply committed to its purposes has played a real part in securing and guiding an agricultural service of wide range and outstanding quality.

The newer Science Consultative Group and Engineering Advisory Committee have an authority and distinction of membership that should give them the same cutting edge.

Alone among all of these outside bodies at present the School Broadcasting Council for the United Kingdom (with daughter councils in Scotland, Wales, and Northern Ireland) has clear and definite delegated powers. Sir John Reith decided early in the development of the service for schools that the BBC was "not a recognized educational instrument" and in 1935 the Central Council for School Broadcasting which had guided the development of the service since 1929 was placed on a new and unique footing. As it now exists the Council has a full delegated authority to determine the broad policy governing school broadcasting; a right (which it exercises fully through specialized sub-committees) to approve all plans; a power of annual request, which the Corporation always tries to meet within the limits of its financial powers; and most significantly, a secretary and a large staff of its own recruited and paid by the Corporation, not involved in the planning and production of programmes, but seconded to the service of the Council "so that there shall be a solid basis of information and assessment to help the Council in its task of guidance and sponsorship".

If a programme service is designed to serve specific aims for a well-defined audience, and if there are authoritative interpreters of those aims, the problem of liaison with the community is straightforward. The broadcasting organization has only to create a machinery which enables the accredited representatives of the Churches, or the schools, or the farmers to determine the broad purposes to be served; to establish departments which are professionally equipped to make a creative contribution to the fulfilment of those purposes; and—most important step of all—to ensure that there is an adequate flow of information from the target audiences about their needs, and the success of the programmes. The problem of maintaining contact with the general public over the general programme output is far less tractable.

Even within the limited field of adult education it is by no means easy to determine the right role for an advisory body. The Further Education Advisory Council of the BBC and the Adult Education Committee of the ITA, representing as they do the main organizations concerned with adult education, can speak confidently for the needs of the committed student. It is not so easy for them to deal with those programmes of informal education which are planned for home viewing and listening, and call for no overt response. There is, as yet, little evidence of their impact and no objective measure of their success. The committee members can see and hear only a fraction of the programme output with which they are concerned. Time does not serve for the detailed consideration of a great mass of forward proposals. The most useful function of the committee is to make the broadcasting organization aware of trends in public opinion and taste which might furnish new opportunities for broadcasting, or call for the revision of established practices. It is a function that can be carried out satisfactorily if the brief of a committee is limited and its membership reasonably homogeneous. In relation to broadcasting as a whole it could not be efficiently exercised by any single body. No organization, or combination of organizations, can speak with authority for the common listener and the common viewer. No committee representing sectional interests could usefully sit round a table weighing one of them against another, or arrive at a balanced overall view of the total programme output. The proposals for a Listeners' and Viewers' Council which have been canvassed from time to time, and which have recently found some support in government circles, are therefore not well-conceived. They could lead only to the establishment of an amorphous body with powers so ill-defined as to be nugatory or so specific as to be an obstacle to considered programme planning. Its functions would inevitably overlap with those of the General Advisory Council, and the benefits which it is intended to secure would flow as readily from a General Advisory Council reorganized on the lines suggested by Sir Ernest Barker as from any new body.

The full and effective influence of public opinion on the broadcasting organizations will be exercised only when the great national organizations representing major community interests are so far convinced of the far-reaching social importance of radio and television that they create organs of their own to channel the views of their members in the right direction and bring an informed criticism to bear on the activities of both the BBC and the Programme Companies. The women's organizations, the Churches, the Trades Union Congress, the teachers' associations, the professional bodies, and the universities should all be concerned with general broadcasting as a mode of public communication that profoundly affects them and their interests, and that ought to be sensitive to their needs, views, and wishes. It is proper that the BBC in particular should be informed, persuaded, lobbied, and generally pursued and pestered by the community that it exists to serve; that there should be a Clean Up TV Campaign and an Anti Clean Up TV Campaign, as well as a wide range of official Broadcasting Committees with ideas to put forward and axes to grind. An *ad hoc* voluntary body, The Listeners' and Viewers' Association, was undoubtedly instrumental in the restoration of some of the cuts made in the Third Programme schedule in 1957. The precedent of establishing organized pressures has been too little followed (except when an inquiry was in progress) by disinterested outsiders.

If criticism is well informed and well pressed home the broadcasting organizations will not only respond, they will have to strengthen their means of response. The most useful step that the BBC could take towards the forging of a closer bond with its general audience would be a massive strengthening of its Audience Research Department, and a redeployment of the resources available. More than enough effort already goes into a continuous, minute, and obsessive analysis of the competitive situation in merely statistical terms. Far too little is available for those basic inquiries which the Department undertakes on its own initiative, or at the request of Departments, into the views, attitudes, and interests of potential audiences, the problems of communication with them, and the impact of programmes upon them. In that field the Corporation should welcome and encourage active partners and fellow workers, from the university Institute of Communications Research to the parent-teacher association with an active viewing group.

In a small country it is possible to involve national organizations directly in the broadcasting process, and even to delegate broadcasting powers to them. The Dutch, through their extraordinary "pillar system" have shown one way in which a sense of national involvement can be achieved. Holland has no less than five separate and competing broadcasting bodies, sharing their studios and transmitting facilities through a national organization, the Nederlandsche Radio-Unie, but each representing one of the main "pillars" of public opinion in the country. The Roman Catholics, the Protestants, the Liberal Protestants, the Socialists, and a

secular cultural group all compete for audiences. They share
the licence revenue and the air time according to the measure
of their success. There is inevitably some duplication; but
perhaps the highest price which the Dutch pay for this form
of participation lies in the acceptance of deep national divisions and the encouragement of a sectional listening and
viewing which is impervious to the other man's point of
view.

Yet another approach is embodied in the report on the
future of Radio and Television in Sweden which was presented to the government in 1965, and which has been accepted as a basis for reorganization. Broadcasting in Sweden is
controlled by a corporation in which other public organizations, and the Press have shares. The new plan provides for
two new radio channels operating "scrambled" transmissions,
receivable only on specially adjustable sets, which will be
available for regular use by approved national organizations
on application to a new Board of Telecommunications.

The size of the United Kingdom and the variety of its
national life makes a plan of the Swedish kind wholly im-
practicable here. The best prospect for broadcasting as an
activity involving the whole community therefore lies in the
development of local stations. We have not enough frequencies available for local television except on a closed
circuit basis, but all of our great cities and many compact
rural communities with strong common interests could have
their own Very High Frequency (VHF) stations, with a range
of from two to ten miles' radius.

The BBC submitted to the Pilkington Committee a plan for
the establishment of eighty or ninety such stations. The
emphasis of its original bid lay on the value of a local radio
station as a focus for the life of the community, and on the
service that it could offer through news bulletins, local
information, and a full reflection of the activities of local

government, the Churches, the sporting organizations, industry and commerce, and the voluntary societies of the neighbourhood. In its later statements the Corporation has given equal weight to the educational possibilities. Since the local programmes of a general character would be transmitted during the daytime, when most people listen to radio, the peak evening hours as well as some part of the daytime could be placed entirely at the disposal of a consortium of local educational interests.

The Pilkington Committee recommended "that one service and one service only of local broadcasting be planned; that it be provided by the BBC and financed from licence revenue; and that the frequencies available be so deployed as to enable it to be provided for the largest possible number of distinct communities". In the two White Papers that followed the Report the government temporized, and stated, first, that it would "prefer to take cognizance of public reactions before reaching a decision", and then that it did not discount "a possible latent demand for local services".

The BBC bid still stands. There is a vigorous rival campaign in favour of local commercial broadcasting; and the issues have been confused by an argument about the desirability of making "pop" music continuously available. Since the local items in a local service would not be continuous there would have to be "sustaining" programmes. In the BBC scheme these would be drawn from the national networks at the discretion of the Station Manager. The commercial schemes would rely very largely on gramophone records. The record companies impose strict limits on the broadcast use of their wares. "Needle time" is rationed. The pirate stations infringe copyright and performing right in a way that no legal land-based operation could. It is therefore very unlikely that local commercial stations would be able to supply what some sections of the public want. It is still more unlikely that they would provide a comprehensive local service. The world can already show a great many examples of enterprises that began with promises of programmes of genuine local interest and settled down to a routine of disc jockeys and syndicated "soap opera", interspersed with questions by telephone from housewives, interviews with local "personalities", and more and more insistent advertisements. The United States has some 3,500 radio stations. "To twist the radio dial today", says Mr. Newton Minow, "is to be shoved through a bazaar, a clamorous casbah of pitchmen and commercials which plead, bleat, pressure, whistle, groan, and shout." In Australia, where the local stations of the Australian Broadcasting Commission compete in many towns with commercial stations, local radio from both sources has proved its capacity to provide a supplement to the national services of real value to the community. The commercial stations have the bigger audiences. It is the public service stations that serve education, farming, and other minority local interests best.

To reject the claims of the commercial lobby is not necessarily to accept the bid of the BBC. The whole point of local broadcasting is that it shall be local. The BBC is a huge national concern with strong centralizing tendencies. Its capacity to launch the new venture is, however, unique. There must be a licensing authority through which local stations are responsible to the government for their conduct of the operation. The ITA has no experience of radio. If the BBC can indeed achieve the act of self-abnegation that it has promised, if it can allow to each local advisory council a large autonomy and power of initiative, and act in the education field as no more than the trustee of the local education authority, the teachers' associations, the university, and the voluntary bodies, it can render them signal service. It can provide the technical and professional help and the sense of standards without which local broadcasting might founder through sheer inexperience and amateurishness. It can support the independence of the Station Manager if it is threatened by pressures of a sectional or party-political kind. It can place the resources and the help of its regional centres at the disposal of local stations.

The weakness of the BBC case lay in its financial provisions. The original BBC scheme called for an increase in the licence fee (though only of some five or six shillings) for the benefit of selected areas. The best hope lies in the establishment of partnerships which need follow no unvarying pattern between the BBC and those local interests which can participate most fully in the operation and which might be able to carry some part of the cost. It is along these lines that the BBC has now been authorized to go ahead (though without any long-term commitment on the part of the Government) with a nine-station experimental project. It is hoped that this experiment will provide a firm basis for a final decision.

If the United Kingdom chooses to establish local sound broadcasting on public service principles as a complement and completion of its existing public service system, and if it chooses to support the Independent Television Authority in its present policy, it will be better equipped than any other country in the world to use broadcasting for educative and for educational purposes.

III

VALUES: TRADITION AND INNOVATION

THE values of a broadcasting organization are implicit in its programmes. The programme structure rests on a complex of value judgements and assumptions about God, man, and the social order which is created by the interplay of all those who work in broadcasting with the world outside. "By its nature", as the Pilkington Report says, "broadcasting must be in a constant and sensitive relationship with the moral condition of society."[1] It is a relationship achieved through a host of individual men and women from the latest trainee to the Director General, each with the strength and the limitations of his age and his social group, each with his own sensibilities and powers of judgement, his own blindnesses and moments of vision. In any broadcasting concern the producers lie at the very tip of the antennae. Their signals penetrate, however imperfectly, to the centre and make their impact. The whole organism makes its moral movements, hesitantly and clumsily at times, and often with a very imperfect co-ordination of its departmental limbs, in response to the messages that come back from its central nervous system, the management.

Every broadcast is a moral act. The sum total cannot be formulated, but each successive Director General must state his own version of the principles that should inform the output. For Lord Reith the overriding obligation was a Christian commitment that expressed itself in what he described as "a definite, though restrained association with

---

[1] *Pilkington Report*, p. 15.

religion in general, and with the Christian religion in particular";[1] in the general tenor of programme planning, and
indeed in a rigid Sabbatarianism that lasted well into the 1940s.

"Christianity happens to be the stated and official religion
of the country", he wrote. It still is; but Lord Reith's own
term of office coincided with that loosening of the fabric,
though not with that "shaking of the foundations" which
has marked the drift of social habit and the direction of
religious thought in our times.

Until well after Lord Reith's departure both religious
controversy and the overt expression of unbelief were expressly excluded from the programmes by the edicts of
successive Boards of Governors. In 1947 they issued a public
statement explaining and defending their decision that the
time had now come for the Corporation to move cautiously
and with "a deep seriousness and high purpose" into both
fields. The highest duty of the BBC must, in their words, be
towards the search for truth. In broadcasts for schools and
young people there must, however, be no relaxation of the
old strict rules.

The motives behind the new policy were mixed; in part,
no doubt, a desire to "meet the needs of the millions of
people . . . hungering after information on spiritual issues";
in part a concession to the demands of anti-religious and
unorthodox groups who complained that they were denied
the freedom of the air. Their insistence was beginning to be
an embarrassment even to the Religious Broadcasting
Department of the BBC, which had no desire to appear as if
it needed protection from any challenge. The new venture
proved to be fraught with difficulties. It was easy enough to
find speakers whose aim was a display of virtuosity, or Christians and scientific humanists who talked past each other; by

[1] ASA BRIGGS, *The Birth of Broadcasting*, vol. I, p. 241.

no means so easy to achieve any real engagement of minds. The reaction of the average listener was bewilderment or a sense of missed opportunities. As was pointed out by a wide-ranging and sensitive report prepared for the BBC by Dr. Kathleen Bliss as an outside consultant, the need at that time was neither for "information" nor for religious controversy in any sense that at all resembled political controversy, with its simplified polemics and clear-cut choice between alternatives. At one level it was rather for fundamental debate; the patient unravelling by men of good will of the tangled skein of their intellectual agreements and disagreements—an enterprise only practicable in Third Programme terms. At another, it was for keeping alive in men's minds some sense that there were in life high issues and questions worth debate—an aim to be pursued for most people through encounter and experience, in drama and in documentary programmes rather than in the unfamiliar terms of theological or philosophical debate.

The cautiously bold new departure had led nowhere so far as programmes designed for a wide audience were concerned.

In any event, there had never been any intention to engage in a major change of direction, or to suggest that British broadcasting was neutral where Christian values were concerned. "Of course it is not", said the Director General to the British Council of Churches in 1948. "There are many demands of impartiality laid upon the Corporation but this is not one of them. We are citizens of a Christian country, and the BBC—an institution set up by the State—bases its policy upon a positive attitude towards the Christian values. It seeks to safeguard those values and to foster acceptance of them. The whole preponderant weight of its programmes is directed to this end."[1]

[1] Sir William Haley, *Moral Values in Broadcasting*, 1948, p. 7.

Sir William Haley was careful to distinguish between the Christian values and the Christian faith. There was a proper place within broadcasting for Christian evangelism; it was no part of the general duty of the BBC to make converts. He saw no reason why faith should not go hand in hand with tolerance.

It was the precarious doctrine of a time of uneasy equilibrium. The Education Act of 1944 had not long before required—and still requires—that every school within the state system should provide non-denominational religious instruction and a daily act of worship. An overwhelming majority of British people subscribed—as they still do—to a belief in some sort of God. The Christian values, however vaguely apprehended, were hardly challenged. It seemed at least possible that men of good will would be able to walk together in charity, if not in faith, and that there need be no large breach of continuity in British culture or in moral standards.

The "preponderant weight" of BBC programmes still rested on the side of tradition; excessively so in the eyes of its critics and of some of its more discerning friends. The Third Programme was its most deliberate instrument of social exploration. As Harman Grisewood, whose deeply civilized influence was to leave its lasting imprint on every aspect of broadcasting, wrote in his testament of farewell to the Third Programme in 1953: "The characteristic of our society is to be speculative, experimental, and daring. Western man does not take kindly to the idea of a static society. He is not willingly subject to formulae. Each of our national groups requires the invigoration of discovery. But these inventive elements in a society are not revered as they work; they are tolerated. That limited concession is part of the experiment. What may be yielded as valuable will be yielded in due time.

"It seemed to me that the Third Programme was gaining a place along with other agencies that were stimulants to this essential element in our society—the element that discusses and revalues; prepares the ground for the necessary new departures and for the equally necessary recoveries to be made from well-tried traditions."[1]

The Third Programme was a compass-needle swinging in new directions, but the whole stance of the BBC in those years invited the arrows of the left. Viewed from that direction its religious policy was the type and symbol of a total attitude. The formula was coherent and complete: establishment values for the populace at large; indoctrination for the young; and a privileged area of debate for a cultured minority, rather on the principle that held the younger Pitt back from the suppression of Godwin's *Political Justice*. A book costing four guineas was unlikely to do much social harm.

Even on the Third Programme, with all its freedom of thought, decorum still reigned, because decorum was still valued and expected. I remember, indeed, how the whole Corporation was shaken by an unsanctioned and uncensored reading of George Barker's *True Testament*. The apotheosis of the four-letter word was still to come. It is, indeed, only through a failure in historical knowledge or imagination that the critics of the BBC can write now as if it could in those days have exercised the freedom that now obtains. The early post-war years were politically an uneasy period of international uncertainties and domestic touchiness: a period when it was not even clear whether Russia was friend or foe, and when plain speaking about Russia or any other country might cause grave diplomatic offence. At home the broad lines of a social policy accepted by both parties had not yet been formulated: my own worst lapse, and one that

[1] H. J. G. GRISEWOOD, "On Hearing the Third Programme", *BBC Quarterly*, Spring, 1953.

evoked a volume of correspondence of a vehemence that presented a problem in public relations with the medical profession, was to allow a speaker to schools to praise too unreservedly the new plans for a National Health Service. The moral consensus was still a real and solid consensus. A public corporation must act within the limits determined by broad national policy and by the pressure of responsible public opinion. It is nevertheless an organism with a will of its own, and a freedom to choose its own emphasis. The BBC chose in 1950 to think of itself as "a bastion against the tide seeking to submerge values in a disintegrating world".[1]

Twenty years after Sir William Haley's profession of faith the accent of everything that Sir Hugh Greene says falls in a very different place. He shares his predecessor's preference for law over crime; kindness over cruelty; education over illiteracy; health over insanitation. He has his own list of "the basic moral values—truthfulness, justice, freedom, compassion, tolerance". He would agree wholeheartedly with Sir William Haley that "the search for truth is endless and an end in itself"; perhaps in little else.

The key words of his own addresses are liberty and scepticism, with a *caveat* against the attachment of "a ubiquitous, unanswered, question mark to everything—in religion, culture, politics or education", but with an unmistakably "progressive" trend in the phrasing and colour in the aphorisms. The obligation of the BBC is "towards the maximum liberty of expression"; its aim is "to widen the area of acceptability". "Outrage is wrong; shock may not be good. Provocation can be healthy, and indeed socially imperative."

It is a doctrine that has, then, its categorical imperatives. "I do not mean to imply", Sir Hugh writes of public service broadcasting, "that a broadcasting system should be

---

[1] *The Beveridge Report*, Appendix H, p. 210.

neutral in clear issues of right and wrong—even though it should be between Right and Left. It can, for instance, encourage the right attitude on the colour bar. . . . There are some questions on which one should not be impartial." The imperatives are self-subsistent, resting on no fundamental commitment. Their existence as absolutes consorts a little oddly with the manifesto in which Sir Hugh sums up the task of the BBC as he sees it.

"The main purpose of broadcasting is to make the microphone and the television screen available to the widest possible range of subjects and to the best exponents available of the differing views on any given subject: to let the debate decide—or not decide as the case may be—and, in Cardinal Heenan's words, 'to emerge with a deeper knowledge'."[1]

In broadcasting, to deal with the widest possible range of subjects is still to apply a rigorous principle of selection and of rejection, of proportion and of emphasis. More entertainment means less education; more Boulez may mean less Bach; more cricket, less chess. Except where the gross size of the audience is the sole determinant of choice some things must always present themselves as more worth doing than others. An undeclared hierarchy of values will inevitably assert itself in the programmes themselves and in the total programme planning. The explicit commitment in Sir Hugh Greene's profession of faith is only to the philosophy of the open forum in the open society. The "preponderant weight" of programmes is thrown on one side of the scales as clearly as ever. The change in programme content is in large part a response to changes in the temper of the times that were bound to affect every aspect of broadcasting. In his own domain, more insulated than most from internal changes and chances, the present Controller of the Third Programme,

---

[1] SIR HUGH GREENE, *The Conscience of the Programme Director*, 1965, p. 4.

P. H. Newby, as deeply concerned as Harman Grisewood fifteen years ago with the delicate balance between change and continuity, and with the need for "recoveries from the past" as well as "new departures", has made his own ironic bow in the direction of the *Zeitgeist:* "We are relativists. We believe the truth is what works. We are sceptical, anti-authority, permissive. We are against cultural dictators. It follows that no Chief of the Third Programme can afford to be too certain of himself."[1]

The ban on religious controversy in school programmes has been relaxed, not by any initiative of the Corporation, but at the request of the advisory Committee that watches over the interests of sixth forms. Whereas once it sponsored Bible Talks for boys and girls assumed to be orthodox churchgoers it asks now for programmes which assume no commitment on their part to Christianity, but which aim at stimulating thought about all those faiths, whether secular or religious, by which men now live.

These are straws in the general wind of change. In the television service for the general public the wind reaches gale force, and it is there that the main social significance of the new approach lies. It is there, too, that the relationship between broadcasting and the moral condition of society is most confused by factors deriving from the nature of the broadcasting organization itself. Television is a young man's trade and fiercely competitive. The young urban intelligentsia is radical in politics and morals. There is a double temptation: to produce for the peer group, and to produce for the news-paper headlines. The machinery of immediate control is much more difficult of application than in sound broad-casting, with its apparatus of scripts that can faithfully enough convey the nature and probable impact of a forthcoming

[1] P. H. NEWBY, *The Third Programme*, B B C Lunch-time Lectures, 1965, p. 9.

F

programme. No departmental directorate in television can see in rehearsal more than a small fraction of the output for which they are responsible. Its character must depend largely on departmental directives and a departmental ethos created within a matrix of intentions which derive from the Director General of the day, and for which the Governors carry the final responsibility.

The issue has been squarely joined in our society between tradition and innovation, authority and freedom; between "Romanitas"—that word which for Mr. Auden stands for the belief that virtue is prior to liberty, and "Libertas" which is in itself "as neutral to values as the 'nature' of physics", and which throws on to the individual "the lot of the wandering Jew, i.e. the loneliness and anxiety of having to choose himself, his faith, his vocations, his habits".[1]

There is a range of balance between these antinomies within which a society can flourish, but outside which it petrifies or loses its cohesion. Broadcasting stands in the midst of the conflict, not as a neutral, because it cannot achieve neutrality; but lending its help to one side or the other; exercising leadership, wondering if *demos* any longer has a need for leaders, or simply carried along by the tide of battle.

Its weight is thrown now, not in any purely intellectual way, but with all the force of the visual and the concrete, of encounter and of drama, on the side of cultural and moral innovation. Its address is no longer *ad clerum* but *ad populum*. It sees its role as that of a catalyst of change. The older attitudes slipped too readily into the rigid postures of a "good form" instinct with the values of what was then the governing class; the new attitudes can be theatrical gestures of revolt, and as empty as the old, produced with less regard for the

---

[1] W. H. AUDEN, *The Dyer's Hand*, 1963.

long-term impact on society than for the short-term impact
on the ratings. In its least happy offerings the BBC used to
play to the stalls; now to the gallery. Moral shock tactics
encourage the shock troops. They rarely make converts,
and always harden the opposition. The story of the BBC's
excursion into a *genre* that is still by the abuse of a useful
word called satire is perhaps a cautionary tale. Political
satire with a cutting edge calls for a committed political
passion; *saeva indignatio* is not to be had weekly for the
asking; social comment must be urbane and polished to earn
the name of satire. *Not so much a Programme* . . . and its
successors found one brilliant mimic with a gift for punctur-
ing the pomposities of politicians of whatever party; one good
amusing comedienne. With far too much space to fill the
programme had not "wit enough to keep it sweet". It was
reduced to charades about clergymen, headmasters, and other
Aunt Sallys of the Left; to interminable and disorderly conversation pieces; and to increasingly crude attempts to shock
the *bourgeoisie*. BBC apologies followed indecencies, and
grosser indecencies the apologies. The public was left in
doubt whether a recurring nastiness was part of a campaign
of provocation which the Director General welcomed as
socially imperative, or whether it simply revealed a disciplin-
ary incompetence which would have seemed ridiculous to
any previous BBC régime.

The new freedom is a clear gain, but not an end in itself
if it means only that "anything goes". However hardly won
or greatly cherished, it is no more than a condition for the
realization of values, which lie beyond the battlefield itself.
There are programmes that are struggling through into a
new dimension of experience. A society owes its continuity
and stability to well-tried and transmitted values. Broadcasting makes its affirmations of faith through many programmes.
It is easy to forget that the great bulk of those that can be so

accepted to go on asserting a quiet and perennial belief in Mozart and in Shakespeare, in gardening and in discussion, in the humour of Tony Hancock or the nature films of Hans Sielmann.

For most people life is neither an unending quest for unattainable truths, nor a series of discontinuous experiments in living, nor a pursuit of sensation for its own sake. Its conduct rests on the firm possession of a few provisional certainties strong enough to survive a lifetime of hard wear. It is within the framework that they provide, or by contributing to its slow organic growth, that broadcasting pursues the greater part of its task of showing men, in Dr. Johnson's phrase, how best to enjoy life or how best to bear it. When Sir Arthur fforde was Chairman of the BBC Governors he circulated a personal profession of faith in which the final accent fell on the word Joy. He could "find no way of sympathizing with the categorical negative, the total rejection of Joy", and for him the ultimate test was whether a programme said "Yes" or "No" to the question whether human life is to be respected and valued. It is a criterion, so far as I understand it, that would admit *King Lear*, reject *Krapp's Last Tape* after a careful heart-searching, and dismiss *The Man from UNCLE* and *Peyton Place* with contempt. It would welcome every programme that ministered to the satisfactions of understanding and of contemplation; to delight in the created world and delight in creative activity; to the love of man, and, as the Christian must add, to the vision of God. Perhaps in the long run they would prove to be the surest agents of the most radical change.

IV

BROADCASTING AND THE NATIONAL CULTURE

To survive and prosper a community must pass on contin-uously the skills which are the basis of its economic life, the bodies of knowledge which it develops for their own sake or for their practical applications, the codes of behaviour and the attitudes of mind which give it social coherence, the arts that it values, and the faiths by which it lives. The social heritage is in great part created, extended, modified, and kept alive for a society by its saints and scholars, its artists, its scientists, its technologists, and its men of affairs. It is sustained by the daily business of living, by the intercourse of equals, and by the continuing existence of social groups of all kinds from families and cricket clubs to public corporations. It is mediated and diffused throughout the community down to the last degree of dilution by the effort of that larger minority which Coleridge coveniently called the clerisy, and which consists both of those who write and those who interpret— parsons, popularizers, journalists, and broadcasters. It must be consciously extended to wider groups, and passed on to each successive generation, through all those institutions and activities which carry on the business of education in the narrower sense and constitute the national system of education.

Broadcasting serves a threefold purpose: the maintenance, extension, and transmission of a culture. It must concern itself with emergent values, but it must concern itself even more with those transmitted values without which no society can achieve continuity and stability. In the historic societies of the West a man's status, vocational opportunities, and chance to share fully in the national culture have, for all but an able and fortunate few, been based upon the accidents of birth. It has been assumed that fine manners, the fine arts, and finesse in personal relationships were the preserve of a governing class. There could be no other assumption in societies living close to the subsistence level, dependent on slowly changing agricultural routines with no opportunities of social mobility and no margin of leisure for the labouring masses. Society could afford for them no more than Gray's elegiac gesture towards the humble dead: "their lot forbade". It was more comfortable to believe that their lot was the measure of their capacities; tempting even for a Burke to dismiss "the swinish multitude".

We face now a radically different situation. In common with nearly every country in the world Britain is deeply committed by the economic needs of a technological society, and by the popular pressure for social justice, to a vast expansion of education. She must go on pursuing the quest for equality of opportunity, however unattainable its perfect realization may be. In that pursuit we have, since the war, been aiming at the achievement of a state of affairs in which children get the kind of education for which they appear to be fitted and then enter the occupation for which it fits them, irrespective of the income and social background of their parents. In the process we have become increasingly aware that there is at present a great difference between those at the top and those at the bottom of our educational scale in verbal facility, in the capacity to handle ideas and abstractions, and in their mental persistence. These academic activities are characteristic of the boys and girls who reach the grammar school after a selection test at the age of eleven, and are further developed by the kind of education that it provides. Further down the scale people tend to be interested in the written and the spoken word only when it deals in concrete terms with their own immediate concerns, or when it has a strong human or narrative interest.

We have thus been moving towards a new kind of stratified society, in which ability, educational background, tastes, and social habits all run together. For the rising generation the kind of job a man will do, the attitudes he will adopt, the newspapers he will read, the radio and television programmes he will hear and see are determined more by the kind of education to which the state assigns him than by the family into which he is born. The gulf between the boy who leaves school at fifteen and the boy from the same social background who follows a sixth-form course is very wide.

We have been running the risk of creating a socially mobile but deeply divided society. In the nineteenth century the leader of working-class opinion at the shop-floor level was, by and large, a man of ability who believed that his class had not only been denied their economic rights, but had been excluded from their cultural heritage. He and his like formed the backbone of the Victorian Mechanics' Institutes, and of the Workers' Educational Association in its creative years. Their politics might be deeply coloured by class feeling, but they were bridges between their own class and the classes above them because they accepted the same values. They believed, in Ruskin's phrase, that civilization must be built on truth and mercy. They had no doubts about the fundamental character of the love of knowledge, the respect for truth, and the virtues which, even when they are not explicitly Christian, belong to the same stream of Western civilization. Unless we order things otherwise their place may well be taken by men of far less native ability who have totally rejected the "upper class" culture which in their own belief rejected them at "eleven plus"; who have ceased to believe not only in the traditional values, but in any order of values, and who find sufficient justification in the flatteries of the mass media and the daily Press.

The gap between leaders and led is already too wide. We can neither stand still nor maintain the fiction that democracy can safely rest on the untutored unwisdom of the ignorant. Russia has become a managerial society of an authoritarian kind using the mass media as a vehicle for all the devices of propaganda, and subduing the popular arts to the same purposes of indoctrination. The United States is in danger of becoming a managerial society of a free enterprise kind, using the popular arts cynically as an opium of the people. The courses on which they are set are not open to a country that believes in a participating democracy. Our only choice is to renew with the missionary zeal of an Arnold (or at least with the enlightened self-interest of a Robert Lowe who knew that we must educate our masters) the attempt to create and maintain a common culture.

If our industrial society is to go forward with the adaptability and appreciation of economic realities, with the sense of responsibility and the sense of national solidarity that we need for survival; if democratic politics is to be a rational choice between sober alternatives; if the things that unite us are to remain more than the things that divide us, there is no more urgent task ahead than that of bringing the skilled workers of the future into the main stream of our culture, as sharers of a common heritage.

It is not a task that can be left to the schools; and there was a time when both for the schools and for society at large it seemed a hopeless undertaking. Only ten years ago a mistaken psychology was insisting that genetic factors were overwhelmingly dominant in the development of ability; that it was "possible at a very early age to predict with some degree of accuracy the ultimate level of a child's intellectual powers", and that there was within the population only a very limited "pool of ability".[1] We know now that intelligence tests measure powers which are related in the last resort to an innate equipment, but which can reveal themselves and develop freely only in a favouring environment. The extent to which they are evoked and utilized by our society depends on the social and educational opportunities that we provide. It is clear that we are not offering full scope to abilities and aptitudes already developed and potent. It seems certain that the capacities and the sensibilities which our culture values are latent in a far wider section of the population than the pessimists would have had us believe. As a matter of theory, we have hardly begun to appreciate or use the full talents of the great majority of our countrymen. As a matter of fact, the maintenance of standards after each successive educational expansion has always confounded the prophets of "more means worse". The sociologists and the psychologists no longer speak of a "pool of ability", but of a "pool of capability" whose full extent we cannot yet discern.

The sharpest limitations of most men at present are the limitations imposed upon them not by nature but by nurture. The most fundamental revolution of our time is the educational revolution, and it is gathering momentum everywhere.

We should be looking forward now to the problem of a wholly new kind of society; one in which the governing element is a complex of professional groups renewed in each generation to a far greater extent than ever before from the great mass of the people. There is a danger that by the very act of recruitment and by their specialized education they will be divorced from all the habits of thinking and all the cultural values of the homes from which they come and that they will be in a new sense of the phrase "two nations".

[1] *The Spens Report*, 1938, p. 357.

Of course, there will always be differences of function in society. They will be correlated into differences of ability. There will no doubt prove to be wide innate differences between man and man in the capacity for logical and abstract thinking, and differences as great in sensibility and the capacity for responding to the arts, in creative gifts and in human sympathies. Nobody who has seen the art room of a good primary school, or watched the adolescent boys and girls of a Glasgow slum school following *The Caucasian Chalk Circle* on the television screen with close attention and heard them afterwards discussing the nature of justice can doubt that these are potentially universal possessions. They are neither the monopoly of the academically gifted, nor even, it would seem, highly correlated with academic gifts.

In the long run the homes will catch up with the schools. In the meanwhile broadcasting can do far more than any other medium to bridge the gap between them.

It is a situation in which a great part of the interminable debate about culture and its extension begins to look faded or irrelevant. There are exquisitely phrased laments from the older generation of literary men for the irrevocably vanished aristocratic culture which shaped their values; there are intellectual card castles with no sociological foundations; there are the mock heroics of intellectual journalists bent on defending a tower of dubious ivory in the midst of a wilderness of fun-fairs. The aphorisms are elegant or incisive, the sentences well turned and gnomic. In the eyes of George Santayana: "Culture is on the horns of this dilemma; if profound and noble it must remain rare, if common it must become mean." "Is it possible", Rostovtzeff writes, "to extend a higher civilization to the lower classes without debasing its standard and diluting its quality to the vanishing point? Is not every civilization bound to decay so soon as it penetrates the masses?" In their wake comes Mr. Dwight Macdonald, despairing of the state of American society: "Up to about 1750, art and thought were pretty much the province of an educated minority. Now that the masses—that is, everybody—are getting into the act and making the scene, the problem of vulgarization has become acute. I see only two logical solutions (a) an attempt to integrate the masses into high culture; or (b) a contrary attempt to define two cultures, one for the masses and the other for the classes, I am for the latter."[1]

In all these writings, in Mr. Eliot's *Notes Towards a Definition of Culture* from the last generation, or Mr. Dwight Macdonald's as typical of the new, one looks in vain for any appreciation of the nature and trend of the educational revolution, or for a plan of action. In the arid and patronizing pages which Mr. Eliot devotes to education he dismisses as a myth the belief "that a great deal of first-rate ability—not merely ability but genius—is being wasted for lack of education".[2] Genius apart, the evidence is now set out plain for all to read.[3]

Mr. Macdonald is entitled to an abstract and personal preference. He does not explain what the role of the schools would be in his ideal cultural oligarchy. Schoolmasters would, perhaps, disseminate the lower culture while aspiring themselves to the higher.

It is instructive to turn from the Praetorian Guard of high culture to the cultural rulers of the new and profitable empire of low culture, and to see how nearly full circle the wheel has come.

In 1960 the National Union of Teachers called together a full-scale conference on "Popular Culture and Personal Responsibility" designed to bring together representatives

---

[1] DWIGHT MACDONALD, *Against the American Grain*, 1963.
[2] T. S. ELIOT, *Notes Towards a Definition of Culture*, p. 102.
[3] See *Ability and Educational Opportunity*, Ed. A. H. HALSEY, 1961; *Higher Education* (*The Robbins Report*), 1963.

of all those bodies concerned with either the conduct or the impact of the mass media.[1] Mr. Cecil Harmsworth King, the proprietor of the *Daily Mirror*, and Mr. Norman Collins, one of the pillars of a commercial television company, Associated Television, were there. It was a conference of earnest and puzzled people, deeply concerned for children and the future, and unhappy about the quality of popular journalism and of television. Mr. Collins said that he wanted to talk seriously to the teachers present since it was quite obvious from the illiteracy of the letters that his company received "that the educational standard of the country is deplorable". He held teachers responsible, in fact, for the quality of the programmes which Associated Television felt obliged to provide. Mr. King said that the *Daily Mirror* had gladly responded to the improvement of cultural standards brought about by Independent Television but his main contribution to the debate was to express the belief that "it is only the people who conduct newspapers and similar organizations who have any idea quite how indifferent, quite how stupid, quite how uninterested in education of any kind the great bulk of the British public are". These are the men who have the power, and the will, to "define" a "culture for the masses". Their ignorance is even more alarming than the vulgarity with which they choose to speak of people less fortunate than themselves. Mr. Collins could have discovered that there has been a steady and continuous rise in reading and writing ability since the beginning of the century as the school-leaving age has risen. Mr. King could have made himself familiar with the basic work of Dr. Joseph Trenaman on the sociology of the mass media.

Dr. Trenaman did not concern himself with either cultural definitions or hypothetical future states of society, but with

[1] See *Popular Culture and Personal Responsibility*, Ed. B. GROOMBRIDGE, for a report of this conference.

the straightforward facts about popular taste as it now stands. His work was concerned in the first place with attitudes towards the broadly educative element in journals, books, films, and radio and television programmes. It showed that nearly forty-five per cent of the population were, in 1957, "resistant to new ideas and higher values". The newspaper preferred by this group was the *Daily Mirror*. Above that level resistance (or at best indifference) changed to "at least a mild curiosity to know more about the world". The potential audience for the abstract and the intellectually complex was a negligible percentage of any group except the ten per cent of the population with grammar school education to at least School Certificate level, and with professional or administrative occupations; a further twenty-five per cent, consisting of skilled workers drawn from the lower levels of the grammar schools, were prepared, in spite of all their limitations of background and vocabulary, to accept the presentation of serious material in a serious way; and yet another twenty per cent, of modest educational backgrounds but engaged in the main on skilled work, were willing to give their attention to similar material if it was presented in terms that were simple enough, and seemed relevant to their lives. Since then, the balance has been steadily shifting with the steady growth of education.

In 1962 the Audience Research Department of the BBC undertook a study of the public "images" of the BBC and of Independent Television. A large and representative sample of viewers was confronted with a list of forty adjectives and asked to indicate those of them which in their view described what they liked about the BBC and those which described what they disliked. They then carried out the same exercise in relation to ITV. The adjectives most used in the BBC's praise were "educational" (by sixty per cent), "interesting" (by fifty-seven per cent), and "entertaining" (fifty-seven per cent). In the words of the report, " 'educational' and 'cultural' are overwhelmingly qualities which viewers *like*, and these adjectives were applied far more often to BBC TV than to ITV."

The correlation between listening and viewing habits, programme preferences and educational levels is high and abundantly documented. The more educated a man is, the less he tends to listen or view; the more likely he is to be selective, to take an interest in "serious" types of programme, and, significantly, to prefer BBC programmes to those of the commercial companies. The average figure of two hours' viewing a day masks a wide variation in terms of educational levels as well as of age. People in the top educational group view on an average less than one and a half hours a day; people in the bottom group more than two and a half. The wider the educational background, the less the appeal of the "undemanding"—of quizzes, variety, crime, and westerns. To take a single striking instance from the field of radio, a BBC Audience Research analysis of the audience for the stream of "pop" music provided by the pirate radio stations showed that it consisted of some seven million listeners, for most of whom it was an addiction. Half of them were between eleven and twenty years old, and this group included half of the school population. Among the general population only one per cent of those educated to the age of eighteen or over— that is, the grammar school "sixth form" group—proved to be addicts, compared with fifteen per cent of those educated to the age of sixteen plus, and eighty-four per cent of those who had left school at fifteen. There are social as well as aesthetic determinants of the habit of listening to pop music; they operate in a conjunction which is a sharp reminder of our present educational stratification.

There can be as little doubt about the changing composition of our society. The majority of men and women in this country had left school by the time they were fourteen. In twenty years' time there will be nobody under thirty who did not continue his full-time education until at least sixteen; most of the age-group will have had part-time education for at least another two years.

Two-thirds of the boys and girls in the sixth forms of grammar and comprehensive schools already come from homes where both parents had left school by the age of fourteen. By 1980 over 20 per cent of the age-group will be in sixth forms. By that time the proportion of the working population who have completed full-time higher education will have risen from 3·4 per cent in 1960–61 to 6·2 per cent. (It will reach 15 per cent towards the end of the first quarter of the twenty-first century.) There will be few homes untouched even during the coming twenty years by the incidence of a new educational and social mobility. That "respect for learning" which Mr. Eliot appears to hope for as an intellectual touching of the cap by those who have none to their fortunate betters will arise, if it ever arises, from the knowledge that learning is open to all, and that every family may be nurturing a "lad o' pairts".

Broadcasting can serve the educational revolution, or can be a brake on its progress. The main responsibility must rest on the public service organization which used to take pride in the charter description of its status as "the national instrument of broadcasting". The phrase has been dropped; the function remains. It is not compatible with a competitive attempt to defeat the commercial enterprise on its own grounds. If the BBC determines to compete with commercial television for audience on either of its channels (and its intentions must be judged not by its protestations but by its programmes), it must accept those conditions of the contest which its rivals are in a position to dictate. It must deplore the growth of critical and selective viewing, and cherish and foster the addictions of the addicted. It must devote its energies to whipping up a wholly factitious enthusiasm for the professionalized spectator sports. "I can assure you", writes the Head of Sound Broadcasting, Mr. Frank Gillard, "that during these summer months, in homes and offices, schools and factories, on trains and buses, in public and private places, openly or surreptitiously, millions of little transistor sets will be flicked on momentarily, and off again, time after time, just to get the score in the last test match. And because of the possibility the BBC will be putting out ball-by-ball commentaries on each test."[1] It is a dubious contribution to the work of either the factories or the schools. Television has concentrated with even more resolve on horse-racing and on football; the BBC spent fifty programme hours in three weeks on the World Cup. It must deliberately set out early in the evening, when the maximum number of children are viewing, to establish an evening audience held captive by inertia with programmes aimed at a lower level of know-ledge, of sensibility, and of discernment than any school need postulate. It must seek out the writer for the market rather than the writer who must have his say. It must scour America for a counterpart to *Batman*, and decide what formula would provide the right successor to *Compact*.

The BBC could already serve a solid majority of the nation with programmes of character and quality placed at peak hours, moving at a variety of levels yet unsegregated from each other, with large marginal groups of the audience moving happily between one level and another. If it aims consistently at the maximum audience for the whole evening and at beating the rival in a purely statistical sense it must deliberately try to bring within the audience for every pro-gramme Dr. Trenaman's bottom forty-five per cent. It must consciously base its plans and policy for "peak hours" broad-

[1] FRANK GILLARD, *Sound Radio in the Television Age*, BBC Lunch-time Lectures, 1964, p. 8.

casting on the tastes of the group that rejects the *Mail* and the *Express* for the *Mirror* and the *News of the World*, and which determines the general colour of peak-time commercial television programmes. A policy which is content with rather lower but steadily growing figures, and content for them to vary largely provided that they command in the aggregate a large and solid body of supporters need not follow Mr. King and Mr. Collins in lumping the whole working-class together as one great cultural proletariat. The BBC must of course continue to offer its great popular programmes as the staple of its fare; its sport and its variety programmes, its *Z-Cars* and its Dr. Finlay, much more dubiously, its Dr. Kildare. It will look for no rival to *Peyton Place*, and it will credit the plain man who has no elaborate education or high intellectual gifts with the power to enjoy those kinds of entertainment that have some of the depth and quality of life itself, and not the glossy emptiness of the merely commercial product. It can assume that he has a sensible concern for his job, for the world, and for the welfare of his family, and a capacity for developing personal interests whether in racing pigeons, in home decorating, or in union affairs, that calls for both thought and effort. It can remember that he wants light relaxation without throwing the weight of the Corporation behind the other forces which suggest that it must be wholly "undemanding". It can bear in mind that his boys and girls in the single living-room are moving at school towards a freer range of thought, a greater width of opportunity, and a wider range of pleasures than their parents have enjoyed. It can refrain from furthering the process by which mass society takes its colour from those who have least knowledge of the past, least sense of responsibility in the present, and least care for the future. As Sir William Haley[1] once wrote: "It

[1] *Moral Values in Broadcasting*, 1948, p. 11.

is idle to believe that Broadcasting on its own can take a nation far beyond the point that the broad base of its social programme has reached in formal education." It has a duty not to hold a nation back, but to be on the side of the future and the young. "It is essential for the preservation of the culture of a minority that it should continue to be a minority culture", Mr. Eliot says. It is a dogma; unargued and unexplained.

We can set beside it, with good grounds for confidence and with new and powerful instruments to serve our purposes, the nobler dogma, the explicit call to action, and the large hope of Matthew Arnold—

> The men of culture are the true apostles of equality. The great men of culture are those who have had a passion for diffusing, for making prevail, for carrying from one end of society to the other, the best knowledge, the best ideas of the time; who have laboured to direct knowledge of all that was harsh, uncouth, difficult, abstract, professional, exclusive; to humanize it, to make it efficient outside the clique of the cultivated and the learned; yet still remaining the best knowledge and thought of the time, and a true source therefore of sweetness and light.

The central tradition of the BBC has been to make "the best" more widely available to those shut off from it by barriers of education, of background, and of circumstance, and to help them towards another level of knowledge, of discrimination, and of enjoyment. It has seen its aim as the creation of "an informed democracy leading a full and satisfying life". It has never argued that the function of its programmes of entertainment was to reconcile the public to the continued existence of an institution which in other ways serves educational ends. It has insisted that it discharged its educational responsibilities and fulfilled its charter obligations through the whole range of its programmes, and that there was a complex interweaving of the three strands of education, information, and entertainment. All of these aims were restated by the BBC in its evidence to the Pilkington Committee.[1] It was in the light of that restatement that the Committee recommended the grant to the BBC of a second television channel.

The Director General "considered that television would be one of the main factors influencing the values and moral attitudes of our society". He explained that "the Corporation regularly and deliberately put on programmes which would appeal immediately to a comparatively small audience, but tried so to present them as to attract and hold wider audiences which did not at first know that they would be attracted by such programmes". He assured the committee that the BBC held it an important part of its responsibility to "give a lead" to public taste.

The Chairman of the Governors stated that the attitude of a public corporation must in the last resort be paternalistic; the Director General, with a characteristic qualification, said that there was in the policy that he had outlined "a risk of paternalism, but it was a risk of which they were conscious, and which they must accept".[2]

During the period of public debate that preceded the appearance of the Pilkington Report the staff of the BBC grew very familiar with the argument that a modern democratic state has no need for a self-appointed class of Platonic guardians, seeking to impose the restrictive and outworn canons of the upper middle class on a vigorous and healthy popular culture. Who, after all, were they to say what should and should not be enjoyed?

The staff of the BBC are not dictators but middlemen. In

---

[1] *See* the BBC memorandum, *Monopoly and Competition in Broadcasting*, Appendix H, p. 196, for the fullest statement of traditional BBC doctrine; *Pilkington Report*, pp. 37–41. [2] *Pilkington Report*, p. 38.

so far as they serve the central aims of public service broadcasting their business is to provide a platform for the views of
that clerisy of which they are a part. The abdication of a
clerisy so unsure of the value of its own possessions that it
no longer wishes to share them does not usher in the reign of
cultural democracy. It prepares the way for the sales talks
of the tough and the cynical. "Never put on the table of
Demos what you would not put on your own", was one of
Northcliffe's favourite sayings. However little one may like
the fare that he provided, it is the only honest counsel for the
masters and servants of the mass media. Its alternatives are a
barren professionalism or an open cynicism. The belief in
"good television" slides easily into the belief that it is enough
for a programme to be "good of its kind". If its kind is the
patently bad produced with a slick professional competence,
the cultured impresario can always claim that it offers a special
kind of enjoyment to those with the tongue in the cheek,
and choose to forget that it is not so enjoyed by the millions
for whom it is concocted. The step to "good enough for
them" is a very easy one. A clerisy that loses faith in a hierarchy of values is impotent, and those who control the great
modern channels of communication have only one choice.
They must be managers or missionaries. "The mass of a
people", Mr. Henry Fairlie once wrote in a diatribe against
Lord Reith, "must find its culture if it is to be real to them at
all, by following their own tastes and their own pleasures."[1]
Like Mr. Dwight Macdonald, he calls for an abdication by
the schools in the name of a mythical entity.

There may have been times when a healthy popular culture
existed side by side with, yet wholly separate from, an
aristocratic culture; it is not easy to discern them within the
limits of our own social history. There is no such possibility

[1] HENRY FAIRLIE, "The B B C", in *The Establishment*, 1951.

now. In an era of universal education, social mobility, rapid communications, and powerful centralizing agencies the mass of people must have a culture that is one with that of the dominant group or a culture that has been commercially manufactured for them. The "pop" cult is the creation not of folk-culture but of modern publicity methods backed by radio and television. Films are made in Hollywood. To treat "pop" music, and westerns, as the modes of a popular art with its own independent being and critical canons, whether as a highbrow game or in the classroom is to confuse the issues. A good teacher can use a bad western that his pupils have enjoyed as a preface to the discussion of high issues, or can help them towards the enjoyment that comes from knowing a good western from a bad one. If it is indeed a good western, it must take its place not in a limbo of popular art, but within a continuum that also holds *Moby Dick* and *War and Peace*; the Beatles must stand judgement not only with the Rolling Stones, but with Bach and Boulez. The central tradition of our culture insists that there is a hierarchy of works within a *genre*; a hierarchy of *genres* within an art. It is at least a pointer to the place of pop music and westerns in a hierarchy that the taste for them diminishes sharply with every step forward in education.

Paternalism as a word is out of fashion, and even those who believe that the schools must stand *in loco parentis* as transmitters of a heritage would hesitate now to say as bluntly as Dr. Johnson: "To be sure, Sir, the vulgar are the children of the state and must be taught like children." The doctrine that the cultural duties of the state stop short with the provision of facilities for formal education is none the less a doctrine that no government anywhere can yet afford to accept. In this country as elsewhere the state supports libraries and art galleries, theatres and concerts, as well as schools. It tries through what it offers to influence the pattern of cultural demand instead of letting it be determined by the existing distribution of educational privilege. It seeks that all its citizens shall understand the political issues that must be faced at home and in the world at large. During the election campaign of 1966 there were complaints that the "party political" programmes, including the speeches of the party leaders, which were carried on all channels and reached ten million homes, were depriving people of their customary entertainment. A letter to *The Times* claimed for the populace the right to a choice of programmes. It was answered by Dr. Jay Blumler, who is engaged at Leeds University on research into the impact of television on electoral behaviour. He pointed out that a decision to carry these speeches on one channel only would certainly lead to a drastic reduction in the size of the audience. During the 1964 election campaign from one-third to one-half of the audience for "party politicals" were viewers belonging to the "unselective" group. They did not switch off, but would not have switched over. These were the members of the public who learnt most, and whose attitudes underwent most change.

No question of individual liberty is involved; nobody need watch television. It is overwhelmingly the most important channel of information about party plans. It presents both sides of the argument equally, whereas the single newspaper that enters the average home is committed to one side or another. The screen shows the possible Prime Ministers as people with a unique force and clarity, and invites a judgement.

The question is simply whether it is more important that the maximum number of voters should be better equipped to decide the fate of the nation, or whether they should be entertained every evening. It can hardly be answered in the latter way in the name of democracy. Every new lease of democratic government begins with the excitement of an election. It does not end there. Any country with a developed television service can ensure that the great mass of its people understand something of the tasks of government in a complex and dangerous world.

The United States has opted for entertainment. "Surely we shall pay", said Ed Murrow to his American audience, "for using this most powerful instrument of communication to insulate the citizenry from the hard and demanding realities which must be faced if we are to survive. I mean the word—survive—literally."[1] In so far as the state must look for the widest possible diffusion among the adult population of information and education as well as for entertainment, it must concern itself deeply with the output of the broad-casting media. The broadcasting organizations in turn must concern themselves not only with the content and character of all that they broadcast, but with the programme structure and its influence on consumption. The story of sound broad-casting and its vicissitudes displays with exemplary clarity the nature of the problems that both media still have to face.

The basis of programme planning in Lord Reith's time was the juxtaposition of programmes of every kind and every level on the same channel, on the double principle that "it is better to over estimate the public's mentality than to under estimate it", and that this was the most effective way of introducing people to new pleasures and new interests. In music, to take Sir William Haley's example: "The devotees of Irving Berlin were suddenly confronted with Bach." It was a principle that took too little account of socially deter-mined and individual variations in capacity for enjoyment and understanding. "The weakness of the process", as Sir William pointed out, "was that so many intolerances were set up." His own approach was therefore radically different. "It rests",

---

[1] In H. J. SKORNIA, *Television and Society*, p. 228.

he said, "on the conception of the community as a broadly based cultural pyramid slowly aspiring upwards. This pyramid is served by three main programmes (i.e. of sound broadcasting) differentiated but broadly overlapping in levels and interests, each programme leading on to the other, the listener being induced through the years increasingly to discriminate in favour of the things that are more worthwhile. Each programme at any given moment must be ahead of the public, but not so much as to lose their confidence."[1] It is a conception which embodies too optimistic a hope of what broadcasting by itself can accomplish, too little appreciation of the limits set for most people by their education and social background. It was nevertheless defensible as the best approach for radio in our transitional era so long as the broad overlaps were maintained. The Light Programme offered to millions not only light entertainment but its broad human popular services (of which *The Archers* still and perenially survives) its admirable *Woman's Hour*, its programmes designed to help young people towards an active understanding and enjoyment of the world, its popular symphony concerts, its documentaries, its plays of quality, and its programmes of current affairs. The Home Service excluded neither the broadly popular nor the demanding and austere.

The policy was implemented by highly intelligent men of the upper middle classes for whom the idea of public service was a daily reality, but whose own education had followed the usual professional pattern and who were singularly ill-equipped to understand the difficulties of comprehension that face men and women of limited educational backgrounds. It was, for them, a natural assumption that anyone who really cared to know more about the world he lived in was capable of following a straightforward talk on current affairs.

[1] SIR WILLIAM HALEY, *The Responsibilities of Broadcasting*, 1948, p. 11.

They might be aware that there were millions of their fellow citizens by no means incapable of taking a lively interest in events for whom the Third Programme was a remote and unattainable Everest. They found it hard to believe that for many such people the average "documentary" and the average Home Service talk were ranges too high to be lightly attempted or easily scaled, and that their assumptions, their range of allusions, and their vocabulary all made them difficult for those who had left school at fourteen. Programmes of entertainment might well have a breadth of appeal that cut right across social divisions. Serious programmes must, it seemed, be couched in the mode and idiom not of the man in the street, but of the man in the club window. I remember one talk for the millions on Malta which began with these words: "To me, the island was not so much a geographical entity as a Platonic idea. . . ." It is not surprising that the Labour Party, in its memorandum to the Beveridge Committee, asked that "the BBC should now be encouraged to broaden its field of recruitment and bring into broadcasting more and more scriptwriters and producers who have been inside factories, shipyards, coalmines, docks, and transport depots, and know how the people of Britain live, how they talk, and how they behave". The British Council of Churches made the same point. "Much that is broadcast, e.g. in the Light Programme News Bulletins, leaves little or no impression because it is couched in terms which are remote from the needs and interests of the listeners."

Lord Reith had from the start been anxious that the BBC should build up in the public mind a sense of its collective personality.

The characteristic symbols of middle-class dominance were the anonymity of the announcer, with "highly individualized announcing in the American style" specifically rejected; his dinner jacket (invisible though it was to the listeners); and his "Oxford accent". During the war years and after these were one by one abandoned as out of tune with the times. In an increasingly egalitarian society the time had gone when a formal dignity could serve as Bagehot thought that "the dignified parts" of the British Constitution did in Victorian times to "incline the people to look above themselves in education and social rank for the leaders by whom they would be guided".[1] Radio Luxembourg in its "pirate" transmissions and commercial television from its inception were consciously demotic; anxious to meet the man in the street on his own terms, appreciative of his habit of seeing everything in sharply personal terms, aware that a Transatlantic or "Mid-Atlantic" accent was neutral and classless, and intent on an intercourse that could always be easy because it need never be demanding.

It is not surprising that when Dr. Trenaman personally questioned some 1,500 people constituting a wide cross-sample of the population in 1958 he found that a very large number of them were convinced (in a quite friendly way) that the BBC was remote, impersonal, and socially alien. It represented the government, the employers, educated people, privileged people, the Establishment. Its links were naturally with the group of which it was the social and cultural expression. It was their view that the BBC (honestly enough according to its own lights) tried to "put across". Commercial television was simply selling something that people were willing to buy. In its best days, under Kenneth Adam, the Light Programme was breaking the bounds of the formal tradition, and achieving a style and stance that served far wider purposes than that of light entertainment. Its achievement was one of the first casualties of the BBC rivalry with commerce.

Under the impact of external competition from Radio Luxembourg and internal competition from television the

[1] R. H. HUTTON, "Walter Bagehot", in *D.N.B.*, vol. I, p. 866.

sound broadcasting service allowed a new doctrine to gain ground. The missionary function of the Corporation as Lord Reith and Sir William Haley had conceived it was by the new lights out of accord with the temper of the times. To survive, the BBC must accept the pressures of the new egalitarian society as these expressed themselves in audience sizes.

It must recognize the realities of a stratified society by a correspondingly rigid stratification of its programme structure. Above all, the Light Programme must be lightened. The educational obligations of the Corporation could still, on this view, be properly and adequately discharged through a reduced Third Programme, through the use of the same channel (instead of the Home Service) to serve adult education and a miscellaneous group of other specialized interests, through the talks, documentary programmes, music, and drama of the Home Service, and through the continuance of programmes for schools. After all, the "serious" material would still be there for people who wanted it. "It's not the policy of the BBC", said Sir Ian Jacob, in explanation of the new policy, "to force education down people's throats."

The new structure invited listeners to find for themselves on one or other of the three networks the programmes that appealed to them. It is a type of invitation which is realistic enough for the better-educated groups, and wholly unrealistic for the rest. It cuts across the social pressures that made it difficult then for a young national service man or a girl on the production line to confess a preference for the Home Service, and that make it difficult now in some worlds to prefer BBC television. It ignores the family situation which prevents a boy or girl from tuning the radio or the television set in the living-room away from the family programme. It is blind to the fact that selectivity is itself a product of education, and it takes no adequate account of the existence of insurmountable educational barriers. To tell the audience of the

Light Programme that they must look for anything further that they want on the Home Service or the Third Programme is to tell them that if they do not like the fare at Lyons, the Ritz is open to all. They cannot pay the educational price.

Radio has found a new role in the provision of daytime programmes to be heard in daytime circumstances, and evening programmes for minorities who already know what they want. The missionary function has passed to television; a medium intrinsically better equipped to discharge it. The Pilkington Committee rejected the suggestion that the third television channel to be sanctioned in Britain should be devoted to educational or narrowly cultural purposes because it believed that the greatest social need was for the widest possible diffusion of material of quality. It recommended that the BBC should be freed by the grant of a second channel from the tyranny of a situation in which it could not take risks or satisfy minorities without losing a dangerously large number of its supporters to the rival. It accepted and endorsed the Corporation's own view that the possession of two channels would make it possible "to increase the number of serious, cultural and informational programmes, to cater more fully for regional needs, to extend educational broadcasts, and to provide more opportunity for programmes of an experimental nature". It agreed that neither programme should be given a minority character, that each should maintain a balanced proportion of light and serious material, and that each should be so planned that "viewers who did not switch would find themselves exposed at some time of the evening to informational material". "Light entertainment programmes", the Corporation promised, "would be divided more or less equally, but not all would be broadcast at peak-viewing hours."[1]

---

[1] *The Pilkington Report*, pp. 238–9.

The recommendations of the Pilkington Report and their acceptance by the government have held open the possibility that Britain may some day have a television service with a sensitive, comprehensive, and single-minded concern for national needs. They have given to the BBC the opportunity of returning with renewed strength to its central tradition. It is moving, hesitantly at times, in that direction. Minorities are being served. There is a closer relationship with the great professions, with doctors and scientists, builders and engineers, teachers and social workers, and through them with those whom they serve. Programmes of professional refreshment are finding a place in peak hours; the programmes of a University of the Air soon may do. The pitfalls will still be where they always were. It would be just as easy in the new medium as in the old, on two channels as on one, in nominally comprehensive as in separate and segregated services, to accept and foster a polarization of the audience between *Monitor* and *Compact*, lectures on relativity or lessons in Russian and the Black and White Minstrels. The greatest social need is that the middle ground shall be well cultivated, that there shall be no great gap between the programmes for the educated and the cultured and those for the groundlings, assumed for the most part to be capable of nothing but inexplicable dumb shows and noise.

If the BBC is to take up the task it must be with a new concern for the problem of communication across educational, cultural, and social barriers.

V

COMMUNICATION: WORDS AND PICTURES

I

FOR two thousand years it has been the business of the Christian religion to speak to all sorts and conditions of men. In our own time some of the best minds in the Churches have been feeling their way towards an appreciation of the problems of communication in a society stratified like ours. It is not, therefore, surprising that one of the most deeply considered documents laid before the Beveridge Commission came from a small Commission appointed by the British Council of Churches. Concerned that broadcasting should "help perplexed men and women to discern the signs of the times", the Commission recommended "that those responsible for programmes which are broadly educational should examine more closely the meaning and character of education in a period of revolutionary change such as our own in order to discover how the BBC can better help listeners *at various levels* to understand and to respond to the challenge of the times".[1]

General broadcasting is addressed to remote, imperfectly known and often very heterogeneous audiences across barriers presented by differences of age, of education, and of social class, which more often than not divide the broadcasters from those whom they wish to educate, inform, or entertain. The strength of those barriers can, as Dr. Trenaman and Dr. Zweig have both noted, render some social groups almost wholly impervious to new ideas; it can never be ignored.

[1] *The Beveridge Report*, Appendix H, p. 417.

In the course of his study of the skilled worker and his interests, Dr. Zweig gave a very simple "cultural test" (based largely on recognition of the names of the great artists, thinkers, and religious leaders) to a wide sample of men with no more than elementary education. "The tests show", he wrote, ". . . that a man's mind is an extremely selective instrument. If a person is not interested in ideas, or they are beyond his reach, names like Marx, Darwin, Buddha or Rembrandt can be repeated to him a hundred times and they will not penetrate the wall of his indifference. One may argue that television could and should aim at higher cultural standards, but the fact is that programmes which are beyond the reach or interest of certain layers of society cannot penetrate these walls."

Some understanding of the nature of those walls is the necessary prelude to purposive broadcasting if they are at any point to be surmounted.

Broadcasting has at its disposal two languages; the spoken word, reinforced at times by natural or musical sound; and the visual image accompanied by speech or sound.

Words are a slippery and indeterminate means of communication with obvious limitations. Pictures, it is often said, speak a universal language. They do nothing of the sort. Their impact is conditioned as much as that of words, by the capacities of the audience. Unless a programme in either medium is adapted to that capacity it will go unregarded, or will be resisted, or will be distorted and used to reinforce habitual attitudes. It will contribute nothing of value to the lifelong business of learning.

To learn is to revise the stereotypes with which life, art, and the formal business of education have endowed us. It is to modify the complex of assumptions and expectations, concepts and attitudes with which we confront the world; which constrains us unconsciously to hear what we want to hear and see what we want to see, and governs our interpretation of all that we do perceive. The building up of that complex begins with birth, and in most homes viewing begins to make its contribution not much later.

It is possible, at any rate analytically, to distinguish two phases in the learning process. From the moment that a child is born he begins to extend his experience of the world through the senses, and however it may be with fishes and dogs, sight is the dominant sense for men. At the same time he begins to impose order on what would otherwise be no more than the "buzzing, blooming confusion"[1] of sense data, to identify, to place in categories, to discern patterns, to establish relationships, and thereby to evolve from immediate experience a framework of ideas, of schematic representations of the world within which all new experience will acquire its meaning. Each of us continually matches the deliverances of eye and ear against his existing store of patterns to see if they will fit.

The business of all education is to present the learner with new experience in broad accord with such moulds, such schemes as he already possesses, yet demanding that they shall, to however small a degree, be enlarged and modified. If the new demands are too great, if the old vessels cannot stretch far enough to hold the new wine, the response will be bewilderment, boredom, or rejection. An Education Officer of the School Broadcasting Council who had spent the whole of one term in studying the response of unacademic boys and girls of fourteen to a series of plays grew familiar with "the worried look of the child who was trying to grapple with something just beyond his experience and comprehension". Galsworthy's *Strife* was rejected absolutely by the less able. It was too close to their circumstances yet

[1] WILLIAM JAMES, *Principles of Psychology*.

too alien for them to penetrate to its timeless elements; too scrupulous in its distribution of sympathies for their black and white moralities.

The experience of a class of ten-year-old children who watched a programme about fishing on the Grand Banks of Newfoundland was more rewarding. "We had to readjust our ideas about seagoing", said a report from their teacher. "Living inland, our knowledge of nautical matters is mostly derived from tatty old television films. Therefore we expect a storm, and to be shipwrecked; it surprises us to find a captain who is not insane or a dipsomaniac, and a mate who is not in the pay of a rival firm or a foreign power. The absence of the beautiful stowaway puzzled us too."

There can be no doubt about the importance of words in the ordering and organization of our experience. Thinking certainly precedes either talking or the understanding of speech. Babies acquire an awareness of sequences, a sense of how things happen, and a capacity for purposive activity before they acquire the first rudiments of a language. They are as capable of direct insights into patterns of relationships in space as Kohler's apes, when they learnt how to fix one stick into another and reach the bananas outside the cage, but even problem-solving of this visual kind soon comes to be fostered and facilitated by language. A young child uses words to isolate and identify the elements of his experience, to retain and to summon up his memories, to tell himself what to do, to ask himself the necessary questions. The further he needs to move from present experience, the more necessary words become. With the help of the simple mono-syllable "cat" he learns to associate the furry domestic tabby on the rug, the neighbour's Siamese, the coloured image in the rag book and the flickering monochrome image on the television screen. He develops a *schema* into which he fits his widening idea of cats, a preconceived notion of what a

H

cat ought to be, adequate for his purposes at each stage of its development. Signs are the necessary tools of conceptual thinking; for most of us words are by far the most significant signs. The complex of experience that we build up from childhood onwards is organized by concepts embodied in linguistic structures. When the need arises we have words (not mental pictures) at our disposal to deal more or less adequately with the causes of strikes as well as with the nature of cats. The verbal component of all our thinking, which extends even to the simple act of recognition, becomes so habitual that for most of the time it goes unnoticed.

Words are the private instruments with which we build our private worlds. They are the public instruments with which we try to share them.

It is indeed doubtful whether men would ever have developed the power of conceptual thought unless they had been gregarious animals with an urge to communicate. As means of communication, words—the instrument through which sound broadcasting works—are conventional and arbitrary. By and large they bear no resemblance to the things they symbolize. Those onomatopoeic words which do bear such a resemblance are an inconsiderable element in the sum total of language. Words are evocative, not representative. They point to common elements in a common world and display them in new relationships. They owe to their arbitrary character their flexibility and speed, and that freedom from the limitations of the particular which enables them to serve as the vehicle of general ideas. At the same time the fact that they are non-representational circumscribes the area within which they are effective means of communication. It is only possible to communicate in words on the basis of a shared experience as well as a shared language.

For an audience which has not broadly the same experience, the same background, and the same linguistic apparatus as the speaker communication always has its concealed as well as its obvious pitfalls. Plato for that reason held that a philosophic doctrine could only be conveyed in its purity and entirety to a single pupil living intimately with the master. As the audience grew and became more remote, so must the chances of misunderstanding and distortion increase. George Simmel has noted how the rapid and allusive conversation of two people who know each other well will change its character if they are joined by an acquaintance, becoming broader and more general, and, as the circle increases, descending to commonplaces and banalities.[1] General broadcasting is a one-way conversation with strangers.

The difficulties that might arise from simple and superficial differences of vocabulary can often be anticipated, and surmounted by a careful framing of the context, a choice among synonyms, or a parenthetic explanation. The major causes of a failure in communication lie deceptively deeper in those gaps between one man's experience and another's which words can only partially bridge. A careful investigation of the vocabulary of boys and girls in the upper forms of the secondary modern schools of Leeds showed that more than eighty per cent of them were familiar with "plugs" and "wigs", only half of them knew "acorns" and "apricots", a third of them "almanacs" and "alligators", one in ten "amethysts" and one in a hundred "dowagers". Nearly half of the boys, but less than one in ten of the girls could attach some meaning to the word "dynamo"; half of the boys, but three-quarters of the girls to the word "jeans"—a finding that illustrates the problems of establishing a common vocabulary for a mixed audience.[2]

---

[1] Cited by R. B. MEYERSON, "Social Research in Television", in *Mass Culture*, Ed. Rosenberg and White, 1957.

[2] D. G. BURNS, *A Study of Vocabulary Achievement in the English Language in Secondary School Children*, Ph.D. Thesis, Leeds University, 1958.

As for those words which are in some sort the vehicles of ideas, Professor P. E. Vernon, using words drawn from the Forces Educational Broadcasts, of whose intelligibility he made a study, showed that less than half of the naval recruits whom he tested could give the meaning of "automatically", "equivalent", "inevitable" or "analysis"; only one in ten that of "function", "arbitrary", "impartial", or "remuneration".[1]

In each of these lists there are words for which others might have been substituted without prejudice to the meaning; but it is unlikely that many of the Leeds children were familiar with acorns under some other name, and certain that none of the naval recruits who were unfamiliar with the word "function" had arrived through other verbal counters at a concept of function of any wide generality.

In some of the listeners to almost every sound broadcast some of the phrases will strike no responding chord; far more will call up images or concepts less clear, less precise, less comprehensive than for the speaker; some will be imperfectly emancipated from narrow personal associations, some will give rise to the wildest misrepresentations. As the words accumulate and are combined in more and more complex patterns, so do the need for interpretation and the difficulties of interpretation grow.

Even where there is a broad linguistic consonance there remain the interrelated factors of "background" and "interest" —of the bodies of knowledge in the minds of the listeners to which new knowledge must be assimilated and the attitudes which will govern the degree and direction of attention. In a study of *Topic for Tonight*, a series of short talks on current affairs for which the target audience was taken to be a broad middle section of the general population, omitting the top

[1] P. E. VERNON, *An Investigation into the Intelligibility of Educational Broadcasts*, B B C, 1950.

fifteen per cent and the bottom thirty per cent on an occupational or educational scale, W. A. Belson came to the conclusion that it would, for example, be unwise for a speaker on the Argentine to assume that the public knew its language to be Spanish, or for a speaker on Australia to assume that they knew it to be a continent with an almost entirely white population, and that "the ideas and information which were understood were not necessarily those which the speaker had in mind as the most important in his script. The quarter which the average man understands is, as it were, a random collection of the ideas presented to him—a collection in which subsidiary points are, if anything, likely to figure unduly".[1] Random, perhaps, from the point of view of the broadcaster, but determined for each individual by a multiplicity of causes of which no broadcaster could take full account.

The working-class audience has a limited background knowledge, and a sharply limited vocabulary. The researches of Dr. Bernstein into working-class language have shown that there is another and even higher barrier between the middle-class speaker and the working-class audience. The working-class language is indeed a mode of communication with a limited number of words, and a shortage in particular of qualifying words of all sorts, and of those that stand for abstractions. More significantly, the whole structure of language in a "working-class" *milieu* is different from the structure used in more educated circles. Working-class language is atomic, and operates largely through simple concrete statements linked by co-ordinating conjunctions. The syntactic relationship between them is no more than that of sequence. The language of educated people uses the subordinate clause as an instrument for making distinctions, and as the means towards a synthesis. It is more sensitively

[1] W. A. BELSON, "Topic for Tonight. A Study of Comprehensibility", *BBC Quarterly*, Summer, 1952.

equipped to deal with the subtleties and discriminations of personal intercourse, and so far superior to "working-class" language in the handling of ideas and relationships that anyone who has not learnt to use it is debarred from the stricter and more complex modes of conceptual thinking. Linguistic poverty is the worst form of cultural deprivation. The man or woman who has only the impoverished version of a language can neither respond to the subtleties of human speech nor follow an argument where it leads.[1]

A radio programme as we experience it is created by each of us to a far greater extent than we commonly realize out of his own store of memories and concepts and habitual responses. For that reason listening can never be passive. Listening to a radio talk is ideally an unspoken colloquy with the speaker. What he says is translated into thoughts or images related to private experiences and memories. It is accepted or rejected and leads to conclusions of which the premises have been established but forgotten. The art of the speaker lies in keeping the mind alert in the quest for attainable meanings and moving forward towards their completion. Any good radio programme builds up patterns as various and individual as the minds of those who listen, yet so controlled by the pattern of the words that there is a full and valid act of communication.

Listening to a radio play is ideally a production, in J. C. Trewin's phrase, of "the drama of the mind's eye".[2] As the Head of BBC Sound Drama puts it: "All that is needed is for one of the characters to say with conviction that he is looking at a landscape of infinite beauty, and every listener who is concentrating will immediately supply his own idea of such

---

[1] BASIL BERNSTEIN, "Social Class and Linguistic Development", in *Education, Economy and Society*, Ed. A. H. Halsey, J. Floud, and C. A. Anderson, 1961.

[2] J. C. TREWIN, "We'll Hear a Play", *BBC Quarterly*, Summer, 1954.

a landscape. Accordingly, it could be said that radio drama is of all kinds of drama the most visually satisfying. It can paint any picture, however complex, however horrible, however beautiful, however fantastic, and will never fall short of doing so."[1] Radio has often and justly enough been commended for its appeal to the imagination, but most often by those who are most at home with words, and whose minds are richly stored with memories. "Imagination and memory", as Bacon has it, "are but one thing, which for divers considerations hath divers names."

A performance in words and sound alone can do no more than throw old experience into new combinations. It is improbable that the boy in Leeds who in some sort knew the word "dowager" would have been able to conjure up at any verbal cue an image of Dame Edith Evans as Lady Bracknell. The listener who can produce in the theatre of the mind a tolerable version of *Mrs. Dale's Diary* may well fall short when it comes to the *Antigone*. Any one of us may find himself doing little more than put his familiar puppets through new paces against a mental backcloth which is the best that we can do, but which would have been better if it had been designed by Visconti.

There are contexts in which it is vital that the mental image should be controlled and precise; other contexts in which an unfettered liberty of interpretation through a wholly personal imagery can create a greater sense of involvement. When a class of backward eleven-year-old children who have heard a dramatized radio programme about Joan of Arc interpret it through drawings of the market-place at Rouen, dominated like the only market-places they know by the great red facia board of Woolworth's, with the soldiers round the stake dressed like the only soldiers they

[1] MARTIN ESSLIN, *The National Theatre of the Air*, B B C Lunch-time Lectures, 1964, p. 13.

know in khaki and carrying Sten guns, they have clearly been unprepared for an exercise of the historical imagination, but not for a story of heroic courage. Like them, we all take from the radio what we can.

Words are symbolic, pictures are representative. Even in a child's crude hieroglyph there are spatial analogues, spatial resemblances between his boundary line with two little circles inside it and the human face. More sophisticated representations are so like the real thing that it is easy to think of a television programme as "given" in a definitive form to every viewer. Not even our direct visual experience of the external world is so given. W. H. Ittelson puts it: "Perception is never an absolute revelation of 'what is'. Rather, what we see is a prediction—our own personal construction, designed to give us the best possible bet for carrying out our purposes in action." Our purpose in watching a television programme is the discernment of meanings; it calls for an exercise in interpretation as continuous and as demanding as does listening to the radio. To see a picture is to make an unconscious judgement of what, for us, is significantly there to be seen.

The work of the experimental psychologists has confirmed and given a new precision to some older insights. Carlyle knew that "the eye sees only what the eye brings means of seeing". Blake was well aware that "the fool sees not the same tree that the wise man sees". The basic act of interpretation is recognition; the identification by analogy of those pictures of an itemized world which constitute the basic vocabulary of television but which, like words, derive their significance from their context. They are very imperfect pictures, offering a little more guidance than the Rorschach blots in which the psychologist invites us to discern some representative figure, but, like Rorschach blots, patient of imposition of our own meanings.

Recent work on communications theory has shown just how far the "information" on a television screen can be reduced before there is any serious impairment of recognition for a competent viewer. We supply the deficiencies of the symbols with which we are presented by assimilating them to *schemata* of our own which have been developed with the aid of contributions from all our senses. We always elaborate and often distort the message as we decode it, and confidently accept an unstable two-dimensional pattern in monochrome framed on a screen of an invariable size as a "window on the world". We forget about the conventions that serve us as canons of interpretation, and the artificialities that have come to be taken as appropriate and normal. African viewers may have so little experience of television, and an experience of life so different from our own, that they are unable, as one careful observer has said, to recognize "a compass or a bus, a rose or a shop window, a tennis racket or a horse".[1] An English film or television programme presents them with a series of puzzles, made still more baffling by shifts of scale that make mosquitoes look as big as bats, by music with no apparent source except the image of the moment, and by the bewildering pace and discontinuity of the succession of shapes before them. Perception is never instantaneous. If they do succeed in isolating the image of a rose from the flux and identifying it as a flower, it must be by analogy not so much with other flowers as with other pictures of flowers; they will still be unaware (in so far as they must rely on the visual impact of the programme) of its colour, its fragrance, and its texture. Their difficulties differ from ours in degree, but not in kind.

The interpretation of still and moving pictures is a skill that must be learnt. In our society (though not in Africa) it is

[1] H. F. KYNASTON-SNELL, "Seeing is Believing", *Times Educational Supplement*, 10th September, 1965.

commonly learnt in early childhood, and rarely thereafter calls for conscious effort. The flickering shadows of the television screen must nevertheless be interpreted in the light of an existing knowledge of the visual world. They impose no single image on their viewers. The relationship that they bear to reality is, however, much more direct than that of words. They are so easily interpreted in their visual aspects by analogy with previous experience that what they show is accepted as a direct transcript of reality, a straightforward extension of experience. Television does indeed offer an incomparable new range of encounters with nature and with man. It brings with it no automatic enhancement of the power to grasp and understand relationships.

As the complexity of the presentation increases, so does the need for interpretation. A village audience in the Congo is ill-equipped to identify a rose; still worse equipped to follow on the television screen the course of the World Skating Championships. Very few of us are capable of identifying on sight the artefacts of another culture, or interpreting its rituals, and, indeed, only the champion skaters among us are likely to "see" the fine points of a sport which belongs to our own. The recognition of familiar objects and the understanding of familiar actions call for no help from words; a narrative sequence of easily identifiable images can evoke a mood. Outside these limits, to discern links between pictures and to read into them a total significance is to bring to bear on them a more or less sophisticated conceptual equipment operating in verbal terms.

Except in so far as there is an art of moving shapes with neither representative character nor logical interconnexion television programmes depend on words to give them meaning and significance.

With the visual aspect of programme-making uppermost in his mind, the television producer is always tempted to

believe that he has been thinking in pictures which individually carry their self-evident meanings, and that a carefully
ordered visual sequence can by itself communicate a train of
thought. It can effectively do so only to those viewers who
are capable of supplying their own unconscious, unspoken,
yet ultimately verbal commentary. Confronted with a picture
of a face or a device that we cannot at first recognize, we
search for a word which will help us to focus our memories
on the image before us and give it meaning. Shown how to
cook an omelet or cast a fly we most of us master and memorize
the action by translating it into a set of verbal instructions:
they serve us better than our visual recollections when we
come to try our own hand. Grappling with a complex series
of pictures we consciously or unconsciously use what verbal
imagery we have at command to guide us towards what is, for
us, the best attainable meaning—"our own personal construction". There has gone to the making of almost every television
programme a conceptual framework, and a verbal substructure
whether it has been made explicit or not. Our thinking is
shot through and through with verbal elements. The more
closely it is controlled by the words of a programme, the more
complete the process of communication is likely to be.

The producer must so devise and order his images that the
attention is visually undistracted and directed towards
essentials. He must be careful that they are in keeping, that
none of them are likely to have associations that will sidetrack
the viewer or a power that will give them undue prominence.
When all these things are done he must decide what for that
specific audience can be left unspoken, and what remains to
be done with words.

The words must govern the direction of attention; they
must point out causes and effects and relations and inter-
connexions, not only between the constituent elements of
the programme, but between these and the viewers' own

experience; they must range from the image on the screen to the images in the viewers' memories. Above all, they must transport the audience from the realm of images to the realm of concepts.

So long as the commentary deals with appearances it has the freedom of a wider vocabulary than a sound broadcast, since the meaning of new words is given by the image on the screen. As soon as it moves away from appearances, however, the television programme faces its central problem. The only image on the screen that is generally appropriate to the process of allusion or abstraction is that of the speaker himself—any other would inhibit the free flow of their own imagery through the minds of the viewers, and tie down the discourse to the individual, the particular and the limited. The television encounter with a man or woman of distinction is fuller and richer in its impact than an encounter through sound alone. Attention to what a man is may still be a distraction from what he is saying.

II

Radio can offer the listener fresh insights into the world that he already in some sort knows. With its power to set the mind questing for the right image, the appropriate memory, the faithful response, it can order and give a new significance to experience. It can concentrate attention on speech itself, on the precisions and ambiguities of words, and the subtlety of their rhythms; it was the perfect vehicle for the Welsh lyricism of Dylan Thomas, the mannered rhetoric of Max Beerbohm, and the splendid comic fantasy of *ITMA*. It can handle ideas and controversy with a range, depth, and freedom that the loosely scripted and image-ridden television programme rarely achieves. It can serve the competent listener as an incomparably rapid and efficient vehicle of information. There was a time when all the powers of radio were deployed for a mass audience, when Wilfrid Pickles and his quiz, *Have a Go*, had a following of twenty million people, and when *Saturday Night Theatre* commanded an audience of ten million, and a series of talks on atomic power ran for eight successive evenings without falling below the seven million mark. Nevertheless, only a handful of speakers ever fully mastered the art of addressing the unseen mass audience. Those who did were men who by artifice or by intuitive adaptations could present through speech alone a simplified, friendly and universally acceptable self, and who moved with authority in the common highways of experience. Mr. Middleton, as friend and mentor, shared with his audience the simple pleasures of the garden. John Hilton became the wise household counsellor, knowing about money and its ways. Dick Sheppard of St. Martin's handled the great commonplaces with what Lord Reith described as a "subtle mastery of humour, and sharp visual imagery and sincerity".[1] J. B. Priestley embodied the dogged resolve and common sense of a nation at war. Churchill lifted it to share his own sense of destiny. Perhaps none of them achieved more success in the sheer art of communication than that great musical popularizer Sir Walford Davies; he had no need to rely on words alone. Once television came there was never any prospect that radio could sustain a mass audience for the spoken word. As Wordsworth knew, the eye is at all times "the most despotic of the bodily senses", and can, especially in childhood, claim "absolute dominion". A listener who loses the thread stops listening; the mere succession of arbitrary sounds has no power to hold him. A succession of moving images has in itself a compelling power. Even for

---

[1] BRIGGS, *The Birth of Broadcasting*, vol. II, p. 228.

the viewer who no longer has any firm grasp of the relationship between them there remain the simple pleasures of recognition, of expectation, of variety, of fragmentary and episodic glimpses of "meaning". So long as he persists it still holds on offer what it has to give—or what he can impose upon it.

In a letter to Sir Harry Pilkington, Sir Kenneth Clark, the first Chairman of the Independent Television Authority, says of television that "there are very few things that it can do well, and those few are rapidly becoming exhausted".[1] It is the comment of a man concerned with the deepening of what is already a wide and varied experience, and who has never had occasion to think how narrow the experience of other people can be.

Most people have little knowledge of the world. Television can familiarize them with the daily lives of men and women in distant continents whose destinies are nevertheless linked with theirs. It can bring release from the bonds of the familiar, and a great widening of sympathies. In every social group travel films are more popular than crime stories. Most people have little opportunity of coming face to face with Harold Wilson or Jomo Kenyatta, with Henry Moore or Francis Chichester, with more ordinary people in all their infinite diversity. Most people have not the mental resources to produce Shakespeare or Shaw in the theatre of the mind. Most people accept and understand life most readily in personal and concrete terms. Many are not interested in ideas or general problems or objective solutions, but in personal relations. Their thinking must be firmly based on individual instances. They live by analogy and intuition, feeling their way from one situation to another, rather than by generalizing or abstraction. Television can show life as a network of

---

[1] *Pilkington Report*, Appendix E, p. 1113.

relationships embodied in actions and people, with something of the warmth of life itself, yet displayed in bold, clear, patterns.

In theory a broadcasting organization like the BBC with both radio and television at its disposal would use each of them to serve those purposes to which it was best adapted. Since the cost of television is from five to eight times as great as that of radio, it would always consider whether the margin of advantage which the visual medium possessed in any instance justified the use of the dearer medium. In practice, considerations of this kind are significant only in relation to institutional audiences and minorities with strong existing interests. Perhaps "a natural division of labour between the media will eventually correspond to a conscious choice between them" and "a really sophisticated audience will make sophisticated choices".[1] In the meanwhile the big audiences are creatures of habit.

So far as the general audience is concerned freedom of manœuvre is sharply limited by listening and viewing habits so strongly established that changes in the pattern of what is offered can do little to modify them. There are still some four million people without access in their own houses to television receivers. They form a large part of the evening audience. They are a group in which old people and others in the lowest income groups are heavily represented. It also includes a residual resistance group of highly educated men and women, but is so nearly a true cross-section of the community that the BBC must still provide a comprehensive radio service. For them, it must offer a duplicate coverage even of those occasions of pageantry which lend themselves best of all to television.

The great majority of people with access to both media

---

[1] MARTIN ESSLIN, op. cit., p. 15.

use radio in the daytime and television in the evening. Half of them never listen at all in the evening. The other half listen selectively, forsaking television only for a favourite comedian, a brass band or a string quartet, a play or a lesson in Russian. Twenty-five million people listen to radio in the course of each twenty-four hours. The really big audiences are all daytime audiences, consisting of men and women who are doing something else at the same time, shaving or eating breakfast as they listen to the morning news, cooking or driving a car as they "eavesdrop" on school programmes. For some of them it is the merest background listening— musical wallpaper as the phrase goes. The local radio station in Australia or the United States often offers little more than a stream of "pop" music punctuated by time checks. We are facing a demand for the same provision. For others it can be deeply attentive listening. Radio allows for routine activities without any loss of concentration. Almost half the women who listen in the evening choose at times to knit or sew, yet prove to have as firm a grasp of what they have heard as the rest. For listeners who cannot choose the time when they begin or end their listening or guarantee freedom from interruption, a magazine programme with its structureless succession of items has clear advantages. It is a form that can hold the wide-ranging topics and pointed comments on the passing world of *Any Questions*, the intent and searching concern for the matter in hand of *Country Questions* and *Gardener's Question Time*, the variety and wide human interest of the breakfast-time magazine, *Today*, and of *Woman's Hour*.

In its other function as a way to meet the needs of minorities who already know what they want, radio is so comparatively cheap that it can offer an incomparable range and variety. At present the BBC offers 374 hours of radio a week. The choice of music is immense and all-embracing. For the selective the spoken word offers an infinite variety, including the whole spectrum of the world's drama. The evening audiences are rarely much more than a million strong. The characteristic audience for talks, of fifty to a hundred thousand, is a very small number compared with any evening television audiences. Sixty thousand listeners to a course of *Beginners' Russian* is nevertheless a large proportion of all those who wish to learn Russian, to hear in sequence the late quartets of Beethoven, or to follow the debate on the relation between law and morality.

The Home Service caters for the residual listener, the Light Programme for background listening. The Third Network with its daytime Music Programme, its early evening Study Session, and, most characteristically of all, its Third Programme, displays most clearly how radio can serve minorities, and what minorities it can still serve.

Because the Third Programme moves within a restricted range, it faces the problems of communication only in its own modified way. There is clearly a class of programmes which would compromise their whole integrity and quality if they were adjusted to any supposed needs but those of the *alter ego* who is the creative writer's ideal audience and most demanding critic. A poem must be what it is—or rather what the spoken medium will allow it to be—and as Miss Gertrude Stein observed, the way to say it is to say it.

There is a further class that is addressed not to an ideal but to a postulated audience, assumed to be receptive towards programmes of a particular kind. The Third Programme has from its earliest days set itself the task of catering, not, as is sometimes thought, for the specialist or for the speaker's peer group, but, as its present Controller puts it "for the layman, for the same kind of people who read the more serious daily or Sunday newspapers, who read *Encounter*, *The London Magazine*, *Twentieth Century*, who read the literary and political weeklies, the people who go to concerts, the theatre and the cinema, and more particularly those people who would go to concerts or to the theatre if only they lived near enough and could afford it".[1] Its planners and producers concern themselves strictly with the needs, interests, and capacities of the target audience, and with clear and effective communication to them in terms of the spoken word. The "good prospects" for the Third Programme (to adopt the terminology of an Audience Research inquiry) constitute a minority amounting to no more than two per cent of the population. While they are much more heavily represented in Third Programme audiences than in the general population, the great majority of Third Programme listeners are men and women with a more modest educational and cultural background who have, nevertheless, been attracted to some item. The greater part of the audiences consists in a sense of eavesdroppers; if the programmes were deliberately adjusted to their powers of comprehension there would, nevertheless, be a loss for them as well as for the target audience. The creative writer thus knows what kind of work to offer to the "Third". The speaker who is concerned to persuade or to inform knows what company he keeps from the list of contributors, and has a type-figure in mind to whom he is speaking, and whose features can at least be more distinctly discerned than those of the typical listener or viewer in other contexts.

Most programmes of persuasion, of information, and of informal instruction are, however, planned and produced on the assumption that there is a broad cross-section of the public which has an existing or potential interest in some topic, which is already "in the market" or which can be brought within it for some kind of programme. They are intended to serve a majority of the actual audience (so far as it can be

[1] P. H. NEWBY, *The Third Programme*, p. 6.

gauged in advance) which will choose to listen or to view on the strength of a descriptive billing. Audiences of this kind may well consist so largely of listeners and viewers of a particular sex, age, educational background, or social grouping that they have a special claim to consideration, but no speaker can know the whole audience. A large mixed audience always poses the problem of communication across barriers.

There is a radical difference between the approach to such an audience with the intention of discovering common ground and establishing a basis for communication and the creation of a mass audience by deliberate calculation.

III

In the very early days of broadcasting Lord Reith drew a distinction between programmes that contributed to education as "a systematic and sustained endeavour to re-create, to build up knowledge, experience, and character", and those that carried out "the great educative work" of making life "more interesting and enjoyable than it otherwise would be". As a reaction against the crude opposition of entertainment and education which he deplored the distinction has too often been blurred. It is of cardinal importance for the future of broadcasting that the differences between two provinces as distinct as North and South America (in spite of the isthmus of Panama) should be clearly recognized. There is one sense in which one learns by leaning over bridges and watching the water flow, by falling in love, listening to Beethoven, and watching the news; a diffuse process like the growth of a coral reef on which each hardly perceptible deposit leaves where it can a trace that will be reinforced by later deposits so that the whole reef grows in conformity with its under-lying structure. There is another sense, in which learning implies purpose and constructive effort. There may be a customary looseness about the common uses of the words "learning" and "education"—there is far less about the word "teaching". Educational broadcasting implies a relationship between teachers and learners in raising a new building on known foundations.

Like other forms of educational communication, educational broadcasts are addressed to defined audiences and have specific ends in view. They are designed for use by institutions forming part of the national system of education, or, if they are addressed to a home audience, are planned—as the official British definition of programmes of adult education has it—"to help towards a progressive mastery of some skill or body of knowledge". A defined audience need not be a narrow one, and the definition of his target as "all mothers of young children" imposes just as strict conditions on a producer as the definition "first year undergraduates reading mathematics at the University of Hull", but the closer the definition and the narrower the focus the more effective the programmes are likely to be. It must be an audience whose common characteristics are known to the producer by direct acquaintance with an adequate sample, or by a full descriptive account, and there must be arrangements for a continuing "feedback" from it which will enable him to adjust the programmes to its needs. But beyond this it must be an adequately motivated audience, which has made a voluntary or constrained submission to the disciplines of learning, which is prepared to follow a series of programmes regularly, is equipped with any necessary handbooks and is willing to make a conscious effort which may extend well beyond the experience of listening or viewing. The audience must in all these ways be committed to the task of learning.

The first concern of committed audiences (bearing in mind that groups of young children or less able students may not be in the sense "committed") is that they should be making satisfactory progress. For them the most important inherent characteristics of the programmes are those that should be common to all modes of teaching; accuracy of focus in terms of audience level; clarity; cogency; firmness of structure; a just judgement of pace and relevant illustration. Their continuity of attention will derive from these, and from the increasing command of the subject that they give rather than from any additional attractions that the programmes may possess. It has, for example, been experimentally shown that neither colour nor professional polish in the photography makes any contribution to the learning process in adequately motivated groups unless they are necessary and integral to the presentation of a subject (as both might be in the recognition of stained bacteria). The more intent an audience is on learning and on the matter in hand, the less tolerant it is of digression and of adventitious material; the more willing it is to accept illustration that is no more than sufficient for the purpose; words without pictures when words are capable of evoking an adequate mental image; abstractions where abstractions are required, and consequent passages of "talking face".

The approach to an uncommitted audience consisting of all those members of the general public with a sufficient common interest in some subject to embark on a programme or series of programmes, but among whom neither regular listening and viewing, nor ancillary reading nor any deliberate attempt to learn can be assumed is necessarily of a very different kind. Programmes designed for that large sector of the general public which Dr. Trenaman found to be "in the market" for broadly educative programmes must be addressed to everyone who has been attracted by the billing in the hope that the attention of the great majority of them will be held. They cannot hope to evoke the same degree of comprehension in every listener or viewer, but must carry as many as possible over passages that might otherwise be tedious for them; they must arouse and not assume a high degree of interest; and for these ends must use variety of presentation, visual and aural devices for arresting the attention, strikingly unusual or strikingly familiar illustrations, and on occasion a degree of bold simplification which would be unacceptable in the context of the Third Programme or of broadcasts contributing to higher education.

Educational broadcasting contributes to a planned and systematic progress. For the home student its contribution may be central and basic; for the institutional student it may be marginal and ancillary, contributing as the broadcasting medium best can to a larger process. A school may wish to expose its pupils to experiences that in another context would be broadly "educative"—to a performance of *King Lear*, to a hearing of the Fifth Symphony, or to a film of travel— but which find their place in the total development of the children under its care. But in so far as educational programmes are designed to convey an ordered body of knowledge, or to teach a skill, or to further an intellectual mastery of some academic discipline, their impact can theoretically be assessed in the same way as other modes of teaching are assessed. The medium may be the message in other fields, but for a man who wishes to master Hooke's law or spot-welding, the medium has significance in so far as it may or may not be a more efficient means to an end, and over a wide field there is little to choose between one medium of instruction and another. The operational result is what matters. A test of recall, a problem to solve, or a practical examination will be a valid index to the effectiveness of the broadcast operation. The common element in the contribution which it has made to each member of the audience is its most significant element —a purposive addition to a known and common possession.

The application of recall tests, which may superficially seem to be relevant to the assessment of an informative programme addressed to a general and uncommitted audience, is a tricky and largely misleading procedure. A general audience approaches a talk on the Common Market or a documentary film about Eskimoes on television with a set of mind entirely different from that of an audience with a specific academic or vocational end in view, and with the expectation of a particular kind of pleasure rather than with the intention of adding to an existing body of knowledge or starting a new structure. A "recall" test which may be wholly appropriate for a student audience will often shift the emphasis from what a programme can most valuably give to the general listener and the general viewer. An unguarded assumption that the ability of an audience to recall a high proportion of the "main points" of a programme is an index to its success can well lead to the conclusion that the perfect programme should be not more than two minutes long, and should tell its audience only what they already know.

The aesthetic and emotional impact of a programme and the swirl of mental energy that it sets up will generally be of far more importance than the deposit of hard information that it may finally leave in the mind. An educated man no doubt has a body of systematically arranged factual knowledge at his command, but he is also a man who moves freely among a certain order of ideas, who is sensitive to the impact of other minds and personalities, and whose convictions have been reached by processes of rational persuasion. Professor Namier once drew a nice boundary line between knowledge and insight. "The crowning achievement of historical study", he said, "is an historical sense—an intuitive understanding of how things do not happen. How they did happen is a matter of specific knowledge."

An "educative" programme may leave with some of its

audience as a more or less permanent legacy a substantial body of ordered information; it will much more certainly leave traces below the threshold of recall, yet capable of being revivified and reinforced by later impressions. Its more significant result may well be a quickening of the intellectual pulses, a broadening of sympathies, and a sharpening of intuitions which lie wholly outside the range of any formal process of testing. An inquiry into the impact of a series of talks on the new astronomy by Professor Fred Hoyle showed that those who had followed them with the greatest excitement scored least on a test of comprehension as measured by recall, and there is nothing mysterious about the fact that test scores may be inversely related to expressed interest. The most interesting of programmes may well be that which best conveys the excitement of roving into worlds half-realized, the thrill that the young R. G. Collingwood experienced when he found himself at the age of eight reading Kant with a blend of utter bewilderment and a sense "that things of the highest importance were being said about matters of the utmost urgency; things which at all costs I must understand". The opening up of new horizons is a task that broadcasting is uniquely equipped to carry out. It allows of no easy assessment. In relation to a general audience the best and most comprehensive index to the effectiveness of a communication is not "recall", but the interest that it has aroused, and a major part of the study of the process of communication must be a study of those ways of arousing and maintaining interest (for an audience of a given educational background) that are integral to the presentation of the matter in hand.

VI

BROADCASTING AS AN EDUCATIVE FORCE

I

PUBLIC service broadcasting should, like the Third Programme, have a special concern for "intelligent, eager, responsive people—curious about the world they live in". Not all of them are potential Third Programme listeners; cultured by background and habit, or aspirants to the traditional culture with its emphasis on music, on literature, and on the adventures of the mind. Only a growing minority have yet had the opportunity of developing "the appetite for such things, and the kind of background of knowledge that this appetite creates".[1] Over against the ideal Third Programme listener stands another archetype: Ferdynand Zweig's skilled worker in an affluent society seven years later, as he appears in a recent survey of his interests and way of life undertaken by the Education Officers of the BBC.

The rumbustious, hard-drinking, cloth-capped British workman—the Andy Capp of the cartoonist—has suffered a further decline. He is ageing, obsolescent, already in many areas a myth. His place has been taken by a younger man with the confidence that goes with full employment and money to spend and the awareness that his generation enjoys a new range of opportunities. The interests of the new skilled worker are centred overwhelmingly on his family, his home, and

[1] P. H. NEWBY, *The Third Programme*, p. 5.

his garden. He is an enthusiast for "do-it-yourself" home decorating; perhaps for woodwork. He owns, or hopes to own, a car. He will certainly take the family away for a holiday, and this year it may be the Costa Brava instead of Wales. Life is very busy, but he may still find time for a hobby; photography, pet or animal breeding, or sport. He is keen on his job, wants to get on, and may even be putting in time at the local technical college, but he has no desire to master any body of knowledge for its own sake. His tastes are not at all academic; nor has he any desire to be in the cultural swim with the readers of the Sunday papers. His own paper is the *Mail*, or the *Express*, or the *Sun*, and he takes a reasonable interest in the news, but his strongest interests by far are those that arise from practical needs and the daily business of living. He is not concerned with psychology in the abstract, but he does want to arrive at a better understanding of his three-year-old daughter or his difficult adolescent son. He is no economist, but would like to know the ABC of investment, and how a pay freeze will affect his long-term prospects. His wife, with new curtains to choose, has been taking a lively interest in design and colour; her cooking and dressmaking are becoming more adventurous. They would both like to know what to look out for in Wales—or in Spain; perhaps to have a shot at a little simple spoken Spanish.

It is for them that the BBC and the programme companies have in recent years been developing a new range of television programmes. These lie within the official British definition of programmes of adult education and rank for additional broadcasting time in so far as they are planned in series, loosely progressive, and sometimes supported by booklets, but since they impose no discipline of response they should rather be thought of as the most systematic part of the "educative" output. With a late-night timing they reach audiences of half a million upwards, who accept and welcome them as part of the general provision; on a segregated "educational" channel (judged by the experience of sound radio, when it was still a mass medium) they might reach no more than a tenth of that number. They offer help towards a mastery of car driving and car maintenance; of gardening, or cookery or flower arrangement; towards an understanding of the intricacies of house purchase or the adjustments called for by retirement; above all, towards a deeper knowledge of children and their needs, and of what the schools are trying to do.

There should be no sharp boundary between programmes like these and programmes designed to open up new horizons. Flower arrangement may be a minor art; it is still an art. The law of house purchase is part of the great social structure of the law. The study of children is part of the wider study of human nature. Science in the garden is still science.

For the middle-class audience radio offers a magnificent range of opportunities to cultivate the major arts and keep abreast of the pure as well as the applied aspects of science. The viewer who has not wholly forgotten his "O-level" grammar school science can pick up the threads again with a television series on gravitation or on human physiology. He can follow a feature programme about atomic power, or a new way of transplanting living tissue.

The challenge that still goes unanswered is the challenge to bridge the gap between those who were given the right kind of apparatus for understanding the modern world and those who were not. It is widest of all in the field of science. Even in the least developed parts of the world the level of man's well-being is increasingly determined by the results of applied science. The fabric of our daily lives must increasingly be sustained not only by highly trained scientists but by a host of technicians and craftsmen with some understanding of elementary scientific principles. Those same principles lie at the base of the whole structure of scientific thought. Television can start with people's everyday interests and arrive with them at a better understanding of the ways of thinking that have shaped our present civilization, and of the great unifying ideas which have given a new order and cohesion to man's experience. It will not reach that destination (valuable though medical programmes may be as a mode of reassurance) through its present obsession with hospitals, or through programmes that too often seem designed to dazzle rather than to enlighten. It will need to approach the task through a patient study of the audience, and with a new simplicity.

For the present the field in which radio and television are making by far their most significant "educative" contribution is the field of politics. The Third Programme listener and the skilled worker are alike voters; both of them, perhaps, politically active.

Political broadcasting reaches everybody. As in the ideal city state, the political leaders of the nation can now address the whole community. The coming of television has ensured that their address will be made in sharply personal terms. When there is an urgent need for national unity under a great leader this new power is of obvious value. In quieter times there may be a balance of gain and loss. A skilful exploitation of the image of authority may give an undue advantage to the man in power. A General de Gaulle can offer himself with masterly dignity and presence as a national figure; a politician above politics. An excessive concern with the electoral repercussions of personal statements of policy to a mass audience may inhibit lesser men from the shaping of bold policies. The emphasis of politics may shift away from resolute leadership towards exercises in the science of political market research as a prelude to the art of salesmanship. The dramatic contest between the rivals for power may divert attention from what they stand for. There can, nevertheless, be no doubt that the British people are, through television, better informed about political issues than they have ever been before, and therefore better equipped to vote on them.

The study of electoral behaviour during the 1958 election which Dr. Joseph Trenaman and Denis McQuail published in 1958 under the title *Television and the Political Image* has been supplemented now by the as yet unpublished survey of two Leeds constituencies during the 1964 election by Dr. Jay Blumler; the findings are wholly consistent. Commentators have too often seized on the fact that neither television nor indeed the political campaign as a whole appears to have been more than a marginal and insignificant factor in determining the considerable changes of political allegiance that took place (though in 1964 there does appear to have been a relationship between the impact made by the television programmes of the Liberal Party on the floating voter and its gain of votes).

As Trenaman and McQuail point out[1] political attitudes are determined over a long period by a multiplicity of social and personal factors. They are, for most people, sufficiently stable to resist an intensive campaign of propaganda, and are as unlikely as any other deep-seated attitudes to be immediately affected by a marginal, or even by a large, increment of knowledge. The fact remains that "there was a significant increase in political knowledge during the campaign and, as far as comparisons could be made, these increases were consistent with the emphasis placed by the parties on different aspects of their policy. It seems, as previous studies have shown, that the attempt to convey information does not meet with the same resistances as does the attempt to persuade,

[1] J. TRENAMAN and D. McQUAIL, *Television and the Political Image*, 1961, pp. 233–4 and *passim*.

but that material designed primarily to influence opinion may also increase knowledge. . . . Of all the sources of political persuasion, only television is found to add significantly to viewers' knowledge." Women learnt more than men, the dubious and uncertain more than the committed party supporters; for the overwhelming majority of people television was the only way in which they were made aware of the views of both parties, and not simply of their own.

The most general finding of all is of good omen for the whole future of democracy. "Lastly, there is fairly strong ground for believing that changes of political attitude are the result of independent, personal judgements acting upon information partly taken in from the campaign. These decisions rest upon assessments of a general nature concerning the case put forward by the parties, rather than upon acceptance of any particular programme or policy advanced. The elector is looking for a coherent and convincing policy for government."

The "party political" broadcasts of an election year must clearly continue to be the responsibility of the parties. The BBC as the proprietor of a well-managed forum may try to persuade them that "confrontations" are a more effective stimulus to democratic choice than exhortations. The tension between the Corporation and the Prime Minister during the 1966 campaign and the admission of the Postmaster General that the possibility of some sort of Council with the function of supervising political broadcasting was being investigated are warnings that there is little room for manœuvre when party feelings run high. The findings of Trenaman and McQuail throw the emphasis heavily back on to the long quiet periods when public opinion is being gradually moulded. It is then that the broadcasting organizations must exercise their own trusteeship most boldly. It is doubtful whether they can ever attain a perfect neutrality. *The*

Economist, making an editorial plea for a liberal-radical policy
which would commend itself to the progressive elements of
both parties, considered that "although the broadcasting
authorities are not supposed to propagate an editorial view,
they quite plainly do so, and in this direction".[1] However
that may be, they plainly have a duty to subject to criticism
and scrutiny the plans and policies of whatever party may
hold power, and to ensure that every issue of public concern
is fully canvassed whether the government so wishes or not.
"All governments tend to believe the BBC is against them",
as a leader in *The Times* put it,[2] and so, within limits, they
should be made to feel. They are a fair target for criticism,
and Mr. Wedgwood Benn as the spokesman of a government at odds with the BBC held it right to speak of "a proper
tension between those responsible for the conduct of affairs
and those commenting". They can properly be called to give
an account of their stewardship at times and in ways that
they would not necessarily have chosen—and can as properly
refuse if they wish. One of the most accomplished masters of
the television interview, Mr. Robin Day, has justly written
of "the value of sustained questioning in a more coherent
sequence than occurs in Parliament", and of the need to
"provide from time to time a topical platform for inquiry
on some urgent issue which Parliament cannot or does not
discuss".[3] An interview so conceived can become a part of
the democratic process. It may offer a temptation to play for
drama. It offers far less temptations than the hustings once
did to those politicians whose instinct tells them, in the words
of the political agent who once explained the art of electioneer-
ing to Mr. Douglas Woodruff, that the audience does not
want to hear their arguments, but to hear them saying that

[1] *The Economist,* 22nd May, 1965.
[2] *The Times,* 14th April, 1966.
[3] ROBIN DAY, "The Television Interview", *The Listener,* 21st July, 1966.

somebody who is not present ought to be hanged on the nearest lamp post.[1]

Radio and television have shifted the emphasis of political controversy in the democratic countries from abuse to argument; the major parties have decided that the appeal to reason will pay them best. The independence of the ITA and the BBC enables them to foster the habit of hearing both sides of every question. The citizen's act of judgement between the two sides can, however, take place only within the framework of his general assumptions and his background knowledge, built up slowly over the years. The implications for the plain man of British policy in the Far East, or a British entry into the Common Market, cannot be left to emerge from the clashes of an election-year debate. They will not, for most people, be made clearer by any discussion that does not start with elementary facts and first principles.

The news reaches the great majority of people by radio as well as by television. It is a welcome item for every class, but nothing is received with a more selective attention. News consists of a series of items; everyone absorbs what he will, or can. The admirable news magazines reach ten million people. Their episodes, too, are discrete, inconsequential. They offer new knowledge and new insights to be related to what is already known, or whet the appetite for more solid fare. For the politically sophisticated there is the wide-ranging nightly radio programme *Ten O'Clock*, with its authoritative comment from all over the world on the news of the day. There are the discussions in depth of the Third Programme, and the systematic surveys of the new Africa or the new trends in economic thought which are broadcast in weekly serial form as part of the Radio *Study Session* hour. In television there are the lively but allusive

[1] DOUGLAS WOODRUFF, "Debates and Discussion", *BBC Quarterly*, October, 1946.

encounters of the late evening programme *Gallery*. There is the statutory account of the day's proceedings in both Houses, *Today in Parliament*, which reaches half a million people. No doubt some parts of those proceedings will soon be broadcast both by sound and by television. The old suspicion that the use of the medium would transfer the scene of debate from Parliament to the country at large, has led the present House of Commons to decide against a trial. The Lords are still discussing the need for experiments, and the need for a machinery of control which will ensure that there is a fair and balanced selection from each day's debates. On occasion such broadcasts may make their abiding mark, as the Senate hearings on Vietnam have done in the USA. To watch puzzled, deeply serious, yet divided men quietly trying to talk their way through a tangle of all-but-insoluble problems is at least to realize that there are no short cuts in statesmanship. Much of what is seen will inevitably be routine and unlikely to command a large audience. There will still be all too little basic material for those who are no surer than in the days of *Topic for Tonight* whether Spanish is indeed the principal language of South America.[1]

Political education must begin with political information, and with the continuing build-up of a coherent body of knowledge in terms that men and women of modest education can accept. Television is the ideal instrument.

We can none of us take upon ourselves the scattered burdens of the whole world; of an earthquake in Turkey today, a flood in China tomorrow. The danger of a vivid and various television journalism is that we shall accept them all as spectacle, with the same absence, or the same indulgence, of feeling, and with no outlet in action. The task of a responsible television service is not only that which it already discharges

---

[1] *Vide supra*, p. 109.

so well of making people aware of problems; it is that of involving us all in their solution.

Nobody is more aware of the long-term need than the Editor-in-Chief of BBC News and Current Affairs. "I believe we must do more research and more discussion in depth", he wrote in 1962. "We must spend less time airing opinions and more time giving explanatory facts. . . . Our duty is not merely to reflect life as it is, but also to inspire a sense of direction and purpose. . . . We want to be a vigorous creative factor in national life. We want to quicken interest and understanding of matters that affect not only us, but our children."[1]

Broadcasting can best serve that national need in two ways. It can, in the first place, concentrate on a few great central issues at home and abroad in all their infinitely various human manifestations—on our own economic problems, on the plight of the poor nations, and on the balance of world power—with the determination that there shall be a full and effective communication to everyone of the basic and enduring facts.

In the second place it can aim at fostering a full understanding by every citizen of those aspects of social policy which most clearly and immediately link up with his home-centred interests and affect him and his children; of education, health, housing, the care of the old, the needs of the adolescent, and the maintenance of law and justice as these come within the province of ordinary men and women. It could show that all these afford opportunities for involvement and service. On the great new housing estates, with their inward-turning family units, there is, nevertheless, an impulse towards community; in young people everywhere there is an impulse to help. If the broadcasting organizations are to play a full

[1] DONALD EDWARDS, *BBC News and Current Affairs*, BBC Lunch-time Lectures, 1962.

creative role they must face far more boldly than at present the need for exposition as well as for journalism; for the study in depth as well as the magazine item; for the series as well as the isolated programme; for continuity and repetition; and for all these at peak times and not in an obscure and inconvenient hole or corner. They must work in closer partnership with the voluntary bodies concerned with adult education and with the great women's organizations to foster among minorities of the audience for these programmes the habit of group viewing and discussion, and to provide chances of further study. The strength of television lies in its initial impact; unless the print it leaves is deepened it is soon effaced. Perhaps in the long run the energies that it calls into play will be most effectively channelled into constructive action with the help of local radio, with its power to focus attention not only on what needs doing, in general terms, but on what can here and now be done.

II

Religion, like politics, calls for a choice and for commitment; an informed choice, or acceptance based on ignorance and inertia. Religious broadcasting reaches two-thirds of the population. Every day more people hear or see a religious programme than go to all the churches combined on Sunday. The Third Programme listener and the skilled worker (who is the heavier consumer of religious programmes) are either Christians or potential Christians. In broadcasting the Churches have their largest educational opportunity. They are aware that it calls for a close partnership with the broadcasting organizations nationally, and for an international awareness of new possibilities. A World Association for Christian

Broadcasting exists to keep the Protestant Churches in touch with each other, and exchanges information with its Roman Catholic counterpart, *Unda*—the wave.

Everywhere the scope and nature of religious broadcasting depends upon these factors; the national attitude towards religion; the view which the Churches take of the opportunities for communication, education, and evangelism that it offers; and the nature and policy of the broadcasting organizations.

Great Britain is still officially a Christian country. The practice of worship and religious teaching are obligations in the State schools; the vigorous campaign against them by the organized forces of secularism and scientific humanism meets with little popular response. According to a survey conducted for A B C Television Ltd. in 1964 by the Gallup Poll organization, almost the whole of the adult population in the three commercial television areas of London, the Midlands, and the North, regard themselves as belonging to a religious denomination; sixty-seven per cent classified themselves as members of the Church of England. More than four in every five of the representative sample who were interviewed believed in some kind of God; only two per cent were dogmatic atheists. Only a quarter of the sample, however, said that they went to a place of worship as often as once a month. It would appear from other sources that about a quarter of the population are committed Christians; and that perhaps half of these are active and well-informed church members. Behind the figures lie every kind of ignorance, inconsistency, confusion, and perplexity. The Christians, whether they go to church or not, are divided between believers in some sort of spirit or vital force and believers in a personal God. There are agnostics who pray, devout Anglicans who think that Christ was no more than a man, and church-going Roman Catholics with no belief in life after death. The general population gives a vague assent to Christianity but has little speculative interest in the content of belief, and is indifferent towards the claims of the Churches. The churchgoers are split between a conformist majority and the questioning minority that gave such a surprising welcome to the Bishop of Woolwich's book *Honest to God*. BBC inquiries in sixth forms and among technical college students have provided some significant footnotes on the attitudes of the younger generation. Three-quarters of them believe in a God; the proportion rises as they grow older. They are better informed than the general population, and far less given to anthropomorphism and crude picture-thinking. The primary question for most of them is not whether God exists, but how he is to be thought about. They are looking for a faith and failing to find answers in the Churches to many of the questions that concern them most.

In all the audiences for religious broadcasting there is a large majority of men and women whose only contact with the organized life of the Churches is through broadcast programmes. It is clear that these audiences consist of two main groups: the committed Christians, and those who stand only on the fringes of religious belief. That fact has been recognized since the earliest days of the BBC.

Since 1922 the policy of religious broadcasting has been guided by an interdenominational body which in its present form, as the Central Religious Advisory Committee, also advises the Independent Television Authority. CRAC represents the major Christian denominations in Britain—the Church of England, the Church of Scotland and the Methodist, Baptist, Congregational, Presbyterian, and Roman Catholic Churches—and recognizes that other bodies, including the Society of Friends and the Salvation Army, belong to the same main stream of historic Christianity, and should have their share of broadcasting time. It has increasingly come to think of the primary aim of religious broadcasting as evangelistic.

Most religious broadcasts are devotional programmes; many of these are broadcasts of church services. They meet the needs of Christians who cannot go to church beause of age, or sickness, or household duties; they reach a vastly wider audience of those who do not care to go. Both the BBC and the Churches have been aware of the danger that broadcasting might do no more than provide a form of sacred entertainment. They have tried to guard against that danger by insisting that religious broadcasting should "reflect and proclaim the Faith of the Church as it is actually found in the Bible and in the living traditions and liturgical life and preaching of the visible Christian Churches".[1]

A long experience has made it clear that the broadcasting of church services offers only an imperfect educative experience and a dubious means of evangelism.

In 1963 (as part of a series of studies of the communication of the Christian faith today), a Christian group at William Temple College, Rugby, undertook a careful survey of all the religious programmes broadcast during the month of June, and a simultaneous survey of the services in a "central group" of twenty-three churches of all denominations. They found that the broadcasts fairly represented the average level of "the worship, thought and action of those Churches which represent the main stream of the Christian tradition in the country",[2] and that they fell far short of the needs of Christian teaching today. The Church as reflected in its run-of-the-mill sermons seemed to them to be inward-turned preoccupied with its own role in the world, yet imperfectly aware of what was going on there. Its hymns, like its homilies, were more often comforting than challenging; its theology untroubled by the findings of scholarship or the crises of new thought; its estimate of human nature low; and its

[1] Resolution of the Central Religious Advisory Committee, 1948.
[2] *BBC Handbook*, 1963.

attitude to the outside world pessimistic, timid, and remote.

In the perenially popular "soap operas", in *The Archers*, and *Coronation Street* religion played no significant part. The American film series *Going my Way* presented a shallow and complacent version of religion; an episode in *The Defenders* equated the belief in the authority of conscience with belief in God. "It is only when the feature programmes, such as *Meeting Point* and *Sunday Break*, are considered", the report of the group concludes, "that some contact with reality is established. There is an acknowledgement that not all the worthwhile people in the world are Christians. There is, too, an honest attempt to face up to contemporary problems, and to present differing points of view in regard to them."

The forces of simple conservatism in religious thought and practice are very strong. The BBC faced an outcry when it changed the title of its early morning religious programmes from *Lift up your Hearts* to *Ten to Eight*, and tried to ensure that they were fresh and challenging rather than anodyne. The schoolmasters who once a week use the religious service for schools (which reaches two million children) have always divided sharply into two camps: those who prefer traditional forms, the English of the Authorized Version, and what their critics call a stained-glass atmosphere, and those who welcome translation of the Bible story into modern terms, and an astringent realism. There has been a sharp tilting of the balance in recent years towards those who believe that the older modes no longer speak to the condition of the young. In general broadcasting as in the schools, religious broadcasting must continue to use the older forms for the sake of many of those within the Churches. It can no longer rely on them for its missionary purposes.

In an interview with Mr. Kenneth Harris, the Archbishop of Canterbury said that in his view religious television should help the committed Christian to "an intelligent and thoughtful commitment instead of an unintelligent one. A commitment that has more thought of obligation to all those outside." For the person on the fringe of religion there should be "programmes that challenge him to decision and help him to make his own faith and decision articulate."[1]

Through broadcasting the Churches can state their challenge in purely intellectual terms. There are contexts in which that is the only proper mode of address. A sixth form boy or girl who is taking stock of his beliefs demands from a broadcast on religion a strict academic rigour and cogency. The young men and women who ask straightforward questions in the television studio about the bearing of Christian thought on the problems of the world and the problems of personal relationship expect straightforward answers.

Neither group is all that inclined to accept what it is offered out of a simple respect for authority. The future of Christianity in our time depends largely on the success of the Churches in appealing to the abler members of a generation that is more resistant to indoctrination and less ready to accept *ex cathedra* statements than any of its predecessors. With the under twenty-fives as his audience the bishop starts at a disadvantage; to them, he represents a vested interest. They are curious about other religions, and about the secular substitutes for religious belief, because they wish to try all things, and are reluctant to commit themselves too soon to any creed. For them, every exposition must be open-minded and open-ended. They are receptive, sceptical, and, for the most part, astonishingly ignorant of Christianity, either in its biblical sources or its historical development. In so far as they are in revolt against any religion it is against the childish beliefs which they have now outgrown, but which represent the only version of Christianity that they know. Few of

[1] *Religion in Television*, 1964.

them come from homes or belong to communities that can help them to make the transition to a more mature understanding. From among them will emerge the *élites* and the leaders of opinion of the future.

Broadcasting can reach them as no other medium can, and presents the Churches with their greatest educational opportunity.

Radio and television can be the vehicles of a Christian apologetics that does justice to the world, the flesh, and the devil; that encounters its friends and enemies in the common market-place of discourse, and that is acceptable for the very reason that it does so. Through them the Churches can ensure that their best mind is fully known, and that those who do ultimately reject religion are not rejecting a feeble or obscurantist version of the Christian faith. They can deploy all their resources of scholarship and intellectual power to make men and women who are outside the range of the pulpit aware of the findings of New Testament criticism, of the explorations of the latest theologians, and of the abiding tradition of the Christian mystics. They can, and must, make known their doubts as well as their dogmas.

This is an age in which the Churches must draw men into a questioning community before it can extend the bounds of the worshipping community. In the last resort no purely intellectual approach to religion can do more than clear away obstacles to belief. The sermon has traditionally three aims: to instruct, to delight, and to influence the will. In so far as religious broadcasting proves indeed to be "the greatest power for indirect evangelism offered to the Church"[1] it will be through its appeal not only to the mind of a puzzled generation, but to its imagination and heart. Television and radio enable the Churches to confront the world through men whose stature commands respect; through Karl Barth

[1] *Towards the Conversion of England*, Church Assembly, London, 1945, p. 105.

or Cardinal Heenan, Pope John or Martin Luther King. They can show Christianity in action at home and abroad. They can enlist the arts to make a direct imaginative appeal.

Christianity proclaims a dramatic history, and uses visible symbols to focus its acts of worship. The Roman Catholic Church has always known the strength of the thing enacted and the thing seen; of the painted Judgement and the mystery play. There can have been few Christians of other traditions who were not moved and involved by the spectacle on television of the enthronement of Pope Paul. Radio has its dramatic resources; television its added visual appeal. The religious service for schools began many years ago to use a dramatic interlude drawn from the gospel or the records of Christian heroism instead of an address. Dorothy Sayers showed with her radio life of Christ, *The Man Born to be King*, that religious drama could capture and hold a vast audience. All over the world there is a search now after new liturgical forms, new modes of mime and drama and song that will revive in the broadcasting media that medieval tradition which spoke more strongly than sermons to a wide popular audience. At the meeting of the World Association for Christian Broadcasting held in 1966 the programmes that were shown included a Dutch ballet on Abraham's sacrifice, a German film of the death of Christ presented in modern reportage, a BBC dramatic version of the story of Job, and a film of Duke Ellington's band in Coventry Cathedral. If programmes like these are to make their full impact they must increasingly take their place (and be produced with a professional skill that enables them to take their place) not in sacred and segregated spaces but as a part of the general programme pattern. They will have their allies in every secular programme which answers Sir Arthur fforde's test and asserts that life is to be respected and valued; their worst enemy in the persistence of a pervasive triviality.

III

Politics and religion already provide a meeting-ground for men and women of different classes and different educational backgrounds. There is an even gradation of interest and concern from one end of the social scale to the other. Our literary culture has great lines of cleavage dividing class from class.

The Third Programme of the BBC began and continues as an act of faith in the arts and in the speculative intellect. For many years it cannot hope to appeal to more than a small though increasing proportion of the population. If, quantity for quantity of pleasure, pushpin is as good as poetry; if Mozart is like claret, no more than a luxury on which the plain man does not want to spend his money, there can be no justification for giving to the Third Programme more than a strictly proportionate amount of the available time and of the licence-payers' money. To do so is simply to yield to a powerful pressure group. The Third Programme can, like everything else in broadcasting, be justified only as an assertion that "some things are better worth doing than others". On its present scale it can be justified as part of the provision for a democracy only if it embodies values that are absolute and universal, and that are capable of being diffused throughout society at every level. Lord Reith never reconciled himself to the segregation of so many of the peaks of artistic achievement from the main stream of programmes; for him the Third Programme was "a disaster".[1] Now that radio appeals only to the residual audience without television or to the selective listener, the old objections have lost much of their force,

[1] LORD REITH, "The Future of British Broadcasting", *The Manchester Guardian*, 29th December, 1960.

and the "Third" pursues its chosen path with a faithful audience.

Its business is to keep alive the music, the plays, and the poetry of the European tradition however uncompromising and austere, while welcoming whatever is new and adventurous in the arts or challenging in the realm of thought. It has sometimes in the past been remote and esoteric, but it has never surrendered to momentary artistic fashion or felt the need to astonish and to startle. Wide enough now to have on offer something for all who already care for the arts and for ideas it broadcasts Bach and Boulez, Shakespeare and Sartre, talks on Plato or discussions of Chinese Communism in a steady stream. Its task is comparatively straightforward. Radio is so cheap, even for dramatic performance, that there is no need to aim at an audience much more than fifty thousand strong. Half of the output consists of music, and a large part of the remainder of talks and discussions. The audience values and welcomes retrievals from the heritage of the past. Television faces the complex problem of presenting the arts to its great mixed audience.

Sir Kenneth Clark urged in his letter to Sir Harry Pilkington[1] that there should be no question of the establishment of a television counterpart to the Third Programme. Overproduction seemed to him the most serious danger to the quality of general programmes. "Ask anyone to produce highbrow television which is hearable for six hours a week, and you will find that he soon runs dry."[2]

The number of speakers who can hold a television audience with a straightforward discourse to the camera is small. Music offers only limited opportunities to deploy the strength of the usual medium. The "musical biography" is marginal to the appreciation of music; the counterpointing of musical

[1] *Vide supra*, p. 118.
[2] *Pilkington Report*, vol. II, Appendix C, p. 113.

sound with masterpieces of painting has its experimental interest, but allows a full attention to neither. The splendid "Master Class" programmes that have shown teachers like Tortelier and Menuhin in action have indeed offered wholly new insights into the interpretation of great works. Watching an orchestra can be an enlightening as well as an exciting experience. When all is said and done television can never compete musically with the incomparable range and variety of sound broadcasting. The visual arts would seem to offer a more hopeful field. Huw Weldon has written of the satisfying completeness and sense of liberation that can come from receiving words and picture together, and of "the peculiar liveliness of the television image".[1] The first experience is by no means peculiar to television. For many years the radio series *Painting of the Month* has been presenting more carefully chosen words matched with more faithful reproductions of pictures than television can offer. The television image is indeed both lively and impelling; it is at the same time singularly coarse—a reminder or a travesty of the Primavera or a Rembrandt portrait.

Two million people watch the programmes of the *International Concert Hall* series; half a million will follow an introductory series on some aspect of the visual arts. The magazine programme *Monitor* brings to an average audience of three million, and a clientele perhaps twice as large, a new awareness of artists as people, the shock of discovery, and fresh lights in familiar places. Television can bring a foretaste of the pleasures that music and painting can offer to those who as yet only stand on the brink of new enjoyments. It can through a lively but inevitably superficial journalism keep a surprisingly large audience in touch with the changing climate of these arts. Its contribution remains marginal. The

[1] Huw Weldon, *Television and the Arts*, b b c Lunch-time Lectures, 1964, p. 9.

dramatic form presents television with its most significant—
and bewildering—range of temptations and opportunities.

As a patron of writers and an intermediary between them
and the public, television shares and accentuates their present
confusions. Its appetite, with three channels to fill, is insatiable.
It cannot afford, as the Third Programme can, to provide a
platform for the private artist concerned uncompromisingly
with his own truths. It acknowledges a responsibility that is
not discharged by the use of writers aiming frankly and
deliberately at the mass market. Its new audience for "serious"
drama has neither the stability nor the assurance of the central
Third Programme audience. Its wares cannot, like printed
books, be left to find their own level. Since they will be
forgotten next week they must achieve their whole audience
now; they must have "impact". The stance of a television
service with a cultural conscience is necessarily as uneasy as
that of the writers who themselves stand poised between
withdrawal and compromise; between the acceptance of a
modish *succès d'estime* and a bid for a "popular" audience.

Mr. Auden has best diagnosed one of the resulting symp-
toms: "Again, in a society based upon mass competitive
consumption, artists are under enormous pressure to provide
the public continuously with something startling or novel.
In the Victorian age they suffered from the prudery of the
public, which made certain topics and expressions taboo.
Today the demand is that we should take our clothes off,
recite the four-letter words like a rosary, and instead of trying
to make enduring objects, invent momentary 'happenings'."[1]

The first temptation of a television service conscious of a
cultural role is to foster the taste for mere novelty; the
collection of plays with the same value and character as the
collections of the Paris couturiers; the apotheosis of the

[1] W. H. Auden, "Nowness and Permanence", *The Listener*, 17th March,
1966.

impermanent. Its natural but excessive regard for the tricks of the trade urges it in the same direction; and a programme that places a modish professional skill at the disposal of a vulgar sensationalism can, like the BBC's "Debussy" film, be resurrected to achieve the qualified immortality of a television "Oscar"—the Italia prize.

Its second temptation is to parade a social conscience through a series of "strong" indictments, exposures, and revelations conveyed in that "urgent journalistic style" for which the Head of BBC Television Drama has recently been calling.[1] Along that line lies documentary feature neither transmitted by the imagination nor faithful to the bare facts, but full indeed of "agitational contemporaneity".

Good plays will be written because good writers wish to write them; there will never be enough. The alienation of some of the best writers from any wide audience is complete. There still remains a gap to be filled by honest writing. Between the new and the experimental on the one hand and the blatantly commercial on the other there is all too little. As Mr. J. B. Priestley puts it: "There is now an enormous gap between a tiny *avant-garde* and the vast mass of viewers and listeners (between people who are happy with a painting entitled 'Won't 'oo kiss doggie?' and the few who can accept 'sculpture' made out of old motor bikes and dustbin lids). It is, I think, the duty of the BBC not to be too Philistine, and not to be too often out in front and 'with-it' but to do everything it can to fill this gap. In music, I think it does, on the whole. In other things, especially on television, it is too fond of the extremes to do enough to fill this gap."[2]

Television has its widest diffusion as a means of entertainment. Its most characteristic offering is the serial drama,

---

[1] MR. SYDNEY NEWMAN, quoted by Maurice Wiggin. *The Sunday Times*, 21st May, 1966.

[2] J. B. PRIESTLEY, "The BBC's Duty to Society", *The Listener*, 1st July, 1965.

ranging from light domestic comedy to those described in
ITV 1965 as "strong melodramatic drama series, some home-
produced, some American. These are essentially action stories
rather than plays of ideas." The soap opera shades into the
cliff-hanger.

Among those which have achieved a following of ten million or more, Independent Television has listed *Coronation
Street, Emergency—Ward* 10, *The Plane Makers,* and *The
Avengers.* The BBC has reached the same figure with *Dr. Who,
Dixon of Dock Green, Z Cars, Dr. Finlay's Case Book, Dr.
Kildare, Perry Mason,* and *Bewitched,* with *The Rogues* and *Compact* not far behind. The aim of all of these is to draw the viewer
into a continuing world and engage him with the fortunes
and emotional vicissitudes of its inhabitants. Sometimes the
world that they present is patently a world of fantasy; more
often an ostensible replica of life as it is lived in a school or a
hospital, a factory or a newspaper office, a Lancashire town
or a Scottish village. There can be no doubt that the compelling images of the television screen play a great and increasing
part in building up for men and women of limited experience,
but most of all for children, an image of the world outside
their own immediate experience. It is at least a reasonable
working assumption, and finds its place as such in the code
of the Independent Television Authority, that "children
acquire their moral sentiments from the society around them,
including its aspect in television".

"We should try always", said Sir Hugh Greene to the
Pilkington Committee, "to do the best we possibly can in
every type of broadcast, without thinking that it is more
important to put our best into information and education.
It is just as important to put the best skills one can into entertainment". The context, with its insistence that the three
elements of information, education, and entertainment, are not
separable forbids an interpretation of "the best" in narrowly

professional terms. It implies a scale of values even in soap opera which is not that of the ratings.

Such a scale of values has been explicitly recognized by the best practitioners themselves. One of the most sensitive writers of comic dialogue for radio, Mr. Eric Barker,[1] long ago claimed for his own art the integrity of all genuine creative writing. "The best humorous script is, as in the case of almost every other written work, one which the author wishes to write, without more than a vague idea that anyone will enjoy it; one in which he expresses his own contemporary point of view; one which is somewhere autobiographical . . . once the commercial angle enters into it seriously, and as a first consideration, it obviously ceases to be a creative art, and falls into line with the invention of advertisements and the design of utility cups." The honest writer of comedy must, as he saw it, be in touch with his audience and its changing moods; sensitive alike to the warmth and solidarity of the wartime years, and to the cynicism of the later 1940s. He must not calculate his humour.

Tom Sloan, the Head of BBC Light Entertainment, has stated both his own view of the elements that make for success, and his own credo. "The viewers like to have a strong sense of personal involvement in this kind of programme. They ought to be constantly reminded of situations and characterizations within their experience, and an element of compassion in the comedy is all-important. 'You gotta have heart' is not only a great song—it is a basic principle in our business."[2] Ted Mason, the creator of the sturdiest and longest-lived of all British radio serials, *The Archers*, which still carries to an audience two million strong its authentic picture of a farming community—and incidentally of good farming practice—has written of the problems of

[1] ERIC BARKER, "Humour on the Air", *BBC Quarterly*, Autumn, 1951.
[2] TOM SLOAN, *Ariel*, vol. 10, no. 6.

achieving "a happy mixture of story development, character-
ization, farming information and country lore, without
weighting any one of these ingredients too heavily".[1]

Mr. Robert Henriques has posed the central problem of
communication to a popular audience with great lucidity,
from the point of view of a writer of prose fiction: "As an
artist, I wish to say things to people with the utmost impact.
This means creating a private world which is true to my
own feelings on human ecology—that is, the relationships
of humans to each other and to their environment—and next
persuading people to enter it, so that, once they are in my
parlour, my private truths become temporarily their verities.
I try to do this by appealing to their minds, and especially to
the recollections of all their senses; and I can succeed only in
so far as my private world is sufficiently related to their own
for them to accept it as *the* world and be tempted to join
me there".[2]

The makers of honest fiction for a popular audience have
known, by intuition, or empirically or as conscious artists,
the limits within which they must move. They have been
aware that the common world of the mass audience must
necessarily be a world of broad and simple stereotypes, and
that their own central characters must move easily and as
familiar acquaintances within that world. As for "uncommon
individuals", they must, according to Mr. Mason, "be consistently drawn and played so that their oddities and idio-
syncrasies make them acceptable by force of repetition."
What succeeds, says Mr. Barker, is "a combination of habit
and familiarity". They have still been able to throw the
new light of a humorist's view of life on familiar scenes; to
widen sympathies, to enlarge horizons, and to show new

[1] EDWARD J. MASON, "Writing a Radio Serial", *BBC Quarterly*, Spring, 1954.
[2] ROBERT HENRIQUES, "Writing for Television: A Novelist's Problem",
BBC Quarterly, Summer, 1952.

possibilities in experience. Authenticity, a finger on the pulse of life itself, compassion, craftsmanship and, above all, honesty of intention, these are qualities to which great audiences have responded whenever they were embodied in work within the plain man's range. They are the qualities that should distinguish everything that is offered to the public in the name of public service broadcasting. At present they do not. There is not simply a graduation from poor to first-rate work. There is an unbridgeable gulf in BBC programmes—as there is in the output of commercial television—between the bad, good, and indifferent work of writers of integrity on the one hand, and the synthetic material deliberately concocted to a formula for the British, the American, or the world-wide market on the other. On the one side are *Coronation Street*, *Z-Cars*, *Dixon of Dock Green*, *Dr. Finlay's Casebook*, *Hancock's Half-hour*; on the other *The Avengers*, *Peyton Place*—that "hothouse mock-flower of pseudo-sex and romance" as the *New York Herald Tribune* called it—*The Third Man* (the BBC's own excursion into the mid-Atlantic market) and *The Man from UNCLE*. So long as three channels compete for the suffrages of the maximum number of viewers the formula most likely to bring in the bottom section of the audience will go on gaining ground. It is a formula that relies deliberately on the exploitation of violence.

The wholesale display of violence was defended by the Independent Television Authority in its evidence to the Pilkington Committee on the ground that television must mirror the violence of our times. "One can only say", comments Baroness Wootton, "that they must have got hold of a sadly distorting mirror, and that so likewise has the BBC. . . . That there is an area of our society in which violence is an everyday occurrence I do not dispute. (With about forty years' experience as a London magistrate who could?) But that this is in any sense representative of society as a whole is a gross travesty of the facts."[1] The world of most people has few points of contact with the world of *The Informer* or even with the world of *Z-Cars*, and the world of television drama as a whole places a heavily disproportionate emphasis on that element of violence in all our lives to which (it might be argued) the screen gives a symbolic expression. Its procedures are justified in the name of catharsis. Dramatic violence, it is alleged, purges and gives a harmless discharge to men's turbulent emotions. Based on an obscure passage in Aristotle's *Poetics* and a dubious interpretation of Freudian psychology this is a doctrine that commends itself with special force to the sponsors of the more pretentious kinds of violent drama, and that can be coupled with an appeal to Shakespeare.

What modest experimental evidence there is suggests that watching violence on television heightens rather than diminishes the aggressive impulse, at least of those most prone to violence.

Shakespeare, as Mr. David Holbrook, intervening in the debate, has pointed out, was concerned neither with the realistic portrayal of a violent world, nor with dubious therapeutics. "Shakespeare had a tragic purpose—to ask, given man's capacity for violence and his mortality, by what values could he go on living?"

Dr. Hilde Himmelweit, in her classic pioneer study of the impact of television on children,[2] came to the conclusion that while television was unlikely to achieve a catharsis, and might well sustain rather than solve the problems of disturbed children, the stylized melodrama, and characteristically the "western", with its setting remote from everyday life and its clearly labelled good and bad characters, was unlikely to have much disturbing effect or much influence on moral

---

[1] BARBARA WOOTTON, "The B B C's Duty to Society", *The Listener*, 22nd, July, 1965.   [2] HILDE HIMMELWEIT, *Television and the Child*, 1958.

codes. Professor H. Eysenck, writing as a behaviourist, has set out in an extremely interesting memorandum to the Pilkington Committee the contrary hypothesis.[1] Looking at conscience as a socially conditioned response, he would consider that the process of deconditioning could theoretically be best achieved by the presentation of behaviour regarded as wrong "in an attenuated symbolic form" and in the agreeable circumstances of a film or television performance. He would expect a course of "behaviour therapy" along these lines to rid the "subject" effectively of his conscience. "In terms of this theory", he writes, "the usual defence put forward by television companies becomes quite irrelevant. It does not matter that virtue in the end triumphs, and that the criminals are finally shot, drawn, and quartered, the very fact that they, too, should come to a violent end further lowers the conditioned response to this type of activity."

Professor Eysenck emphasizes that he is simply presenting a theoretical account which may or may not be true. He insists that "in a matter of such great importance to the moral well-being of the nation neither the BBC nor the commercial television companies should be allowed to sit back in whatever comfort they may derive from a verdict of 'not proven'", and calls for a major programme of research.

That research is now under way both in America and in this country. Mr. J. D. Halloran, the newly appointed Director of our own research project has insisted that there is as yet an insufficient body of knowledge. "People talk in blanket terms about the bad effects of television on children. We simply do not know."[2] He has himself presented what we do know, not only about the effects of violence but about all

[1] H. J. EYSENCK, "Television and the Problem of Violence", *Pilkington Report*, vol. II, Appendix E, p. 1116.
[2] J. D. HALLORAN, *The Effects of Mass Communication with Special Reference to Television*, 1965.

the ways in which television may have a bearing on the development of moral concepts and social attitudes, in a lucid, wide-ranging and comprehensive summary.

A sense of concern is naturally greatest where children are concerned, and the superficial facts about their viewing are well established. They view now for thirty to forty minutes longer each day than when Dr. Himmelweit undertook her pioneer study in 1958. Only one household in three makes any attempt to control viewing, and large numbers of young children are still watching long after 9 o'clock. Children are selective viewers, switching over from one channel to another in search of westerns, crime stories, comedy, and family serials. With them as with the general audience demand is a function of supply, and they have come to like the kind of fare that is most often provided. There is no very significant learning from their general viewing; its nature forbids that there should be. In so far as television contributes to a wider knowledge of the world it offers most to the younger and less able children, who gain least from their reading. Television interferes less with their more active pursuits than it does with those of older people. The time that is now spent on television was once spent on cinema-going and light reading, and there is at least some justification for the attitude of the boy who said: "It wastes my time, but what else would I be doing? If I was reading a book I might be wasting my time, mightn't I?"

The bare facts are meagre and unenlightening. Beyond them lie only pointers to the need for further investigation, clearest perhaps in their indication that it is the neurotic and the maladjusted, the frustrated and the insecure—the misfits and the unhappy whose problems society has failed to solve—who lie widest open to such harm as television can do.

Every attitude is shaped by a multiplicity of long-term factors. The effects of television cannot easily be isolated.

A total study of its impact on society calls for a study of all those mediating factors, both social and psychological, which help to determine its influence. Until that study has made further progress the community must make its interim judgements. To most people concerned with children it seems self-evident that they should not be exposed night after night to experiences that no sensible parent or good schoolmaster would choose for them. It is just as self-evident that they should not be offered in the guise of an enlargement of their experience of the world a false and silly image of society with an implicit scale of moral values wholly at variance with the values of the schools.

Both the BBC and the ITA have codes[1] of guidance for producers governing the display of violence and horror. The ITA Code concludes, sensibly enough: "When in doubt, cut. The risk is not one that can be decently taken." Codes are mainly negative instruments. "Children", the ITA Code says more constructively, "acquire their moral sentiments from the society around them, including its aspect in television. They tend to model their own conduct on the conduct of those they admire, and shun the conduct of those whom they feel to be bad." It is, at least, the safest working assumption.

The irony and the folly of our present situation is that society has allowed itself to be diverted into preventing television from doing harm, instead of supporting the great range of educative opportunities that it offers.

[1] *See* the *Pilkington Report*, p. 48, for the BBC Code and *ITA 1965*, p. 19, for the Code of the ITA.

VII

EDUCATIONAL BROADCASTING

I

THE Organizing Committee of the Third World Conference on Educational Radio and Television, which will be held in Paris during the spring of 1967 has adopted four characteristics as those which distinguish programmes which can in the full sense be called "educational" from those that are broadly educative. Their purpose must be to contribute to the systematic growth of knowledge; they must form part of a continuous provision and be so planned that their effect is progressive; they must be accompanied by supporting documents; and whether they are received individually or collectively, under supervision or by home listeners and viewers, there must be an active response from the audience, and the impact of the programmes must be supervised and checked.

The main business of educational broadcasting so conceived is to serve those institutions that carry on the business of education in the narrower sense, and together constitute the national system of education; schools and colleges of further education; training colleges for teachers (or colleges of education as they are now called in the United Kingdom); universities and colleges of advanced technology; professional examining bodies, and industrial schemes; university extramural courses, and classes organized by voluntary bodies. It can also, by its very nature, go far to serve the adult student engaged at home in the disciplined and systematic pursuit of knowledge; and further still if his studies can be supported by correspondence tuition.

Educational radio and television can reach the student now in either or both of two ways: through public, "open-air", services, and through "closed-circuit" systems using cable or microwave links for the transmission of programmes to a restricted audience in a single institution or in some larger area.

Until recent years "open-air" broadcasting held the field alone. Every major broadcasting organization in the world developed and still maintains a national service of school broadcasts, among which those of Great Britain, France, Italy, Sweden, Australia, Canada, and Japan are pre-eminent in range and scale. Many of them have moved, at least experimentally, into the field of higher education. Great Britain pioneered the way and the BBC now provides sixty-three radio programmes a week during term-time, including some provision for the national cultures of Wales and Scotland. The programmes cover nearly all the subjects in the curriculum and use every radio form from the straightforward talk to the full-scale performance of orchestral music and of drama.

Many schools in Britain have tape-recorders, and since the contractual difficulties preventing schools from tape-recording the programmes were removed, radio has shown a remarkable strength as a cheap, flexible, and efficient instrument for fulfilling certain educational purposes. It is especially strong in the presentation of literature, music, imaginative experience, and ideas, and in enlisting the active participation of the audience. The programmes now reach well over 32,000 of the 37,000 British schools.

The newer service of school television at present provides fifteen weekly programmes, all of them repeated in the same week since the classroom recording of television programmes is not yet practicable. The major commercial television companies between them provide and network as many more.

These services are exploiting the medium to offer children an extension of their experience in time and space, to bridge the gap between the schoolroom and the outside world with programmes on current affairs and vocational guidance, and to bring new resources to bear on the teaching of music, geography, science, and mathematics. The number of schools equipped to receive the programmes stands now at 14,000 and is steadily increasing.

The whole cost of school broadcasting, amounting at present to roughly £2 million a year, is met by the BBC from its licence revenue.

Every week in term-time NHK (Nippon Hoso Kyokai) broadcasts eighty-four radio programmes for Japanese schools, and one hundred television programmes. Those for the kindergarten classes are in full colour. Some 60,000 schools are equipped with radio receivers and more than 50,000 to receive television, usually in a number of classrooms. The scope of the service is wide enough to include moral teaching as well as mathematics. It makes provision not only for normal children, but for the mentally handicapped and the deaf. For boys and girls who enter industry instead of going on to the senior high school there is the NHK correspondence high school, with opportunities for the further study of a wide range of subjects by sound and television linked with tuition by correspondence and short periods of school attendance. It is a service whose range and volume is all the more astonishing in so far as the Japanese commercial broadcasting companies make their own additional contribution to the work of the schools, as they do here.

As the world shortage of specialist teachers has grown more acute there has been a steady growth of closed-circuit systems, which offer one important technical advantage over broadcasting in so far as they are capable of carrying a considerable number of simultaneous transmissions. The pioneering work in this field was carried out at Hagerstown in Maryland, where forty-four schools serving the 20,000 pupils of the county are linked with a television centre run by the school board so as to place the best local teachers at the disposal of the entire school population. For the past eight years Hagerstown has been a place of educational pilgrimage from all over the world, and has served as prototype for the installations of Britain, as of other countries. The first of these is already in operation at Glasgow. A start will soon be made at Hull; and the decision of the Inner London Education Authority to go ahead on the same lines with a six-channel system (including two channels reserved for colour) providing for the whole great metropolitan complex of educational institutions within its jurisdiction, has ensured that closed-circuit television will play a major part in the development of British education at all levels up to that of the university.

The advance of closed-circuit television in the universities has been even more striking. Almost all of the thirty-five British universities and eleven colleges of advanced technology are preparing development plans. Some of them are already making provision for intercommunication between the campus studio and the major educational institutions in the area. In Glasgow, it is intended that the studios of both the city's universities—Glasgow and Strathclyde—should be linked to the local education authority's schools studio, and through it potentially to three hundred schools; that there should be two-way communication between the universities and the Jordan Hill College of Education (which is also linked to the school system), and that the seven local teaching hospitals should also be included in the network.

Closed-circuit television is not, strictly speaking, a form of broadcasting, but its advent and expansion have radically transformed the context within which the educational broadcasts of the BBC and the independent programme companies must operate. The growth of cctv presents a new problem in relationships, in the proper distribution of functions, and in the proper allocation of national resources. In the long run there must be a co-ordination of effort and a freedom of exchange between the various agencies involved that will eliminate waste and duplication. From a national point of view the efficiency and economy of the whole complex of operations will be enormously increased if facilities can be developed for recording programmes on magnetic tape and film, so that they can be used many times and in wider contexts than those in which they originated.

There is an urgent need for a new national body to watch over and guide the progress of educational broadcasting in all its forms, to serve as a link between national and local operations, and to establish a national library of recorded programmes which will make the best material from every source available to any broadcasting organization and to schools and universities for direct classroom use. There is a model in the regional libraries now in the course of establishment by the ETV stations of the United States. In this country an authoritative Committee set up jointly by the University Grants Committee, the Department of Education and Science, and the Scottish Education Department has stated fully the need for a National Centre which would serve this whole range of purposes.[1]

From whatever source they may come radio and television programmes have well-marked common characteristics.

To think of the educational powers and possibilities of broadcasting in terms of ordinary classroom practice is to ignore both the wealth of resources and the obvious limitations of the media. A broadcast can stimulate, but cannot itself undertake, the dialectics of the classroom. The interrup-

[1] *Audio-visual Aids in Higher Scientific Education*, H M S O, 1965.

tion of its progress by question and answer is technically practicable, but can never offer a sense of participation to a large audience. Experiments with small closed-circuit audiences have failed to establish its value even in that context. A television programme as a teaching instrument has more affinities with the formal lecture than with the conventional lesson in so far as it is a one-way communication going inexorably on, and allowing neither opportunity for questioning nor pauses for reflection. It must therefore depend entirely for its effectiveness on sustained and continuous voluntary attention for a determinate period. The degree of attention that it evokes will be determined by the pre-existing interests and motives of the audience; by the span of attention before fatigue sets in, which will be related to their age and general intelligence, and by its own intrinsic qualities. In any learning situation the most important of all programme qualities is structure. A programme can best achieve its educational aims, whatever attractions it offers by the way, through a compelling coherence, through the boldness and clarity of the main design, through the strength of what producers even of programmes in pure mathematics like to speak of as "the story line". A broadcast so conceived presents a pattern that can be grasped as a whole (whether it is the pattern of the binomial theorem or the pattern of the *Antigone*) and leaves its audience with at least some enhancement of the power to see such patterns for themselves. The strength of the broadcasting medium lies in synthesis. The task of the producer of educational programmes is to subdue all the various means at his disposal to the needs of his theme so as best to display coherences and relationships, whether in practical, imaginative, or intellectual terms. To show caterpillars and carpenters as part of a single ecological complex; to shift from the jib of a crane seen against the skyline to a diagrammatic representation of the triangle of forces that it exemplifies; to go on from the exposition of an irregular verb to the human situation in which it is used; to place the day's events in the perspective of history—these are characteristic achievements of the broadcasting media. An educational broadcast may be primarily an example of "programmed" instruction, compensating for the absence of immediate feedback by the careful breakdown of an argument into a series of steps, and using its own means of compelling and directing attention to keep the mind actively moving forwards in response to the whole carefully ordered sequence of thought. It may, to use a convenient cliché, be a "window on the world", offering an ordered extension of experience in time and space. It may have the character of a work of art in so far as it ministers, in Santayana's phrase, to "the contemplation of things in their order and worth".

At one end of the scale lies straightforward lecturing; at the other, a full-scale performance of *Hamlet*. Looked at from the point of view of the schools, broadcasting offers either "direct teaching", taking over entirely some or all of the burden of instruction in a curricular subject, or it offers "enrichment" which gives a new dimension to the customary work of the classroom. Historically, these are the two poles between which school broadcasting has moved.

Educational broadcasting began with the service of radio programmes for schools which the BBC started in the early 1920s and which was to establish a model throughout the world for the first phase of school broadcasting. At that time secondary education for all was no more than the aspiration of a band of pioneers, and the elementary schools, which provided for the great bulk of the school population, were only slowly moving away from a tradition which saw their function as that of equipping boys and girls, who would end their formal education at fourteen, with the few basic skills and the minimum of useful knowledge that would be called for by a narrow range of occupations and the daily conduct of restricted lives. The ghost of Mr. Gradgrind with his bleak insistence on hard facts was not yet wholly exorcised. As long ago as 1904, Sir Robert Morant's New Code for the Public Elementary Schools had taken a wide and liberal view of the scope of compulsory public education. Twenty years later the supply of teachers who could arouse "a living interest in the ideals and achievements of mankind" was still limited by the narrowness of their own training. The period of school attendance was still all too short; school buildings all too often grim and discouraging. Between the elementary schools and the grammar schools there was still a great gulf, and the ladder between them was still neither wide nor easy to climb for a child from a working-class background. But the President of the Board of Education, H. A. L. Fisher, had spoken of education, when he introduced the Education Bill of 1918, as "one of the good things of life which should be more widely shared", and Sir Henry Hadow was already at work on the first of the great Reports of the Consultation Committee of the Board of Education that bear his name, when the BBC in 1925 appointed Miss Mary Somerville to its educational staff, with a special responsibility for broadcasts to schools. Her vision and energy were to forge a wholly new educational instrument. The Hadow Report on the Education of the Adolescent called for a universal secondary education which should be closely related to life outside the school walls yet breathe "the free and broad air of a general and humane education", the Hadow Report on the Primary School for a curriculum designed "to develop in a child the fundamental interests of civilized life so far as these powers and interests are within the compass of childhood". Mary Somerville saw the new medium as serving these ends by placing at the disposal of the teacher an instrument that would neither do his work for him nor even share with him the burden of his straightforward curricular teaching. Its task would rather be that of bringing to every child in every classroom a kind and quality of experience that would be otherwise unattainable. The task of the school broadcasting service that she created was to enlist the inspired speaker who could share with children an enthusiasm or an idea, the traveller with a tale to tell, the journalist in touch with the news of the day; the skilled and imaginative script-writer, and the first-class professional performance of music and drama. The business of broadcasting was not to teach, but to throw its weight on the side of the new movement. The Board of Education stood aloof, but Fisher and Hadow became staunch supporters of school broadcasting.

In one mode, broadcasting was to bring a new realism to the classroom, helping to make older boys and girls aware of the world of work and the world of affairs as the living concern of men and women, whose voices could be heard in their own classroom. In another mode, it was to be a contribution to Whitehead's phase of romance in learning, to that delighted awareness of new worlds that must, in his view, precede and give the impulse towards the later phases of precision and generalization. Because of the limitations of radio, but even more because of its strength and opportunities, these other phases were to be left as the teachers' province, a division of labour illustrated nowhere more clearly than by the dramatized history programmes that were perhaps the most characteristic of all the early inventions of school radio. The teacher must still concern himself in his own way with the manor and the three-field system. Through the broadcast children should know Piers Plowman in his habit as he lived. The plaque that commemorates Miss Rhoda Power, the greatly gifted pioneer of this new kind of writing, bears the words of G. M. Trevelyan: "The criterion of historical study is truth; its impelling motive is poetic."

If we did not feel, we could not think and should not act. As Mary Somerville saw it, a good radio programme should appeal not only to the intelligence, but to the emotions. It should be concerned not only with facts, but with values. It should impose unity on the facts, order the emotions, and give full weight to the values. Because it was not merely an exercise for the logical understanding it could do all these things in some measure for even the least academic of children.

It would be a profound mistake to think of school broadcasting so conceived as having served its term and outlived its function. All over the world, and on both sides of the Iron Curtain, it is still helping to transform arid and narrowly intellectual modes of approach to the traditional subjects of the school curriculum. In the words of the President of the Polish Radio and Television Organization: "Radio can play an important role in the very process of teaching, by stimulating and developing one of the most important functions of the mind—the imagination. Imagination is not only a precious ally in the study of history. . . . It is the condition of progress in all fields of human activity. Thanks to competitions to which we are trying to attract the best writers of our country, we are systematically enriching the repertory of the imaginative theatre conceived in the form of broadcasts on problems which interest our children and our young people. . . . Our dearest concern is not so much the enriching of the students' knowledge, as the complete psychical involvement of the listener in perception of the works presented."[1]

All over the world school broadcasts are being used not only to appeal to the imagination, but also to enlarge the bounds of the curriculum. The television medium offers

[1] WLODZIMIERZ SOKORSKI, "Function and Position of Educational Broadcasting in Poland", *Proceedings of the Second International Conference on School Broadcasting, Tokyo*, 1964.

M

new opportunities, and the steady raising of the school-leaving age presents new needs.

In Poland, in France, and in the United Kingdom, major educational reports have stressed the need to revise the whole concept of secondary education for the less academically gifted adolescents who are now coming within its scope, often reluctantly, and still more often from homes that set little value on the educational process. The earlier onset of physical maturity throughout Western Europe, and the earlier social maturity of both boys and girls brought up in an increasingly egalitarian society, lead them to think of themselves not as children but as young adults. They have one foot already in the world of easy money and early marriages, of advanced technologies and confused purposes, of mass entertainment and of menacing world events. Faced with a merely academic curriculum or with merely authoritarian methods, they rebel. It is not only in Poland that "the younger generation of today is in violent revolt against the boredom of school routine". If any sentence of the Newsom Report has acquired any general currency, it is the retort of the boy who was asked by his headmaster what he thought of the new school buildings, and who replied: "It could all be of marble Sir, but it would still be a bloody school." In Britain, the Schools Council is already at work on the problems that will face the schools in 1970 when they will be retaining for a fifth year of secondary education 60,000 more of the fifteen to sixteen age-group than now stay on voluntarily, and when there will be a consequent rise in the school population of 350,000 pupils in a single year. It is beginning to look for a new unifying principle for the curriculum in "the study of Man, and of human society, needs, and purposes", and for new ways of helping young people towards some understanding of themselves, of the social order and their own place within it.

For these older pupils a radio or television programme has a value that ranges well beyond the pedagogic effectiveness of the broadcast mode of presentation. It comes from the world outside and points to that world. Using a medium to which they are accustomed outside the classroom, it offers a shared and at times an unpredictable experience, to be enjoyed or criticized by class and teacher together, and establishes between them a happily informal relationship. It makes its impact in sharply individual terms. For that reason, it has perhaps most to offer to those whose responses and habits of thought must be based on what they have heard and seen and felt for themselves, and who may never move easily in the realm of generalization and abstraction.

They want the work of the school to be related, in ways that they can themselves understand, to the life of the world outside the classroom. They are interested in jobs, the headlines of the newspaper, the mass media, the daily business of living and enjoying life, and, above all, in personal relationships. Television can help them to measure themselves against the range of vocational opportunity, and at the same time to appreciate the other man's skills, and the interdependence of all those who contribute to the running of a complex modern community. It can interpret work as vocation through men and women who understand it so. It can present the skills and arts of the home to girls who will, most of them, find their vocation in home-making and half of whom will be married before they are twenty-five, and in the hands of a sensitive teacher can, better than any other medium, help towards an understanding of the physical and the emotional problems of growing up and starting a family. It can by example encourage an adventurous use of leisure at home and abroad. It can show the events of the day in the perspective of those world problems of colour and creed, poverty and plenty, war and peace, which most engage young people's interests and sympathies, or in the long perspective of history.

"They laughed at the early shots of Hitler", wrote one teacher, after a series of programmes using archive film to present the story of the last sixty years, "just as their fathers laughed at the early 'thirties; then came deepening concern and realization. The development of events caught them, and they sat stiff, a little more upright than usual, with unbroken intentness."

The problems of the world will soon be theirs. Their immediate and urgent problem is to manage the new complex of human relationships that late adolescence brings, and to negotiate new and disturbing acts of moral choice. To help them to do so through broadcasting is a challenge that must be faced. It may seem easy to present for discussion a dramatic situation that poses a moral problem, but broadcasting is a general medium addressed to schools everywhere. Dramatic situations belong to a sharply individual social context. A programme that speaks of the condition of boys and girls in Bermondsey or Brighton may seem as remote as the tribal life of Borneo from young people of the same age in rural Devon. And if the fable and its characters are generally acceptable and offer opportunities everywhere for self-identification, another problem arises. The presentation of a "slice of life" without comment suggests an absence of standards, but direct precept sets up resistance, and implied comment through the words or actions of wise or sensible characters walks a tight-rope over an abyss of priggishness. All these are nevertheless difficulties that at least one broadcasting organization has successfully surmounted. In Japan, the government, alarmed by the drift away from traditional values and social habits, has made moral instruction a compulsory subject at every stage of school life, and the Japanese broadcasting organization has produced, to reinforce the new curriculum, a series of little masterpieces of sympathy and artistry. In Britain there has been more encouragement in the responses to broadcast literature in both media of a quality that might have been thought well outside the range of tough and unliterary adolescents. The *Antigone* of Sophocles and Betti's *Queen and the Rebels*, *Volpone*, and *The Good Soldier Schweik*, have alike shown their power to offer a wider insight into the tangle of human motives and passions—a way into the discussion of divided loyalties or the nature of justice, and something of that "habitual vision of greatness" without which Whitehead thought that moral education was impossible. The need for enrichment has not ended, but grows.

The educational situation has nevertheless undergone a radical transformation.

Over the whole range of formal education this country, like its Western European neighbours, has embarked on an unprecedented programme of expansion. Like them it finds that the task is complicated by a rapid growth of population. By 1970 school numbers in Britain will be nearly eight million; by 1980 nearly nine and a half million. The nation is committed by the Education Act of 1944 to the provision of full-time education for all up to the age of sixteen, and continuing education on either a full-time or part-time basis for a further two years. During the past decade a series of major educational reports has set targets for the period between now and 1980, which have been approved in principle by every political party, and has laid down the guiding lines that should determine the nature and content of the education to be provided. We have for the first time the broad outlines of an educational strategy for ten years ahead. The new Schools Council, representing every branch of the educational profession, is a wholly new instrument for the modification of the school curriculum.

The White Paper on Technical Education of 1956 insisted

on the need to educate for versatility in an age of technological change, envisaged an expansion of technical and commercial education at every level, and established the colleges of advanced technology which in 1963 achieved full university status. The Crowther Report of 1959, on the education of boys and girls between the ages of fifteen and eighteen, showed conclusively how many of them failed to go on to a further education commensurate with their abilities because of the pressures of their families and environment, and advocated a plan which would, by 1980, bring half of the boys and girls of the country within the range of full-time education until the age of eighteen. The number of pupils in sixth forms has continued to grow steadily, and is nearly double what it then was, establishing a steady pressure for more and more places in universities and other institutions of higher education. The Robbins Report on Higher Education of 1963, acknowledging that pressure, "assumed as an axiom" and justified in terms of social justice and economic need "that courses of higher education should be available for all who are qualified by ability and attainment to pursue them and who wish to do so". On the basis of a thorough statistical inquiry, the Report called for the provision of 35,000 new places by 1980 so as to raise from eight per cent to seventeen per cent the proportion of the population profiting from higher education. The first phase of this massive expansion is in full progress; the training colleges for teachers have almost doubled their numbers; and ten new universities have received their charters and begun to build. The Industrial Training Act of the same year, concerned with the less academic boys and girls, placed on industry a new responsibility for the training of young workers, gave to the Ministry of Labour a statutory power to set up training boards for each industry, and looked forward to the achievement by 1980 of a state of affairs in which all young people up to the age of seventeen would be thought of as learners, not earners. Finally, the Newsom Report of 1963 showed how far we are from realizing the full potentiality of the boys and girls between thirteen and sixteen of "average and less than average ability" with whose education it was concerned, and persuaded the government that the age of compulsory school attendance must be raised to sixteen. It will be so raised in 1970, bringing us into line with France, with its *explosion scolaire*, its school population amounting to a quarter of the whole, and its inadequate teaching force. Like France we are faced with an educational problem that includes but goes far beyond the problem of sheer numbers.

The central problem is the achievement of a vast programme of expansion without any loss of breadth of approach or humane values.

The task is a formidable one. It is estimated that if we reduce the size of classes to thirty and raise the school-leaving age to sixteen, we shall need 650,000 teachers instead of the present 350,000. The problem of teacher recruitment is further complicated by wastage; with the present trend towards early marriages the mature working life of a woman teacher cannot be estimated as more than five years; and already there are more trained women in the home than in the schools. In some subjects there is a shortage of specialist teachers so acute as to be a serious threat to the maintenance at their highest level of those technologies which are most essential to economic prosperity and to economic advance— a problem common to all the "over developed" countries, to the United States, France, Sweden, and ourselves.

Expenditure on education may well be the best national investment but it is, by its very nature, a long-term investment. When the birth-rate is rising, the school population increases before there is any corresponding rise in the working population and sets up a demand for buildings and teachers which can only be satisfied by a rise in productivity or by the allotment to education of an increased share of the national product. Britain is now in just that situation. The share that goes to education has risen since the war from three per cent to five per cent. Current and capital spending on education is running at well over a thousand million pounds a year, and is scheduled to rise yet more steeply.

The targets that we have set ourselves in the National Plan can be attained only by a realization of the growth-rate postulated by the plan, by a rise in taxation, or by cuts in some other form of government expenditure. It has become imperative to look for economies in the use of buildings and even more in the use of the scarcest and dearest of all resources, specialized teaching skills. The problem for as far ahead as can be foreseen will be to make the best possible use of a teaching force that will fall far short of an ideal requirement.

At the school level the Minister of Education has adumbrated a new role for the teacher as "a manager of the revolution in the technology of education".[1] This, he said to an audience of teachers, might sound airy-fairy, but the Nuffield Foundation inquiries might soon bring it down to earth. The Nuffield Foundation, in partnership with the Ministry of Education, is engaged in an investigation into the effectiveness and comparative costs of all the new media. Across the channel the findings of an inter-ministerial committee have led to the establishment of a joint bureau of the French Ministry of National Education and Radio-Télévision Française charged with the task of inquiry, not only into the value of these media in education, but also into the question of how their exploitation should be divided between local and central organization; public and closed-circuit

[1] C. A. R. CROSLAND, as reported in *The Times Educational Supplement*, 15th April, 1966.

radio and television; radio, television, and film. The concern is world-wide, and UNESCO, seeking to apply the experience of the more-developed for the benefit of the less-developed countries has in hand a major inquiry into the cost-effectiveness of radio, television, and programmed learning compared with conventional methods of instruction.

Everywhere there has been an inevitable shift of emphasis away from "enrichment" and towards "direct teaching"and other ways of using broadcasting to help the schools with their central curricular concerns; make scarce teaching power more widely available, and diffuse new knowledge and new approaches.

School broadcasting services were built up on the basic assumption that their function was not to replace the teacher, but to put new tools in his hand. The urgency of the present situation has called even this assumption into question. There is no longer any doubt that broadcasting can, for reasonably mature students, take over the whole burden of instruction, calling for no more co-operation at the receiving end than a general administrative supervision of the exercise. In Italy, where a legislative raising of the school age outran the national capacity to provide school buildings and qualified teachers, especially in the mountain villages, the national broadcasting organization—Radiotelevisione Italiana—in partnership with the Ministry of Education, decided in 1958 to provide courses covering the whole of the three-year curriculum of the junior secondary school and addressed to boys and girls for whom there are still no schools. They are assembled in private houses or at some public or religious centre, by teachers unqualified for secondary work, or even by friendly adults who would make no claim to be teachers. The methods used are largely those of the classroom, with a small class in the studio to encourage a sense of participation, and to provide models of activity for the viewers. The children are furnished with textbooks edited by their "television teachers", are expected to undertake exercises to be marked at the centre, and can in due course proceed to the school-leaving examination. Within its own terms, the "Telescuola" has met with unqualified success, not only academically, but as an exercise in group work and social training for adolescents. It is, however, a success dependent on circumstances that impose clear limits on its range of applicability as a model. A television teacher needs just as much time to cover his subject as a live teacher does. "Telescuola" was conceived as an emergency service to meet a specific and limited need by a country with large resources and a highly developed broadcasting organization. To cover the restricted curriculum of one narrow age-group it broadcasts for seven hours a day throughout the week. A service that tried to offer a complete mathematics course for each year of the English grammar school, including the sixth form, would use up all the time available during the school day on one channel. The future of exercises demanding such a large allotment of time must be with closed-circuit installations using multi-channel facilities rather than with broadcasting organizations operating on a national scale. In the new situation as it has developed in most countries, the function that broadcasting can best discharge is to provide for the imperfectly equipped or non-specialist teacher a basis for his work, which determines the broad context of his teaching just as a textbook might do. The broadcasts present a topic with the maximum impact, but invite the full co-operation of the teacher in taking his pupils on from the point at which the programmes leave them. It is on these lines that France, with a third of the science teachers in its *lycées*, and a half of those in its modern schools not regularly qualified, has (at the insistence of its inter-ministerial commission) launched a four-year plan using both television and radio, and designed to lead by 1967 to the provision of a complete framework for the teaching of science, mathematics, modern languages, and French. The schools with non-specialist teachers have all been equipped by the government with television and radio receivers. The school principals have been instructed to ensure that the relevant programmes are used, and to return regular reports on their success.

In Delhi, where the number of students in the higher secondary schools has doubled in the past five years, and where there is a shortage of well-equipped laboratories as well as of teachers, a television project financed by the Ford Foundation is covering those topics in the science syllabus which the teachers cannot themselves cover for want of resources, time, or adequate training. In Japan, the various grades of the *Science Classroom* series reach more than half of the primary school population—amounting to more than six million children. In Britain, there is a steady trend in the same direction. Primary schools base their science teaching on the radio series *Junior Science* and secondary schools base their first year's work on the series *Discovering Science*.

It is a trend that calls for a new and closer type of partnership with the teacher. There is a renewed need to enlist the interest and sympathy of the teacher force, and to make them feel that broadcasting is not an alien element from outside the school, and still less a usurper of their own position but an instrument to be used. It is wise for any country introducing a new school service or radically revising an old one to hold seminars for teachers (as Ghana and India most effectively did) to make them aware of the character and limitations of the broadcasting media, of their own role in the classroom, and of the importance of preparation and follow-up work. "The trouble in Thailand", as the Thai delegate told the World Conference on School Broadcasting held in Tokyo in 1964, "is that the teachers will turn on the sets and go fishing".

It is vital for the future of the service that the training colleges for teachers should themselves use broadcasting techniques, and should show their students how to make the most effective classroom use of them. The active help of teachers must be sought in the planning, and in the assessment of programmes. Perhaps the impulse towards a closer co-operation is symbolized most strikingly by the great annual convention held each year by Nippon Hoso Kyokai, the main broadcasting organization of Japan, attended last year by 17,000 teacher members of local Educational Broadcasts Study Groups; it was exemplified in this country by the nation-wide meetings of teachers held by the BBC as a prologue to the launching of its basic "radiovision" course for teachers of French. It must be made effective primarily by a large-scale provision of ancillary literature, planned and written as an integral part of a single educational exercise. If a teacher is to base his work on the broadcast provision he must have long-term information about the general character of each series. He must be equipped in good time with a close and detailed knowledge of the content and purpose of each programme, and of the part that he has himself to play. There must be handbooks for the teacher. There may be picture-books and textbooks for the pupil. There may well be a need for recorded material on film strip or on magnetic tape as a component part or as a permanent record of a presentation. Each year the BBC now distributes to the schools some fifteen million copies of some three hundred different publications, making a massive addition to the impact of the broadcasts and their own distinctive contribution to the work of the schools. The booklets published by the Swedish broadcasting service set a standard of typography and illustration that is in itself an educational force. The teaching skill and care that must go into literature of this kind, and that can help to raise the work of the modestly equipped teacher to an altogether new level, is equally exemplified in the simple duplicated booklets of Tanganyika or of Thailand.

The basis that broadcasting provides for the work of the teacher must be in harmony with the best thinking of the educational profession, and with the latest advances of knowledge. In every school subject new knowledge goes on accumulating. In some of the most important, new teaching techniques have revolutionized the whole pedagogical approach. A series of school broadcasts can introduce the teacher, together with his class, to new facts, new ideas, and new methods of imparting them. There is a development everywhere of programmes designed for this same purpose, but addressed directly to the teachers themselves. They may offer him an opportunity to hear informal discussion of the latest educational developments to organized listening groups, as the "Teachers' Radio Conference" does in Denmark, and the radio "Teachers' Forum" in Tanganyika. They may offer him a refresher course in his own subject. They may make available to him model lessons, demonstrations, and pedagogical advice, as a French venture in the training of young teachers does. They may be linked with a broadcast series for schools, and show the teacher how to make the best use of it, like the series which accompanied the first television English lessons of All India Radio. They may help women who left the teaching profession for marriage to keep in touch with the problems of the classroom. The BBC programmes designed for just that purpose reach an audience of 150,000, including half of the women in the target group. They may serve at the same time a wider range of these purposes.

These broad new tendencies—the provision of a core for the teacher's work through school broadcasts and the diffusion of new approaches through broadcasts to teachers—find their main exemplification in three fields, all of cardinal importance. No school subjects have undergone more radical change than mathematics, science, and linguistic studies; none are more vital to economic and social well-being and progress; none are more gravely affected by the shortage of qualified teachers. All of them lend themselves to effective broadcast treatment at every level, from the primary school to the post-graduate seminar.

The need for scientific education both at the level of general enlightenment and at the level of academic, professional, and technological specialization is patent and universal. The foundations of scientific understanding must be learned in the schools, starting at the primary stage. Nowhere in the world are enough scientists coming forward to meet fully the needs of both industry and the teaching profession.

Radio and television can help to break the vicious circle by which inadequate teaching now ensures that the supply of teachers will still be inadequate in the future. Television has at its disposal not only the whole range of existing laboratory equipment, including the equipment of the great specialized centres of research, but such specially made models, charts, animated diagrams, and films as may be required, and an instrument with an unrivalled capacity for close and detailed demonstration. A model of Hero's aeolipile or Herz's apparatus, an automatic telephone switchboard or a twenty-foot wind-tunnel are as readily available on film or on the studio bench as Wheatstone bridge in the average school laboratory. Animated diagrams have a unique directness and clarity. The more complex the process or system of concepts involved, the greater the service they can render. A verbal explanation must often be cumbrous and involved, or even distort the facts, because of its linear character, since, as Von Haller put it: "Nature has linked her kinds into a net, not into a chain; men are incapable of following anything but a chain, since they cannot express in words more than one thing at a time." An animated diagram showing a feedback loop in a self-regulating system, or respiration and photosynthesis in plants, can display simultaneous processes. Again, there are many contexts in which analogical diagrams and models have an expository value. Lord Kelvin, who was "never happy until he could make a mechanical model of a thing", and for whom model-making meant stringing together little balls and beads with sticks and elastic bands to illustrate crystalline dynamics, would have been the ideal exponent of a medium which offers unlimited scope to those whose teaching gifts and ingenuity in creating visual devices go hand in hand. There are, of course, pitfalls along this path, and fields in which a physicist nowadays may be unwilling to use visual analogies because of the dangers of conveying a false or over-simplified impression through the presentation of abstract relationships in concrete terms. The "models" which he uses may be purely mental constructions, and the inferring techniques on which he depends may make use of a sophisticated mathematics. Those who would follow him beyond a certain point must leave picture-thinking behind. Television can still offer a vastly wider audience for a lecturer and his blackboard.

A medium so equipped has something to offer to the new teaching of the sciences at every school level. One of the traditional approaches to scientific thinking in the primary school has always been through natural history. The school televison programmes of many countries, whether they deal with the coral reefs of Australia, the sand-dunes of Belgium, or the beavers of Canada, are grounded in the new ecological approach to nature study, and exploit the opportunities of television to present a web of relationships. They all aim at producing a stimulus to, and not a substitute for, first-hand observation of the natural world, and reinforce that aim with guidance for class and teacher.

A new approach to the physical sciences at the same level has been gaining ground in the United Kingdom, based on

simple experimentation by the pupils with everyday household objects, designed to throw into relief broad scientific
principles, and using simple apparatus like string telephones
or pocket-torch batteries. This approach is supported here
by a radio series which takes advantage of the power that
radio has to call for overt activity by the children during the
broadcast. On the other side of the world Nippon Hoso
Kyokai serves the same aims. In the middle reaches of the
schools, television provides a solid basis for the teaching of
the new physics. At the sixth form level there are three tasks;
the opening up of new horizons for the science specialist;
the building of bridges between the science and arts sides;
and the scientific education of the arts pupil. To the science
specialist, television can offer the latest findings of research
interpreted by the pioneers in the field, who can convey to
him not only the rigours but the imaginative quality of scientific thinking. It can help him, as no other medium can, to
appreciate the intellectual as well as the social significance of
the new technologies that stand in such urgent need of able
recruits. For the whole sixth form together it can provide an
introduction to fields of discourse such as evolutionary theory
or atomic physics which still find no place in the conventional
syllabus, but which are socially or philosophically of wide
significance. For the arts student it can provide an introduction to scientific thinking, and so relieve an overburdened
science staff of some part of the task of spreading "numeracy".
For the non-specialist, a broadcast series may be focused on
science in its social context. It may embark on a study of
the strategy and tactics of science as embodied in some of the
classic researches. It may go at least half-way to meet the
views of those who believe that the most valuable provision
for the arts student is a modicum of straightforward scientific
teaching. There can obviously be no substitute for individual
laboratory work, where the making of scientists and scientific

technicians is concerned, but most of us will never in that sense be scientists, and it is perhaps worth remembering that a committee headed by one of the most distinguished scientists of this century came to the conclusion that "the view that experiments by the class must always be preferred to demonstration experiments leads to great waste of time and provides an inferior substitute", and that in Sir William Ramsay's opinion "it is possible to have quite an intelligent idea of chemistry without ever having handled a test tube or touched a balance".

In the field of mathematics, a sophisticated use of the television medium is even more effectively keeping pace with the development of the subject. The new need is for a stimulus in the primary school to a discovery by the children themselves, in their own environment, of properties and relationships, and for a cultivation in the secondary school of the power of generalization and abstraction. The new content of mathematics takes within its scope from the earliest stages number notation and two-state systems; graphs and statistics; number patterns and shapes; sets, relations, and functions. The new visual techniques can show congruence or variance through the superimposition of images; develop geometrical ideas through the movements of translation, rotation, and reflection; show how a point generates a line; or facilitate an analysis of groupings and a search for common elements.

They can convey with dramatic impact the intellectual excitements of a logical argument; or they can show how a statistician uses his statistics. How far they may even offer an altogether new way to an understanding of mathematical and scientific concepts by a direct presentation of spatial relationships, or by a visual use of common experience to children and adults who have been handicapped by a lack of verbal ability, we do not yet know. A BBC programme which set out to explain the difference between a statistical

N

average and a distribution pattern may illustrate the kinds of possibility to be explored and tested. It asked a group of thirty schoolboys to try on shoes from a heap of "sevens"— the average size for their age. It showed them in hopeless confusion cramming their feet into shoes too small, and slopping about in shoes too large, and then, issued with shoes of the right size for each of them, sitting down in orderly rows according to their shoe sizes. On top of them, as they sat, the conventional diagram for a distribution pattern was neatly superimposed, and the stage was set for a straightforward exposition.

The Nuffield Foundation and the Schools Council in England, and the Curriculum Study groups in the United States are fostering the new teaching, but science knows no frontiers. Mathematics is the purest of all international languages. The reform of the curriculum in these subjects is going ahead on similar lines in Sweden and France and the United Kingdom, in Canada and Australia, in the United States and Japan, and in all these countries, is finding, in the broadcasting media, powerful means for the spreading of new ideas and the establishment on a national scale of new teaching norms. It is a world-wide movement that offers real opportunities for collaboration and common effort. In Europe, the Organization for Economic Co-operation and Development (OECD) has given a lead through the establishment of international working parties drawn from teachers of physics, chemistry, and mathematics, and charged with the duty of considering the aims, content, and methods of school sience teaching. A special committee dealing with audio-visual aids has provided a forum for professional discussion. A Committee of the European Broadcasting Union has gone beyond discussion to energize a proposal for the co-operative creation of filmed sequences illustrative of mathematical ideas, and available to all EBU members. A growing awareness of common problems should lead to a continuous pooling of ideas on a still wider basis.

Another curricular field in which broadcasting has already become a major force is that of language teaching. Every programme using a language other than the vernacular increases the listener's command of that language. Broadcasting still makes a characteristic contribution to language teaching by providing opportunities for classes to listen with their teacher to the Comédie Française playing *L'Avare*, or to a German commentator discussing the Bundestag elections. Throughout the world, however, a revolution in the teaching of languages is shifting the emphasis away from the formal teaching of grammar, and from traditional methods of "teaching about a language", towards the more natural process of language learning through the constant and progressive hearing, understanding, and use of language in contexts that give it significance. Nobody who has heard a class of far from academic primary school children improvising a dramatic scene in lively idiomatic French can doubt that a second language might easily become an almost universal possession, as invaluable in a multilingual Europe moving towards close integration as in the developing countries. The deployment of the new methods is still seriously impeded, especially at the vital primary school stage, by a shortage of teachers who themselves have an easy, correct, and idiomatic mastery of the language they teach. Broadcasting is an ideal means for their diffusion.

Nearly twenty years ago Professor Bruce Pattison of the University of London and a group of his colleagues, in close partnership with the staff of "English by Radio"—a BBC enterprise concerned with the teaching of English to overseas audiences—carried to completion a remarkable pioneer venture. *Listen and Speak*, the course of 150 English lessons for beginners that they brought into existence, was perhaps the first language course in any medium to exploit fully the methods that are now universally accepted. *Listen and Speak* was designed to teach by familiarizing the learner with the structural patterns of the language, displayed in living contexts, and so graded that he would steadily increase his power, not merely to repeat sentences, but to construct his own by analogy and use them when called upon in the course of the programme to do so. In the early stages of language learning the physical context and references to the visible world provide the most unmistakable clues to meaning, but radio is in itself a blind medium. Professor Pattison and his collaborators overcame that handicap partly through ingenuity in the use of sound effects and partly through the provision of a simply illustrated handbook. Television has brought its own strengths to the support of "audio-visual" language teaching, but without in any way superseding these earlier methods. In the first stages of teaching, radio, accompanied by illustrated booklets, wall pictures, or film strips synchronized with the broadcast can be fully as effective as television, perhaps even more so, since it can strip down the visual component to its bare essentials, and give the listener time to focus his attention upon it without setting up any expectation of visual excitement and change. In the later stages it is vital to train the habit of interpreting a foreign language—as it must, for the most part, be interpreted in actual use—in purely aural terms. Television has perhaps its greatest value in the middle ranges, and for adult audiences without the strong motivation of the committed student, for whom the attractions of the visual medium are in themselves the main reason for watching.

The BBC in radiovision with its *Joseph and Sarah* series; the Centre for Educational Television Overseas with animated cartoon film; the school radio services of Ghana and Tanganyika with the aid of pupils' pamphlets, are developing the new approach for schools in Africa. France, Japan, Sweden, India, the United Kingdom—indeed, all the great developed broadcasting services of the world—are developing more complex and sophisticated radio and television courses for adult students, as well as for the schools, making full use of dramatic techniques.

For the mature and committed student capable of organizing his own work, a broadcast language course supported by booklets and by gramophone records or tapes can be wholly self-sufficient. In the schools, as with the teaching of science and mathematics at any but the highest levels, the task of the language-teaching programme can only be that of initial presentation. Consolidation and assessment, and steady practice of what has been learnt, must lie with the teacher. With a modest linguistic equipment he can successfully manage the necessary drills; and in the United States it is estimated that more than three million children are already learning in just this way from imperfectly qualified teachers. But the teacher must have the support of literature. He can be helped still more by programmes designed to increase his own facility in the language and his own professional skills, as many countries are discovering. All India Radio accompanied its experimental programmes of English teaching by television with programmes for teachers showing how to use them. Algeria has begun to develop French lessons for primary school teachers supported by correspondence tuition.

There is no longer room for doubt that the broadcast as instruction is a valid and fully effective means for the basic presentation of these and other subjects. It may call for further effort by the individual home student; it may, for him, need, or benefit enormously from, the support of correspondence tuition. It may be incomplete without the disciplines of the classroom, the dialectic of the seminar or tutorial. Within its own limits of one-way communication it can carry the main teaching burden as surely as a live teacher can. Theoretically, and without any regard for the special advantages of the medium, there is no reason why a televised lecture or demonstration should have more or less teaching impact than a "live" presentation of the same material using the same resources. Empirically, the facts are that through television and radio, listeners all over the world achieve fluent English; children in half a dozen European countries acquire a first knowledge of binary notation, students in Chicago earn degrees, and old peasant women in Calabria manage to write for the first time to their sons in America. It is by no means easy to eliminate all the variables so as to enable valid comparisons to be made between live and broadcast teaching, but there is now a great body of readily accessible research, mainly American, but accepted as valid and satisfying the strictest criteria by British workers in the field, to show that the advantage is by no means always with the live teacher. Judged by all the ordinary tests of achievement the television class and the home student sometimes do rather better, sometimes rather worse, than the matched group receiving conventional classroom instruction; overall, there is no very significant difference. Among the more revealing experiments to determine the value of television programmes as component parts of a course was the Turkish[1] experiment with the well-known Harvey White physics course, consisting of one hundred programmes addressed to senior high school students, which has been recorded on film for classroom use, and was so used in this instance with the full support of teachers' guides and pupils' textbooks. The students of the very best teachers, using what aids they wished (but not the Harvey White films), scored slightly higher marks than those home students and others who had only seen

[1] Turkish Ministry of Education, *Istanbul Physics Film Report*, Ankara, 1961.

the films; but there was no significant difference at all between the scores of students with experienced and students with less experienced teachers when the films were used by both groups. So far as the use of television programmes as a vehicle of instruction for older pupils is concerned, it is now safe, in the light of evidence from many sources, to generalize the findings of an Australian comparison between the live and the tele-vised teaching of mathematics,[1] and to conclude that "a good teacher on television can achieve results which are comparable with those of the good teacher in the classroom, and which are better than those achieved by a weak teacher in the classroom".

There is no further need of research to determine whether broadcasting can serve the central purposes of education. What is now needed is research to discover how it can best do so. In view of the fact that educational television may cost up to ten times as much as educational radio there is no field of inquiry that calls more urgently for cultivation than the comparative value and effectiveness of the two media in various educational circumstances.

II

The effectiveness of a school broadcasting service depends entirely on the support of the educational authorities, both central and local, and on the good will and understanding of the teachers who use the programmes. It is therefore of vital importance to establish a relationship between the broad-casting organization and the educational system which allows

[1] Victoria School Broadcasts Advisory Committee, *Report on Experimental Mathematics Programmes*, Melbourne, 1961. For a full and recent critical survey of American research see the articles by A. A. LUMSDAINE and W. J. MC-KEACHIE in *Handbook of Research on Teaching*, ed. N. L. Gage, Chicago, 1965. Other references are listed in the bibliography of this book.

the service to develop as a true working partnership. The ways in which this can be done inevitably vary from country to country. Federal states like Nigeria and Canada must allow for devolution, and for a co-ordination of effort between the central and the regional authorities which is unnecessary for a small unitary state like Malta or Denmark. Some educational systems, like those of France (and nearly all of the developing countries) are highly centralized, with a national curriculum determined and closely supervised by the Ministry of Education. In them it is natural that school broadcasting should be controlled and planned by a branch of that Ministry. In the United States, where education is the concern of the separate states, and is organized on a local basis, and where the great national networks are in commercial hands, school broadcasting is commonly planned and provided by local education authorities. Some of them, like Hagerstown, have set up stations of their own; others depend for studio production or for merely technical facilities on local commercial stations. A country where the government is itself a broadcasting authority needs no special machinery of educational control such as is necessary where broadcasting is in the hands of independent corporations or companies. Circumstances vary. Everywhere the basic problem is that of reconciling educational control with the specialized professional competence which can alone ensure the fulfilment of educational purposes.

The broad control of policy must without question be in the hands of the competent educational authorities. Broadcasting will inevitably modify the curriculum and colour the ways in which each subject to which it contributes is taught. No broadcasting organization can properly determine the age at which children should be introduced to a second language or to the facts of human reproduction, the significance of a new way of teaching physics, or the time when a course of

Christian apologetics for sixth forms should give place to a wider treatment of belief and unbelief, of secular as well as religious faiths.

The Ministry of Education must clearly play an important part. The arrangements must also allow the teachers who will use the programmes to have a share through their representatives in determining their general character. The detailed planning must be done by men and women who are firmly grounded in education but equipped with a high degree of skill as radio and television producers. It is not practicable for a group of people unfamiliar with the opportunities, the limitations, and the practical problems of the broadcasting media to plan series of programmes round a table and hand over the plan to a producer without educational experience; nor, on the other hand, is it wise for even the most experienced of educational producers to rely wholly on his own judgement within the terms of a wide and general directive. Plans need a close and critical scrutiny, and a realism that can only be achieved if both those responsible for policy control and those who actually plan and produce the programmes have a first-hand knowledge of the schools, and a steady flow of information about conditions in them, and about the impact and success of the service. There must be opportunities for the planners and producers to discuss their problems with practising teachers. The teachers themselves must be instructed in the proper use of the programmes, and given every kind of help in using them well. In Britain there has been no central control of the curriculum by the Ministry of Education. Each local education authority and each individual school has traditionally enjoyed a large measure of curricular freedom. In a system so decentralized it has not proved easy for the BBC to integrate its broadcast provision with the needs and activities of the schools; and the machinery that has been evolved is of some complexity. Educational control is secured not through a direct relationship with the Ministry of Education, but through the School Broadcasting Council for the United Kingdom, and its daughter Councils for Scotland and Wales, which share in the oversight of the United Kingdom service and exercise a delegated responsibility for programmes transmitted only in their own regions. The formal duty of the Council is to guide the BBC in the provision of a service for schools and technical colleges, to stand sponsor for that service with them, and to act as the official link between the BBC and the world of education in all matters relating to the service. Its constitution makes specific provision for the representation of every major educational body, and in particular of the Ministry of Education, the local education authorities, the professional associations of teachers, and the university departments and colleges of education. It is not merely advisory, but has real delegated powers. It has a right to consider all plans for school programmes, an absolute power of veto, and authority to determine through its written directives the aims and general character of each programme series. These directives are drawn up by programme subcommittees, each of them representing the interests of one age-range, on which practising teachers (other than Council members) are heavily represented. Those directives owe their realism in large measure to the fact that the Council has at its disposal a full-time professional staff (at present some eighty strong) recruited and paid by the BBC, but seconded to its service. Their business is not with the planning and production of programmes, but with the establishment of a firm basis of information on which the Council can exercise its judgement. The School Broadcasting Department of the BBC in sound and television carries the whole responsibility for planning and producing the programmes in conformity with the general policy and specific requests of the Council.

It is a machinery that has worked well in the past and has ensured that the diagnosis of educational needs and the assessment of the extent to which broadcasting has met or might meet them has rested firmly in the hands of the world of education while leaving open for the planners and producers a wide area of creative freedom. It belongs in the last resort to an era when the BBC held an unchallenged supremacy, commanded an adequate licence revenue, and was offering a programme service conceived mainly as an enrichment of the work of the schools.

The situation has been changed by the growth and evolution of the service itself, by the new emphasis on more direct forms of help with teaching as a response to new national needs, and by the trend towards greater centralization within the national system of education. It has been complicated by the entry into the field of independent television. Each of the companies that produces school programmes now has its own advisory body, and since 1964 the Independent Television Authority has been under a statutory obligation to maintain an Educational Advisory Council of its own as a co-ordinating agency.

There is a useful, but loose and informal machinery for achieving some relationship between the output of the BBC and that of the ITA through staff conversations; it falls far short of joint planning. The system, if system it can be called, has reached a point at which it makes large demands on the time of busy and responsible people in the world of education without ensuring that the best national use is made of scarce broadcasting resources, and that there is no unnecessary duplication. It is no longer capable of serving a comprehensive national effort, and any large expansion of the school broadcasting services would need to be accompanied by a radical reorganization and simplification of existing practice.

III

It was Dr. Johnson's conclusion that "nothing can be best taught by lectures, except where experiments are to be shown. You may teach chemistry by lecture. You might teach making of shoes by lectures." The lecture has survived his strictures by some two hundred years as the principal method of university teaching even in the arts subjects, and is strongly defended on the grounds that it is the simplest and most effective way of offering to the first-year undergraduate a broad and up-to-date conspectus of some field of knowledge, and to the more advanced student a survey in greater depth of its frontiers and growing points. The sciences which call for a movement of eye and mind together, and the manipulative skills that serve them, have since Johnson's day assumed an altogether greater importance as advanced studies. Nevertheless, as the Hale Report on University Teaching Methods shows, the lecture and the lecture-demonstration are little studied as means of communication and so uneconomically used that "if during the forthcoming period of expansion the standard of university education is to be maintained, and if at the same time no more than legitimate claims are to be made on the national revenue and path of ability, then university buildings and plant, and the time of University lecturers will have to be better used". Some thirty per cent of all lectures are given to groups of nine students or less, who may indeed have highly specialized needs, but needs that are paralleled elsewhere. The use of the new methods of telecommunication and the new recording techniques could undoubtedly enable lecturers to save time which could be devoted to seminars, tutorials, or research. The Brynmor Jones Committee on the Use of Audio-Visual

Aids in Higher Scientific Education has argued that it is now possible to think in terms of a nation-wide pool of specialized teaching abilities.[1] The universities have already gone a long way towards implementing the recommendations of the Brynmor Jones Report through the establishment of central service units and closed-circuit television installations; the exploration of ways in which they might co-operate has begun. Developments have followed a common pattern with local variations. A medical school or a science department has begun to use television as a way of showing a large group of students the details of an operation, or the Brownian movement seen through a microscope. The group has grown larger still, and the demonstration has been relayed to an "overflow" meeting in another room. The lecturer has seen the advantages of modifying his own lecturing technique so as to use the television medium to the best advantage, has made a practice of recording his complete presentation of the subject for future use, and has, increasingly, begun to wonder whether it might have wider uses.

It is certain that there will be a large-scale expansion of university television, and possibly of university radio, during the next few years. It is unlikely that broadcasting proper will play any very significant part in the use of either medium for the benefit of the internal university student. There are differences of approach to the same subject which make a selective rather than a national use of the same lectures more likely, and even if a universally acceptable course of lectures should be recorded, perhaps co-operatively, to deal with common subject-matter, a simultaneity of transmission and reception would impose on the users a rigidity of time-tabling which would sharply limit the possibilities of development. Since there is no perceptible difference between the

---

[1] *Audio-Visual Aids in Higher Scientific Education*, H M S O, 1965, p. 31.

impact of a live and a prerecorded lecture or programme, both of them having equally the feeling of intimacy and "immediacy" which distinguishes the experience of watching television from that of watching film, the obvious way forward is through the development of university machinery for the co-operative production and exchange of recordings, and ultimately through the establishment of a national library of recorded material. University closed-circuit television will, however, have a twofold importance for "open-air" broadcasting. It will bring into being not only programmes of a highly specialized character, but also programmes likely to interest a widely cultivated audience; the brilliant inaugural lecture, the *colloquium* on some subject of general interest; the exposition of research in progress with far-reaching social or intellectual implications; and the systematic basic course. It will increasingly bring to their making the only fundamental kind of professional competence—an absolute regard for the material and its integrity expressed in television terms.

A still more significant development will be an acceptance by the universities of radio and television as neither the eccentric interest of enthusiasts nor the province of showmen, but as normal and natural modes of communication useful for intra-mural purposes and capable of linking the academic community more closely with the outside world. There has been a wilful academic conservatism, deeply entrenched in France and in the United States, as well as here, which has chosen to think of television and its characteristic devices as no more than what Sir Joshua Reynolds called "a provision of endless apparatus, a bustle of infinite inquiry, employed to shuffle off and evade real labour—the real labour of thinking". It has sometimes been allied with the conservatism of those whose passionate concern for the maintenance of the republic of learning has led them to doubt the wisdom of any large-scale diversion of university energies into schemes of popular education, and to distrust those colleagues who most regularly take their wares into the market-place. As more and more men and women of academic distinction become familiar with television as a part of their own world, more and more of them will be equipped to interpret their developing bodies of knowledge to the educated layman, and to make them, in Matthew Arnold's worlds, "efficient outside the clique of the cultivated and learned". More and more of them will be willing to devise new approaches to their subjects which can be of service not only to their own pupils, but to those more mature students who will be committing themselves to unfamiliar academic disciplines through "the University of the Air".

The intention to make study of a university level possible through broadcasting is by no means new. The first BBC Director of Talks, J. C. Stobart, addressed to Sir John Reith as early as 1926 a memorandum on "The Wireless University" which envisaged a large-scale provision of two-year courses for the serious home student. "No one", as he put it, "need be prevented from learning science by inability to pass in Latin."[1] Broadcast adult education in Britain developed on other lines, and the pioneering work in this field has been done in France and in America. Since 1947 the Sorbonne, which has always admitted the general public to some of its lectures, has been providing some thirty-five one-hour lectures each week for listeners to "Radio Sorbonne". The operation has been thought of as a wider offer of an existing type of facility rather than as a new teaching venture. The English Faculty of the Sorbonne has taken the further step of accepting up to two hundred students for courses using both radio and correspondence tuition; and, significantly, the students have begun to make their own recordings of the broadcasts for use at their own

[1] ASA BRIGGS, *The Birth of Broadcasting*, vol. II, p. 188.

convenience. An altogether more comprehensive combined service, operating at many levels and offering help to the pre-university student working for his baccalaureat is provided by the Ministry of Education through the Centre National de Téléenseignement, and its work for those who for one reason or another cannot undertake full-time attendance at an educational institution is now supplemented and continued by the universities themselves. In 1963 a number of them were persuaded by the Ministry of Education to make a new contribution to the expansion of higher education through a scheme to be operated by regional groupings of some twenty of the provincial universities, and designed to provide through correspondence tuition, through radio and television, and through personal contacts, a new approach to the examination covering the two years of university general studies which link the achievement of the baccalaureat with the start of degree studies proper.

The experiment was accepted under government pressure rather than welcomed as an opportunity. It encountered a conservatism even more rigid and more firmly wedded to traditional university properties and procedures than our own. It was hedged round by the Deans of many of the participating universities with restrictive practices designed to ensure that it should provide neither a supplementary nor an alternative method of study for anyone at all capable of attending conventional lectures, and that it should be confined to a limited group prevented from so doing by illness or occupation. Its use of the broadcasting media was hampered by doctrinal disputes about their proper use, which some academics wished to confine strictly to the provision of a service of guidance and handicapped most of all by a widespread unwillingness to think of communication by radio—so far the principal broadcasting means—as an art to be mastered rather than a mechanical means for the distribution of lectures conceived in other terms. It is a witness to the strength of the broadcasting medium that the scheme has nevertheless survived and grown. Its continuance is assured, and its regional scope is in process of enlargement. In the United States the system by which students accumulate "credits" through the successful completion of the component parts of a course has made it possible for local stations, and even for the great national networks, to offer programmes contributing by arrangement with colleges and universities to the progress of their registered external students. The National Broadcasting Company thus had its "Sunrise Semester" from 6 to 7 on weekday mornings, with accredited courses accepted by some three hundred colleges in subjects as various as American Government and Contemporary mathematics; the Columbia Broadcasting System has its similar lunchtime "College of the Air".

By far the greater part of the audience for "Sunrise Semester" amounting to some 100,000 viewers consisted of men and women with no examination in mind, but there was nevertheless a keen and reasonably successful quota of some 1,300 registered students. A far more comprehensive provision is still made by the city of Chicago, which has for many years been offering on television the whole of a junior college curriculum, with facilities not only for the marking of papers, but for the consultation of lecturers by telephone at regular hours. The external students have achieved results that fully stand comparison with those achieved by students on the campus. In Japan, as a sequel to the success of the full-scale Correspondence High School a modest start has been made with courses designed for students registered with the correspondence departments of universities and colleges. These are officially recognized as constituent parts of the curriculum; are planned by a joint committee of NHK and university representatives; and are accompanied by textbooks specially

o

written by the selected lecturers. In Poland the state broad-casting organization and the Ministry of Education, supported by UNESCO, have this year launched a similar scheme designed to cover the first two years of engineering studies at university level. In this country there has, as yet, been no direct contri-bution to the work of the external student for a university degree, but there have been significant experiments in the opening up through broadcasting of new approaches to higher education. The extra-mural department of Nottingham University has been responsible for one very successful venture, working in partnership with the Midland Company, ABC Television to provide a course in economics on a regional basis. The National Extension College has, together with the BBC, made available a course in advanced mathematics using the same resources. The present British scheme, origi-nated by Mr. Harold Wilson before he became Prime Minister and energized since then with single-minded resolution by Miss Jenny Lee, is the boldest and most comprehensive project that has yet been planned, gathering together threads from many sources and combining them in a new grand design. The end in view is the provision of a new high road to degrees, universally available and open to all without any barrier to admission, for mature men and women who are not in full-time attendance at any educational institution. It is to be achieved through the establishment of a "University of the Air"—or "Open University" as it has come more properly to be called—with the weight and authority of a national institution and the "feel" of a corporate body of which the students are full members. The academic standards of the new university will be guaranteed as the standard of other new universities have been by an academic council widely representative of the world of higher education. The scope and content of its courses will be the concern of its academic staff. Its combination of teaching methods is new and eclectic, its first criterion is that the fundamental and necessary instruction should be available universally, and not confined to the already fortunate urban areas.

It has been recognized from the first that broadcasting could not possibly carry the main teaching burden of even a carefully restricted national operation for sheer lack of available air-time. A modest-sized regional technical college may provide 35,000 hours of teaching in the course of a year, spread over a quite modest range of subjects; a single television channel could not provide a tenth as much at times when its audience might reasonably be expected to be at home. The only method of instruction capable of being made available everywhere and capable of indefinite expansion as new needs arise, is correspondence tuition; and, as was reported by the Robbins Committee on Higher Education, correspondence tuition (without the assistance of broadcasts) has already been used in Russia as a main agent of university expansion. Some forty per cent of all Russian students in higher education there follow correspondence courses supervised by institutions of higher education. The broadcasting media must be reserved for those functions which they are best equipped to perform; for making available the leading authority and the inspired lecturer; for offering demonstrations and illustrative material; for establishing the officers of the university as personalities; for introducing the tutor to his students, and providing students with a stimulus and a sense of "belonging" which could not otherwise be evoked. The broadcasting side of the operation will nevertheless be its most novel and dramatic element, and the amount of broadcasting time available will do much to determine the scope and scale of the total enterprise.

The present plans have been drawn up on the assumption that every course will have the support of both radio and television. The support by broadcasting of a conventional honours degree course would be impossibly expensive in air time owing to the need for a cumulative three-year period of study. The choice of a limited number of disciplines for such treatment would be wholly arbitrary, and would sharply limit the number of potential students. The model chosen for the early operations of the new institution has therefore been the general degree course of the Scottish universities. This offers a wide range of choices, and calls for the study of three subjects for one year, and two more subjects for two years. The appropriate courses may be taken in any order, and the system thus has affinities with the United States "credits" system. The student of the "University of the Air" will be able to choose from a steadily increasing range of subjects, each of which offers a first-year and a second-year course; to take as many or as few subjects at a time as he wishes; and to take as long as he likes over any one of them. In order to cater for the largest possible number of students, yet without dilution of the concept of a university, each component part of the total degree course will have a value in its own right for the serious, registered and committed student, for whom it can lead to a single-subject diploma.

The absence of any qualifying test for admission is basic to the whole conception of an open university. There must therefore be a thorough service of guidance and advice, and, in the long run, preparatory courses for those who lack the instrumental skills that they will need. There must be a central, national, and self-sufficient provision of basic teaching, with supplementary help of every kind that any locality can provide. It must indeed be a condition of entry to some scientific courses that facilities for laboratory work should be available to the student in his local technical college or elsewhere; while the university extra-mural departments and voluntary bodies can be expected to undertake tutorial work in subjects like Economics and English Literature, and to co-operate in the arrangement of vacation courses. Since such ancillary courses will be sporadic there is an absolute need to ensure that all courses (except those in the sciences) can be successfully undertaken by a resolute student with no other help than broadcasting, private reading and correspondence tuition, and that all these are available. Programmed text-books will have to be written in association with the planning of some of the broadcast series; correspondence tutors will have to be available, perhaps through a consortium of the university extra-mural departments. Evening study centres will have to be provided with library facilities and premises suitable for discussions and seminars as well as for viewing and listening. Major centres of this kind will need to be equipped with tape-recorders, and with video-tape recorders.

The undertaking is large and complex. Its critics doubt whether it can reasonably be expected to attract a large enough student body, and to provide economically for their needs. It is not intended primarily for young men and women who have failed to secure university places on leaving school, for whom there is the possibility of full-time courses at the technical colleges now designated as centres for degree work, but for people with jobs and family responsibilities. Many of them will undoubtedly be women, drawn from that large reserve of graduates, trained teachers, and professional workers who left their professional careers for marriage, and who now, with family cares diminishing, have intellectual energies to spare whether or not they are thinking of returning in the near future to work. Others will be married women who want to equip themselves for the first time to teach or to make a career in social work. Some will be young people born a little too early to profit from the great post-Robbins expansion of the universities, or from the change of social habit which has led to a steady increase in the number of boys from working-class homes who go on to universities. Some in the same age-group will have developed unsuspected interests, capacities and ambitions, and be anxious to equip themselves with professional qualifications; some will already have made a start towards a graduate qualification and secured a diploma or other qualification. There will be engineers and laboratory technicians, librarians, accountants, teachers—professional men of all kinds who are unable to proceed by the conventional path to the further qualification that they desire. There will be graduates who wish to broaden their qualifications by adding another science or other language to what they already possess. All these will have a strong and direct vocational incentive to study. There will also be at least some housewives, some mature men, some retired people who wish to take their studies seriously simply for their own sake.

Graduation in these days is not enough. In an age when, as Sir Eric Ashby put it, every professional man needs a renewal of his licence every ten years there is an unprecedented need for refresher courses, and for the diffusion of new knowledge and new techniques. Both the BBC and the independent television companies have made a start in this field. They provide programmes for general medical practitioners, programmes for business men about the use of computers and methods of management, and programmes about new materials and processes for builders and engineers. The "Open University" will be able to build on the foundations that they have laid.

The public reception of the scheme has so far been hostile or hesitant, and for the most part ill-informed. Some of its critics dwell on the limitations of the broadcasting media. They are rarely aware of the experience that has already been gained in the combined use of broadcasts, handbooks, correspondence tuition, an advisory service, and occasional opportunities for meeting. Some point out the high cost of television, and at the full BBC estimate of £5,000 an hour a lavish use of television programmes for direct teaching would indeed be prohibitively expensive. As one element in a combined course of instruction the cost of each programme for a student audience fifty thousand strong would be no more than two shillings a head. For some courses there would certainly be a large "eavesdropping" audience. Half a million viewers followed an austere and demanding series of talks by Professor Bondi on relativity, at a cost per head of roughly twopence halfpenny a lecture. The strongest criticism of all comes from those who doubt whether there is a sufficient body of students whose needs are not met by conventional methods to justify a large new enterprise. Only the event can show; but if the government has the will and determination to see the scheme safely through its early difficulties, and if the new institution bears constantly in mind the strength and the social importance of the vocational impulse, there is good reason to hope that it will serve as a new and powerful agency for the mobilization and fuller use of a great reserve of national ability.

No doubt there will be a high rate of fall-out, and far more people will initially register for each course than will persist as committed students. The results of the Nottingham experiment suggest that the "wastage" will be no greater than in other forms of adult education. It is a clear advantage of the scheme that viewers and listeners will be able to move easily and without any sense of final failure from the "committed" to the "uncommitted" category, and back again. They will be able to sample courses and measure their capacities against them in the year before enrolment. The registered student will have to surrender the liberty of the ordinary correspondence course student. He cannot be allowed to work at his own pace. The University must insist (as Birkbeck College does) that he is a serious university student, working for regular hours throughout a forty-week year, and keeping pace with his radio and television lectures as well as with his correspondence tutors. If he falls by the wayside there will always be another chance.

There can be no future for a University of the Air conceived as a partnership between academics who are ignorant of broadcasting and a broadcasting team drawn from the ranks of general producers. As in every branch of educational broadcasting there will be a need for men and women who are first and foremost specialists in an academic subject and in methods of teaching, but who have acquired a complete professional mastery of the broadcasting skills, and can therefore help others to make the most effective use of radio and television. Initially the educational departments of the BBC, as the only large groups of people with the requisite double qualification, must inevitably play a major part. As the scheme proceeds it will have to enlist the help of the rapidly developing closed-circuit systems of the universities, and (if they so wish), of the commercial television companies. The most important task of its own staff will be the establishment of a new and close working partnership between the world of higher education and the world of broadcasting. If the plan is implemented—and the present government has stated its intention of going ahead as soon as it can—it must be as a combined operation drawing strength from all those in both worlds who believe in the vital educational importance of the second chance.

VIII

BROADCASTING IN THE DEVELOPING COUNTRIES

THE United Nations define a "developing" or "underdeveloped" country as one in which the average *per capita* income does not exceed 300 dollars a year. Two-thirds of the world's people live in such states.[1] They include China and India, all of the new African states, a large part of Latin America, and even a small group of European countries. Eighty per cent of the population in these countries live in rural areas. If there is a characteristic inhabitant of the planet Earth in 1966 he is an illiterate peasant living just above the subsistence level, imprisoned within the narrow and conservative limits of local and traditional ways of living and thinking, ill-equipped with even those vocational and domestic skills which would enable him to make the best of his present circumstances, and without any regular way of keeping in touch with the wider world. As U Thant, the Secretary General of the United Nations, sees it, the gravest problem that the world now faces is not the clash between East and West, but the growing gap and the growing tension between the haves and the have nots.

In 1962, the General Assembly of the United Nations unanimously accepted a resolution expressing its concern that the survey which UNESCO had just completed on its behalf showed that seventy per cent of the population of the world were without adequate facilities for information.

[1] *See* UNESCO, *Statistical Year-book*, Paris, 1966, for the most recent figures.

The standard of adequacy had not been set unduly high, and the first target that UNESCO has indicated calls for no more than ten newspapers, two cinema seats, five radio sets and two television receivers for every hundred inhabitants of each country. A free flow of information intimately linked with and contributing to a vast programme of educational expansion is a prerequisite of social change. Effective communication lies at the heart of the process which is turning inefficient primary producers into efficient primary producers, bringing industry to pre-industrial societies, replacing the technologies of immemorial custom and the habits of thought that have gone with them by those of applied science, welding congeries of tribes into nations, carrying isolated communities into the main stream of the national life, and linking the old and the new nations together in a complex pattern of economic and professional relationships that cuts across the more obvious lines of political affiliation and division.

The major task of governments in the developing countries is to speed the process of change, to help these peoples to overcome fatalism, incuriosity and the fear of innovation, and to involve them in their own destinies. The older generation, wherever they live, must learn to think in national terms, must be made aware of their rights and duties as citizens, and must be prepared to co-operate in campaigns for the improvement of agriculture and the furtherance of health and hygiene. The children must be so educated that there is a universal understanding of the new order and its opportunities, a general level of literacy appropriate not merely to the needs of the moment but to the needs of the next fifty years, and a wide field of recruitment for those professional *élites* which must everywhere take over the full burden of leadership from foreign officials, advisers, and experts. The needs are insistent and the resources to meet them desperately small. It is not surprising that there is a growing awareness of the possibilities of radio and television as instruments to be used in the service of national development, and that the more far-sighted governments are beginning to see those possibilities in the context of their total national plans.

The strength of the broadcasting media in this time of transition lies first of all in the simple fact that they can jump the barriers of illiteracy. In places where an oral tradition embodies the wisdom of the tribe, where there are few readers but many ready listeners, and where there is still a lively habit of story-telling or of discussion around village fires they come as a straightforward extension of the dominant mode of communication. They can be adapted to familiar patterns, as in Ghana, with its imaginative plan for the establishment of viewing posts with specially trained group leaders who will take the role of the traditional story-teller and recite the stories as the pictures unfold. In village and town alike they can bring the illiterate into an equal dialogue with his literate neighbour. They have both now been made free of the wider world.

Of the two media it seems clear that television has a far stronger appeal to the illiterate and a greater power of motivation. A visual presentation is of key importance in the teaching of reading and writing and of vocational skills, as well as in extending experience of the world. The choice between the two must, however, be largely determined by practical considerations, and radio will for many years be the medium best suited to countries with mountains and great rivers, slow and inadequate transport, and strictly limited economic resources at both the transmitting and receiving ends. It is relatively cheap and simple to operate. Although UNESCO has not yet achieved its aim of energizing the manufacture and distribution of a five-dollar radio set, cheap transistorized receivers are nevertheless pouring into even the least developed countries. Japan alone is exporting to African

countries north of the equator some twenty million a year.
There is still an enormous discrepancy between the United
States and Africa with 2·3 per hundred but during the past
ten years the number of radio sets in the world has risen from
237 million to 490 million. The African figure is doubling
every year, and by 1968 Africa will have reached the first
UNESCO target.[1] There will be a set for every four families.
In the villages of the world the bicycle and the transistor
radio are the symbols of emancipation, the index of the
revolution in communications. For families directly linked
for the first time with the outside world news flows as it has
never flowed before through the market-places of Africa and
the bazaars of Asia. Faced with the problem of breaking down
the almost complete isolation of mountain villages whose
archaic routines were hardly touched by the weekly visit of
the mailman, the Tunisian Government found in radio its
most effective instrument. Kenya, with the task of reaching
the mass of the people in a country where eight out of ten
can neither read nor write, and where eighteen different
languages must be used for effective oral communication, can
still, through radio, achieve a comprehensive and universal
service of information. The horizons of the illiterate need
not even be bounded by the national frontiers. Radio has no
inherent limitations, and the BBC Director of External Broadcasting has told how he discovered that the hundred or so
inhabitants of a mud-walled hamlet near Homs on the fringe
of the Syrian desert, most of them illiterate, were listening
regularly on a handful of local sets to programmes from
Damascus, Aleppo, Cairo, and Moscow, occasionally to
programmes from Peking.[2]

[1] *See* WILBUR SCHRAMM, *Mass Media and National Development*, 1965,
pp. 90–133.
[2] E. TANGYE LEAN, *The Revolution Overseas*, BBC Lunch-time Lectures,
1963.

Television has a prestige value that has proved irresistible to most of the developing countries. Its present use to them is far more dubious than that of radio. A television service makes heavy demands on technical and financial resources and on skilled manpower. The total operating cost per hour is variously estimated as something between five and ten times the cost of radio. A transmitter has a maximum range of only sixty to seventy miles. The cost of additional transmitters to serve scattered populations soon becomes prohibitive. Even in a small country like Britain the cost per head of television transmitter coverage, which starts at £0·046 for the London area increases to £20 for parts of the Scottish highlands and islands. A purely commercial operation will inevitably confine itself to the urban areas. It may be difficult for a public service to achieve much more.

The technical problems of transmission in even the wildest terrain may be solved, and the costs reduced. Building on the experience of the Midwest Programme of Airborne Television Instruction the U S Government has this year made possible the establishment by the government of South Vietnam of a nation-wide two-channel service transmitted from two specially equipped aircraft circling above Saigon. The problems of reception are less tractable. The individual set-owner must inevitably be a man of means, with access to other modes of information. There is a real danger that television will serve only those who need it least. As an instrument of social development its future lies in a planned and purposive use with communal groups, or in schools and colleges. In Vietnam, United States agencies have agreed to supply at least 2,500 sets with 23-inch screens for community viewing.[1] In Delhi every secondary school has been equipped

---

[1] See *CETO News*, June, 1966.

with a receiver. Before television can be so used in the vast non-electrified country areas of the world a way must be found to provide a power supply from motorized generators, or through the harnessing of the wind or water.

In every developing country the government has been faced with the double act of choice: whether to have a television service, and if so, what to do with it. In a world where the possession of a television service is a conspicuous badge of modernity it is not easy for any of them to hold back. The splendid new stations at Accra and Kuala Lumpur are assertions that Ghana and Malaya are in the van of progress—at a cost of £2½ to £3 million for each of them. There is an assiduous, seductive and highly competitive wooing of even the smaller states by the high-powered salesmen of Britain and West Germany, Japan and the United States. All too often the United States contract offers a package deal in which the programmes go along with the hardware and the skilled manpower. Where there is a final freedom of programme planning the space must still be filled. The mounting costs must be met and advertising is an easy way to meet them. The advertiser looks for a mass appeal even more crude and blatant than our own, and finds it in imported violence or vacuous imported comedy. Even the public corporation or the government-sponsored service looks, in the absence of a clear directive, for cheap programmes. Nothing with a wide appeal is cheaper than old American films. Their sale abroad may amount to as much as 100 million dollars a year. Television in Manila, as an affiliate of A B C International receives *Maverick*, *Restless Gun*, and *Gunsmoke*. Hong Kong television, in the hands of a British company, offers *I Love Lucy* and *Have Gun, Will Travel*. In Beirut Tele-Orient (also under British control) offers *Rogues* and *The Untouchables*. *Bonanza* is the world's most travelled television programme.

Night after night and in every continent the Western world

presents a false image of its past as an archaic world of horses and violence—and it would be foolish to look for a historic sense in the new audiences of Africa and Asia—or a false image of its present as a world of easy affluence and easy crime, waste, luxury, dissipation, conspicuous consumption, motor cars, and violence. Whether the way of life of this show-business world is envied by the many, or despised by the more discriminating few, the present traffic is damaging to the long-term interests of all the countries that engage in it.

The first step towards nationhood is the assertion of a central authority in terms of personal leadership. It is easy to forget how great the physical difficulties of that assertion have been in the developing countries. An American investigator found in 1956 that there were villages within thirty miles of Poona where most of the inhabitants did not yet know that India was independent. In the village of Patna, seventy-two miles from Poona, only the Headman had heard the name of Nehru. As distance from the towns increases, the flow of information dwindles and dies out; and a survey undertaken in Brazil in 1960 showed that there, too, there was a massive difference in political awareness between the urban and the rural population extending even to the name of the President.[1] Broadcasting offers now an incomparably rapid way of establishing the claims of a new régime or consolidating the hold of an old one. A control of the nation's broadcasting facilities has become the first target of the aspirant to power. The world has become familiar with the *pronunciamento* delivered while the revolutionaries still command little more than the station from which it is made. The strong military guard on the broadcasting station in Damascus and in Lagos bears witness to the troubled politics of the emergent countries and the key importance of a control of communications.

[1] SCHRAMM, op. cit., pp. 69–72.

Authority is most intelligible when it is most forcibly expressed in personal terms, and the leaders of the emergent world have been quick to seize on the importance of broadcasting as a vehicle of personality. It can carry far and wide the image or the utterances of the charismatic leader. Nkrumah's broadcasts according to one of his associates were "one of the principal means of exploiting our country's greatness at home and overseas".[1] It can give the spellbinding force of personal conviction—real or assumed—to a "dynamic" policy, as it did to the aggressive nationalism of Sukarno. It can confirm the immense prestige of a father-figure like Jomo Kenyatta, with his discreet and casual mastery of the television occasion; or of an adroit and sophisticated politician like Lee Kuan Yew of Singapore, whose interest in broadcasting techniques is a facet of his interest in the arts of leadership and whose easy command of them is equally displayed in English, Tamil, or Malay, and in either medium.

Within the Commonwealth the broadcasting organizations have commonly retained that status as independent public corporations which was a legacy of British rule, and elsewhere there is often some degree of freedom from direct government control in the shaping of the programme pattern. Whatever the formal position may now be that freedom does not extend to politics. In Tanganyika as in Thailand, in Egypt, and in Ecuador the content of political broadcasting is determined by the government of the day. It may be either hortatory or expository; it will not be controversial. There is no scope yet for the view of the official opposition, or for the "probing" interview with the man at the helm. Broadcasting in the developing countries is inescapably a political instrument. The dividing line between them cannot

[1] KENNETH ADAM, "Commonwealth Broadcasting from Singapore to Antigua", *The Listener*, 23rd June, 1966.

be drawn in terms of the freedom that they allow to broadcasting, but only in terms of the statesmanship with which it is used. On the one hand are those countries that think of the broadcasting media as useful tools of government in the narrower sense, but show no concern for the character and level of general programmes. On the other are those whose leaders have already seen a clear role for broadcasting in the task of nation-building.

In Israel and in India television has been dedicated strictly to the service of education. In Ghana, Dr. Nkrumah insisted that its paramount objective must be education, that it must not "cater for cheap entertainment or commercialism", but must "assist in the socialist transformation in Ghana".[1] His intentions have survived the fall of his régime. In Pakistan, where a pilot service of television was started in 1966 with transmitters in Lahore and Dacca, President Ayub Khan, himself an impressive master of the medium, has imposed upon it his own version of its task. It will be a general service organized by a Television Corporation in which the majority of the shares will be held by the government. It will, so it is hoped, achieve financial self-sufficiency through the sale of advertising time, but its aim will not be profit. Through communal viewing it will help to build up village democracy. In the words of the Director of Programme Planning: "Television in Pakistan has been conceived as an instrument of education, as a vehicle of good taste, as a medium of sober entertainment, and above all, as a public service worthy of the traditions of the people of Pakistan. It is hoped that this medium will act as a means of promoting moral values, civic consciousness, national integration, and pride and faith in our nation. In short, the purpose of television in Pakistan is to create an awareness of the general range of worthwhile

[1] GENOVENA MARAIS, "The History of Television in Ghana and its Future Plans", *Proceedings of the Tokyo Conference*, 1964, p. 215.

P

activity and experience in consonance with the best of our traditions."[1]

To achieve national integration is to achieve not only an identity, but also a status among the nations. "An awareness of the general range of worthwhile activity" is an awareness of what men have done abroad as well as at home. The most straightforward of all the educative functions of broadcasting is the provision of news. In the developing countries the business of a service of news is not simply to report political events or to serve the immediate purposes of the Ministry of Information. It is to satisfy the keen but unfocused curiosity of men and women who before the advent of broadcasting had little chance to acquaint themselves with even the commonplaces of the outside world. In the early days of the Lusaka radio station one listener spoke in a letter for the millions who can now transcend the limits of their immediate experience. "My brother has bought a new model wireless", he said. "I and my brother have learnt a great deal of things that we never knew before in our poor lives through it." In 1956 a survey by the Indian Institute of Public Opinion showed that illiterates who listened to radio liked best to hear music; then dramatic programmes; then news.[2] There is everywhere a real hunger for information. It is satisfied in part from local sources, but even more in many parts of the world by the external broadcasting services of the great and not so great powers.

The growth of external radio services is largely a post-war phenomenon, though characteristically the Soviet Union was first in the field. As far back as the 'twenties it was broadcasting in all the major world languages, whereas the BBC had to make a start in English with no official backing, and, as Lord Reith put it, in the face of "little encouragement;

---

[1] A. F. KALIMULLAH, "The Future of Television in Pakistan", *CETO News*, March, 1965.　　　　　　　[2] E. TANGYE LEAN, op. cit., p. 4.

colossal indifference; some opposition". Only in 1938 were foreign language broadcasts sanctioned as a part of the preparations for war. In the post-war years the BBC gained an undisputed primacy. Now it has been outstripped at least in so far as its total of 600 broadcasting hours a week is concerned by Moscow with 1,000 hours (and a further 1,000 from its Eastern European satellites) by the USA and by China, with Western Germany and Egypt in close pursuit. In 1965 Moscow added Khmer, Laotian, Malagasy, Malayalam, Marathi, Quechua, and Zulu to the forty-six languages it already used; Peking added Mongolian and Esperanto; West Germany Urdu, Amharic, Kuoyu, and Hindi. Cuba ventured into Guarani. Even in the least regarded corners of the earth the ether is thick with competitive bids for political influence and economic advantage.[1]

Until recent years the overseas services were addressed primarily to the cultivated or to the politically conscious listener, and their vehicle was short-wave broadcasting supplemented by the export to friendly countries of recorded programmes for local use. The BBC provided, and still provides, an admirable and comprehensive projection of British culture. The coming of the cheap transistor has brought new needs and new opportunities. It is normally a medium-wave instrument and there is an urgent rivalry now in the construction of powerful medium-wave stations.

A transistor radio is the proud possession of the poorest owner, and the illiterate is just as likely to tune in to foreign stations as to the local transmitter provided only that they offer what he wants to hear. In the Arab world, the BBC is still dominant with an output in Arabic of ten to twelve hours a day, with a better chain of medium-wave relay stations than its rivals, and with a postbag of nearly forty

[1] For an account of the BBC and other Overseas Services see *BBC Annual*, 1965–66, pp. 83–99.

thousand letters in Arabic each year from the literate part of its audience. To hold its own it must offer a stream of quarter tone music, tales and discussions, feature programmes, light entertainment, and news of the Arab world as well as of the West. It must not only maintain a strong Arabic section in London. It must also record a flow of programmes in its Beirut studio and undertake recording tours throughout the Arab world.

An overseas service so conceived is, at the least, a supplement to the local service that opens up other and wider horizons. It may be the only reliable service of some kinds of information. The five great Press agencies—Associated Press, United Press International, Tass, Reuters, and Agence France Presse—are firmly based on the great powers. The world flow of news is concentrated on their activities, with only a patchy, capricious, or sensational attention to the rest of the world except in so far as the interests of the great powers are involved. There are still forty countries that have no national news agencies of their own. In Africa the telecommunication network is so inadequate that news of one country can often reach its neighbours most readily and cheaply through Paris or London. The best chance of knowing what is happening in neighbouring countries—and indeed in one's own—may well be to listen to the radio, an increasing practice in Africa, or to a disinterested radio service that covers their activities. *The Voice of America* (the US government radio service for overseas) offers a straightforward and authoritative exposition of American policy and the American point of view. Moscow and Peking offer slanted news and the customary gospel of directed hatreds. The achievement of the BBC in maintaining its independent and faithful news service at the time of Suez consolidated its hold on the world's attention. Even in Egypt it now ranks for twelve per cent of radio listeners as the most reliable source of news. With the resources of a monitoring service that listens to the whole world's radio at their command the external services can offer comprehensive news of the five continents.

For most of the developing countries there is no more urgent task than the establishment of a national language, both for the conduct of the ordinary business of life and for the creation of any effective sense of national unity. India has seventy-two languages that are spoken by more than 100,000 people, and in Africa some 700 tribal and linguistic groups meet and intermingle within and across the political boundaries of the new and artificial states. There are three million or more speakers of Yoruba, of Igbo, of Swahili, and of Hausa; less than 10,000 speakers of perhaps a hundred languages. A typical East African country like Kenya with an immigrant Asiatic population to add to the linguistic confusion must use eighteen languages in its daily broadcasts. A tribal vernacular may serve for the traffic of the marketplace and the talk of neighbours. A popular lingua franca like Swahili may be adequate for a wider commerce. A command of the national language is the necessary passport to the world of public affairs, and the key to higher education. Without it a man is denied the full benefit of the mass media. It may be an indigenous language, but neither Arabic nor Hindi will carry a man far without the complementary possession of one of the great world languages. There are many areas where the command of a single major language will not be enough. In Europe, a multi-lingual area moving towards closer integration, every country teaches a second language in its secondary schools. French-speaking Africa and English-speaking Africa are separated now by a linguistic barrier, but Ghana has already begun to use radio for the teaching of French as well as English; and the version of *English by Radio* prepared for those whose basic language is French is broadcast now by every country of French-speaking Africa.

For the rulers of the new Africa a weak tribal language is an obstacle to progress. A strong tribal language is a menace to unity; a symbol of the forces that Ghana has gone far towards breaking, but that may still tear Nigeria apart. There may come a time when the new nations have outgrown the loyalties of the tribe, and can safely foster a diversity of cultures embodied in a diversity of tongues. There may even come a time when they can afford to maintain for each major linguistic group within their boundaries a broadcasting system, a Press, a cultural *élite*, and the costly machinery of higher education. In the foreseeable future the language of the former imperial power must serve both as the bond of nationhood and the path to learning. The fundamental task of the educational system is first to teach good English—or good French—as a second language, and then to use that second language so effectively as the medium of instruction that its use becomes a second nature.

The contribution that broadcasting is uniquely equipped to make, whether it is used as an instrument for the teaching of English in schools and to adult groups or as the major language of general programmes is the establishment and preservation of a standard. There was a time when the language of Tyneside or the Gorbals was as opaque to the Somerset farm-labourer as any foreign tongue. There can be little doubt that general broadcasting has been a normative influence more pervasive than any other. Where there is no central tradition of English speech, the provision of models is all-important. It is tempting for an African who has only reluctantly accepted the absolute need for an English-speaking culture to maintain that there is a native African eloquence, a natural African rhythm which should be allowed to achieve its own phonetic nuances until there emerges a West African English as valid and distinctive as Australian or Lowland Scots. The present danger is that of encouraging modes of speech that will hardly be understood in the next town and not at all in the neighbouring country. The French-speaking African intellectual may pursue the quest of negritude, of a quintessential expression of the African heart and mind. He is prepared to pursue it in the French of Paris, and to value the purity of French as a true world-language. It is the good fortune of Britain that her own spell of power and the technological ascendancy and world-wide interests of the United States have given English a long lead over our old competitors and a very long start on our new rivals. In West Africa French has its last firm strongholds. The old areas of French cultural penetration in the Levant and in South-East Asia are turning more and more to English in one of its two forms. More than half the technical journals of the world are in the English language. It is not surprising, therefore, that the language laboratory of the new Technical Institute of Damascus should be equipping its students to read them. Since English as an official language is a legacy of the Raj it is not surprising that Chinese by radio from Peking finds it harder to establish an audience in India than English by radio from London.

The accidents of history and the spread of broadcasting have conspired to present us with an unique opportunity. Through the *English by Radio* programmes which are now broadcast in ninety countries (including the whole of French-speaking Africa and the whole of South America), with their supporting textbooks in languages that range from Arabic to Urdu; through the general English programmes of the BBC Overseas Services; and through the help that we give to the educational services of the developing countries we can set English still further on the way to being a universal language.

Radio and television can give a new freedom—and a new language—to men and women who can neither read nor write. There is no longer any doubt that they can teach people to do so. According to the UNESCO definition: "A person is literate when he has acquired the essential knowledge and skills which enable him to engage in all those activities in which literacy is required for effective functioning in his group and community, and whose attainments, in reading, writing and arithmetic make it possible for him to continue to use those skills towards his own and the community's development." By that standard forty per cent of the world's adults are still illiterate, and the number is growing. In the long run the remedy lies in universal primary education. The population explosion has made the hope that every country could provide enough primary schools by 1980 look wildly optimistic. In the meanwhile broadcasting can at least ensure for a fortunate and growing number, for an old peasant couple in Calabria or Guatemala or for a young unemployed immigrant in the United States that it is never too late to learn.

"Non è mai troppo tardi"—that is the title of an enterprise that has set a pattern for the world. In 1960 the Italian broadcasting organization, RAI, began to reinforce the national campaign to put an end to illiteracy with a series of television programmes designed for adult viewing groups in the villages of the south, gathered together around communal receiving sets and guided by the local teacher. From the first the programmes had their strong appeal for many adults who would have hesitated from shame to go to school; they were not so much a class as an audience, watching a programme so carefully designed that it did not alienate them either by condescension or by schoolroom methods. The television teacher was easy, friendly, with a gift for blackboard drawing. The approach was lively and varied, and beneath the surface was a firmly structured teaching plan. Soon there were 4,000 viewing groups, and a total of more than half-a-million viewers including those at home—a quarter of the remaining illiterates in Italy. They learnt. Among those who stayed the full course there were few failures. The farmer read his newspaper for the first time, and the mother wrote in a bold hand to her son in the U S A.[1]

Like the "Telescuola", the Italian use of television in its literacy campaign represents the effort of a rich and developed country with a highly efficient broadcasting organization to deal with a residual social problem and speed its solution by the use of modern techniques. In the United States the television series *Operation Alphabet* (an E T V series shown locally on a number of stations) has used a similar approach for the individual illiterate in his own home in cities where there are still large pockets of illiteracy; but even in the most depressed of these areas seventy per cent of the homes have television receivers, and there is the stimulus of a literate and competitive society. The situation in the developing countries is of another kind. Old people everywhere, but most of all in a tribal society, are immobile, set in their ways, and inflexible. There is little incentive for them to learn, since they will never change their jobs. It may be almost as difficult to convince the middle generation that they have anything to gain from the acquisition of a new skill that may cost them 200 hours of patient effort. Their literacy will not necessarily contribute either to productivity or to human happiness. Resources of teaching and organizing manpower are desperately scarce. For many good judges of their own countries' needs the wise course is to undertake only a highly selective campaign for adult literacy, concentrating on rural adolescents with no future on the land and no vocational training; on young men in the cities with their working lives before them (who may already have made a start during a few years of primary

[1] *See* NAZARERO PADELLARO, "Illiteracy, Italian Society and Television", *Proceedings of the Tokyo Conference*, 1964, pp. 445–6.

education), and on those who are already grappling with work that calls for those skills of literacy which they do not possess.

However that may be, UNESCO has called on all member states to give a high priority to literacy campaigns in their national development plans, and in a statement made in 1965 to the Second Committee of the United Nations General Assembly, M. René Maheu, its present Director General, declared that "for the first time the world appears to be materially, technically and psychologically able to eradicate illiteracy in a relatively short time, perhaps within our generation."

The period 1966–70 is to be devoted to an experimental literacy programme as the prelude to a full-scale world campaign. During those four years UNESCO will lend all its support to pilot projects in eight areas of strong motivation; Algeria, Ecuador, Guinea, Mali, Pakistan, Tanzania, Iran, and Venezuela. In all of these projects the use of the mass media is to be integrated with the other elements of a comprehensive scheme. The plan for Iran is a characteristic example. Two regions have been chosen for pilot schemes. The first will be rural, and will be based on ten villages with an illiteracy rate of eighty to eighty-five per cent in the Greater Dez Irrigation Area, where a large-scale experiment in the improvement of agricultural techniques is already in progress. The agricultural instructors are handicapped now by the fact that what they teach orally and by demonstration cannot be consolidated by the use of printed material, but only by time-consuming repetition on the spot. The literacy teaching will be aimed at younger groups between fifteen and thirty-three. It will use audio-visual techniques in the classroom, and what is learnt there will be supported by radio programmes every night.

The second scheme will be urban. Isfahan, with a growing population of 300,000 and with industrialization under way, suffers from a great shortage of skilled workers, and a still greater shortage of foremen capable of understanding printed instructions. There the literacy teaching will be factory-based, strongly supported by television.[1]

There can be no doubt about the universal need for fundamental education. As long ago as 1949 UNESCO described its context in a monograph, and urged that in addition to skills of thinking and communication, domestic skills, and skills used in the arts and crafts it should include knowledge and understanding of the physical and human environment, sympathy and understanding with a different point of view, and a concern for ethical ideas.

In one country or another broadcasting contributes now to all those aims. Perhaps the best developed activity yet is one that will hold its primacy, and agricultural broadcasting must serve here as a type of what the new media can do. In almost every country the largest single vocational group consists of farmers. The developed countries long ago discovered that the agricultural community with its strong shared interests was an audience that radio was well adapted to serve. Television has brought a new contribution, but there is no need to show a dairy-farmer a picture of a cow as an accompaniment to the current fat-stock prices, or to a discussion of the latest legislation about foot-and-mouth disease. A radio service for farmers, whether it is the responsibility of a government department as in Ireland, of a public committee as in Denmark, or of the professional broadcasting organization with the help of an agricultural advisory committee as in Britain and France has a great and proven value as a rapid way of disseminating information. If it can involve the farmers in a dialogue, so much the better. The 6.15 a.m programmes for farmers in Jordan owe their success to the

[1] *See* "Iran: Literacy Teaching in Rural and Industrial Areas", *UNESCO Chronicle*, March, 1964. (Reported in *CETO News*, June, 1966.)

fact that they are firmly based on farmers' questions. "What do I do about the insects that make the bark of my orchard trees fall off?" "How do I treat the sickness that makes my cow have a calf before her time?"[1] In Britain the success of *The Archers: A Story of Country Folk* which has been running now since 1950 has shown how effective a dramatized serial story can be in spreading new ideas, fostering an understanding among townsmen of the country way of life, and modifying at least some attitudes.

It was the Canadian Broadcasting Corporation in partnership with the Farm and Fisheries Department and the Canadian Association for Adult Education that first took a further step that has acquired a universal significance, began to encourage community listening by farmers, explored empirically the psychology of small groups, and discovered that the key to successful group listening was to link it with decision-making. As CBC has put it, the *Farm Forum* groups with their motto, "Listen, Discuss, Act", "provided new ways for people to meet and act together, offered an ideology of adult opportunity, and were rare examples of an educational programme and not a pressure group becoming a social movement".[2] The Canadian example was followed with characteristic and impressive thoroughness by Japan. Faced by a large-scale drift from the land and an urgent need to use rural manpower to the best advantage, NHK began in 1955 to provide systematic agricultural education for young farmers under the sponsorship of the Ministry of Education and the Ministry of Agriculture and Fisheries. For two hours every weekday *Radio Agriculture School* offers a basic course in rural science and its practical applications, with a Sunday session on

[1] SCHRAMM, op. cit., p. 151.
[2] *See* "Adult Education Broadcasting in Canada", *Proceedings of the Tokyo Conference*, 1964, pp. 439–41. *See also* J. NICOL AND OTHERS, *Canada's Farm Radio Forum*, UNESCO, 1954.

problems of farm management. Some 330,000 farmers listen, and for those of them who are enrolled in one of the 15,000 listening groups and supplied with manuals there are supplementary training sessions on the land arranged by the local farming supervisor. Each day there is a half-hour television programme which takes young farm owners as its target, and concentrates on new machines and new techniques. Each day there is a magazine programme in each of the media carrying reports, personal experiences, news of pioneer ventures, explanations of administrative policies, discussions of "rural culture and the art of living" and, as a counterpart to *The Archers*, "serial dramas full of the vigour and good sense of farming people".[1] Perhaps the most striking of all the developments of the original Canadian idea in its communal implications is taking place in India, which already has 3,500 village forums and hopes to add 5,000 a year. Its significance is twofold; first, in the finding that increase in knowledge derived from radio in the forum villages is spectacular, but negligible in those where there is only individual listening, and secondly in the fact that the forums "developed rapidly into decision-making bodies capable of speeding up common pursuits in the village faster than the elected panchayat. The forums then became an important instrument of village democracy, and enabled many more people to partake in the decision-making process in the village."[2]

The experience of the farm forums has demonstrated beyond a doubt that broadcasting linked with group discussion can play a vital part in social development. A group experience that begins as a social occasion involving wives and

[1] "Adult Education Programmes Broadcast in Japan", *Proceedings of the Tokyo Conference*, 1964, p. 443. *See also* UNESCO, *Rural Television in Japan*, 1960.

[2] J. C. MATHUR and PAUL NEVRATH, *An Indian Experiment in Radio Farm Forums*, UNESCO, 1959.

children as well as heads of households can lead to a real involvement. The loudspeaker or the television screen can, as the UNESCO report on the first Japanese experiment tells, help farmers "to open their mouths, to express their thoughts, and to learn that it is not, after all, such a difficult thing to talk in the presence of other people". Information that would have gone unregarded and proposals that might have been resisted as propaganda by the individual can become the possession of the group. The man who would never have ventured on a new course as a lonely pioneer can gladly be carried along by the feeling of the meeting. New knowledge can be translated into fruitful action; and the tyranny of custom can be broken.

It has lain heavy in the past on women, even in their own province of child-rearing and the arts of the home. In the great poverty-stricken belts of the world, in the diet-deficiency region of beri-beri and kwashiorkor, in the lands of the parasitic diseases, of bilharzia and river blindness they are the custodians of the health of the coming generation. There is no more urgent task for broadcasting than helping them to raise the level of health, hygiene, and the care of children. It must begin in the simplest terms; there are still areas where instruction in midwifery must, to be useful, tell how to cut an umbilical cord safely with broken glass.

Women are the custodians of the home. The time has gone when any country can afford to think of them as restricted to it. There is still a long way for them to go in many countries. When television was introduced into Kuwait the agreement of the religious leaders was secured only by an assurance that women should not appear on the television screen in any capacity that did not show them as subordinate to men. When the first woman did appear, there was grave rioting. Its ringleaders were executed. In Northern Nigeria the boys in primary schools outnumber the girls by three to one;

in the secondary schools by seven to one. Old attitudes are hard to change. Radio and television are a powerful instrument in the hands of governments determined to change them. In Japan women were until the war confined by tradition to the home, with limited topics of conversation seldom extending beyond their personal affairs. Since the war they have been given the franchise and equal educational opportunities. Today a quarter of a million of them are enrolled in listening and viewing groups which follow programmes designed to lead to an active interest in social problems and their solution.[1] In Algeria (as in Japan) there are radio and television programmes for women dealing with child-raising, and with cooking. There, too, broadcasting serves a wider purpose in making women aware of their civic rights and duties and bringing them into the main stream of public life. It is the most powerful tool and ally of "the militant and dynamic 'Women of Algeria' organization."

In the long run the key to development lies in the balanced expansion of every part of the system of education in harmonious relationship with the national plan of economic development. "No educational explosion without an economic explosion", is a counsel of perfection. In the short run, as the pressures for more education of all kinds increase, the developing countries are confronted with an inescapable choice between priorities. In some of them less than five per cent of the boys and girls are being educated; in most of them less than half. As communications develop, as new opportunities arise in the towns, and as the level of expectation steadily rises there is a clamour for more and more school places. The total educational expenditure in the undeveloped world is rising from two to four times as fast as the national income. The new national leaders are well aware of the

[1] See "Adult Education Programmes Broadcast in Japan", *Proceedings of the Tokyo Conference*, 1964, p. 456.

need for universal education. The village illiterate is tribal, conservative, and incapable of thinking nationally; but the most urgent and immediate need is to replace the professional *élites* as the expatriates go home. The higher education that produces doctors and lawyers, engineers and teachers must rest on a broad global education. There is a general consensus that resources must for the next decade be concentrated on the secondary schools and the teacher training colleges and that universal primary education—for girls as well as for boys—should be the target for 1980.

The problem of teacher supply is crucial. In many parts of the world the primary school is now manned by teachers with no higher qualifications than those to which their pupils aspire. In South America as a whole, forty per cent of the primary and seventy per cent of the secondary teachers have no proper qualifications whatever. In Africa the teaching profession is too often thought of as no more than a stepping-stone to commerce or politics. The present primary teachers of the undeveloped countries are in general ill-equipped with a knowledge of the subjects they teach, unfamiliar with modern techniques of teaching, and working within a tradition that lays an almost exclusive stress on factual information, on rote memory, and on the passing of examinations. There is little appeal to the imagination and the heart. It is not in Nigeria only that old men lament that young men have lost the old tribal loyalties and customs and acquired in their place only a superficial cleverness. There is a drift to the towns of young men ill-equipped to achieve their ambition to be clerks, and little care for rural education. Technical and practical education and the education of girls are gravely neglected. At the secondary level the supply of teachers of science and mathematics is pitifully inadequate. The needs that broadcasting can meet are those that we face, but greatly intensified. The possibility of meeting them by conventional means is even less. The prototype services already in operation show clearly what can be done.

In Colombia seventy-five local experts and seventy-five volunteers of the US Peace Corps are already offering full-scale basic programmes for primary schools in their five main subjects, with a careful regard for the evaluation of results, and plans for secondary teaching and literacy campaigns are far advanced. In the provision of a comprehensive basic service it is, however, Samoa that offers the model laboratory experiment. In this self-contained area with a population of some 22,000, aiming now at universal secondary education and replacing its old grass-roofed village schools with modern buildings, the new Governor found in 1961 that progress was being held up by the limitations of the 300 local Samoan teachers and their imperfect command of English. Many of them were men and women with twenty years or more of service. Faced with the alternative of dismissing them and starting afresh with American teachers or of helping them in new ways he decided on a major television operation. It uses six microwave channels and covers the whole curriculum with courses so structured that they carry the main burden of the teaching in every subject, yet leave a role for the native teacher. "In-service" training is a vital part of the scheme, and the whole operation is phased for transfer to Samoan personnel.[1] The concentration of effort in the Indian pilot scheme which has been operating in Delhi since 1960 with the help of the Ford Foundation and the British Council is on the teaching of science and English at the secondary level. Each of the 240 secondary schools in the city has been equipped with at least one receiver. Here there is a wider liberty for a better equipped teaching force than in Samoa and a partnership has been established in which

[1] *See* "Educational Television in American Samoa", *CETO News*, September, 1965.

the teacher has a creative part to play at the planning stage as well as in his own classroom. The success of the experiment has indeed derived from the closeness of that partnership, from the creation of an atmosphere of confidence in preliminary seminars for the teachers concerned, and from a machinery of consultation designed to involve the largest possible number of them. There were resistances; they are disappearing. It is significant that they came neither from the good teachers who were glad to have the command of new resources, nor from the bad teachers, who welcomed help though reluctant to acknowledge that they needed it, but from the obstinately mediocre clinging to their self-sufficiency.[1] In Nigeria a nation-wide service of radio programmes for schools was started in 1966 by a team drawn equally from the Nigerian Broadcasting Corporation and the BBC. Since then television services have been established at the centre and in each of the regions. The progress of Northern Nigeria illustrates what can be done by a planned co-ordination of the resources of the two media.

Throughout the developing countries broadcasting could do more than any other agency to help the poorly equipped teacher, to achieve economies in the use of specialist teachers, and above all to set new standards in the schools of what good teaching should be, and diffuse new ideas and new attitudes. The successful establishment of a specifically educational service in a developing country calls for the same measures as have proved their value elsewhere. Without help from outside they may be impossible of achievement. The first need is for a clear definition of educational purposes and educational priorities which can only come from the competent education authorities, but must be made in the light of a realistic

[1] See B. P. BHATT, "Report on School Broadcasting through Television", *Proceedings of the Tokyo Conference*, 1964, p. 91, and J. G. MILES, "The Delhi CLT/TV Project", *CETO News*, June 1965.

assessment of what broadcasting can and cannot do. There must be an agreement and co-ordination between the various ministries concerned—the Ministry of Education, the Ministry of Native Development, the Ministry of Information (or whatever organ of government is in control of broadcasting)—which is all too often lacking. It is not enough for the Ministry of Education to give its blessings or its rulings. It must be deeply committed to the broadcasting venture and take full responsibility for it, while including the teachers through their organizations in its control and conduct. Ideally the broadcasting team of planners and producers should constitute a section of the Ministry of Education, working in close touch with colleagues in other branches. If they work within the framework of a broadcasting system organized as a public corporation, or as a commercial venture, or as a branch of some other ministry, they must nevertheless think of themselves as teachers, belonging primarily to the world of education. All experience suggests that they should be drawn from the ranks of teachers, and given a mastery of broadcasting skills, rather than from the ranks of general broadcasters. There must in those circumstances be a firm and unambiguous concordat between the educational authority and the broadcasting authority over the air time and technical facilities to be made available.

Above all, the Ministry must concern itself with the receiving end. Sets must not only be installed. They must be serviced, and teachers must be shown how to place them and how to tune them. A costly service can come near to shipwreck through a neglect of the simplest technical needs; through a shortage of batteries, a dearth of agents capable of carrying out simple repairs, or ignorance by teachers that the aerial must be duly connected. The worse the teacher, the more help he needs if the programmes are to have their intended effect. The provision of advance information, of teachers' guides, of pamphlets for the pupils must be generous and carefully planned. The training colleges for teachers must know how to prepare their students to make the best use of the media. For the established teaching force, there must be a campaign of in-service training. A regular flow of reports from the schools and from teachers' conferences must be contrived, and there must be a systematic evaluation of the impact of the programmes.

All this amounts to an enterprise which absolutely demands experienced help in its early stages rather than a long and costly process of trial and error. UNESCO is deeply engaged. It has in hand through its International Institute for Economic Planning a study in depth of the economics of all the new educational media. Its pilot project for the use of audio-visual media for adult education operating under joint UNESCO-Senegalese auspices in Dakar is concerned both with educational values and with cost-effectiveness. It is assisting a score of countries from Algeria to Zambia to use the new media in adult education, and collaborating with the Mass Communication Institutes at the Universities of Manila and Dakar. It hopes to share in the establishment of permanent training facilities in television production in South America and in West Africa. From its conferences and meetings, continent by continent, the outlines of concerted and co-operative policies are emerging. The third World Conference on educational broadcasting to be held under the auspices of the European Broadcasting Union will have a special regard for the problems of the developing countries. There is a growing international fraternity of men and women convinced of the educational value of broadcasting and determined to use it for educational needs. The resources of UNESCO are, however, limited. It can do little more than arrange conferences, supply expert advice, and energize pilot projects. In this widening context there is still an urgent need for bilateral help.

Within a limited field it is programmes of the right kind at the right price that are needed. For many years the general programmes of the smaller services must rely largely on imported material, and as Sir Hugh Greene put it: "In the countries of Asia, Africa, and Latin America there are thousands of young idealistic people who want more from television than the ideals of Tombstone and Dead Man's Gulch."[1] The financial needs of the BBC have forced it into a position in which it must think of its overseas sales organization, Television and Radio Enterprises, as a source of revenue. There is a danger that its best productions may soon be priced out of the markets that need them most, and that it will itself plunge further into the manufacture of synthetic "Mid-Atlantic" best-sellers, with all the glossy nullity of *The Third Man* or the bogus and faceless sophistication of international show business. In Hong Kong the BBC Director of Television reflecting recently on a week's viewing which included *Attenborough and the Animals*, *The Black and White Minstrels*, *The Seven Faces of Jim*, *Maigret*, *Hugh and I*, *Robin Hood*, *William Tell*, felt, inexplicably, that "the face of Britain was reasonably presented in this paternalistic atmosphere", but finally and with deep seriousness asked himself: "Is that enough?" In a city only recently torn by riots it was clear to him that "going home to watch *The Avengers* or *The Man from UNCLE* will not keep the lid from blowing off again" and imperative that television throughout the world should build "bridges of understanding".[2] The overseas radio services have faithfully projected an image of Britain. Television might foster a fuller and deeper knowledge of what we are and stand for. The audience for much of the best that Britain is offering and that other countries are using is

---

[1] SIR HUGH GREENE, *The Broadcaster's Responsibility*, 1962, p. 10.
[2] KENNETH ADAM, "Broadcasting in a Colony", *The Listener*, 16th June, 1966.

necessarily limited. *Wuthering Heights* can have only a limited appeal in Uganda, and *Our Mutual Friend* in Pakistan. They lie outside the range of simple people. The lower down the educational ladder, the greater the need for general programmes made on the spot and grounded firmly in life as it is lived there.

At the higher levels and in a limited range of subjects education itself has a universal character. The symbols of advanced mathematics speak the purest of international languages. Engineering science in every country presents the same practical problems against the same background of theory. In the training of doctors there are large overlaps and only relatively small areas of difference. In fields like these an educational television programme may call for no more than a translation of the sound-track to be valid everywhere. For young children and for simple people most programmes must be couched in terms of a specific environment and culture, and so firmly grounded in the life they know that they can only be effectively made on the spot. There are differences of circumstance. The planner of a course of elementary science for eleven-year-olds in one country must think in terms of tadpoles, in another country of locusts. There are deep-seated differences of custom and habit. Everywhere in the world babies must be bathed; in Uganda the head must be washed first. A story may speak out clearly to an Indian villager if it tells of a moneylender; to a villager in Uganda if it tells of a bride-price. There are problems of comprehension and problems of acceptance. Acceptance is easiest where identification is most complete. The Centre for Educational Television and the BBC have both found how hard it is to devise even a simple "audio-visual" course in English for young children. The life of England and its children is too remote. The life of an Ibo village may, for children, seem distractingly different from that of a Yoruba village. A generalized picture of "West African" children in wall-pictures or animated cartoons can never have the compelling power of a sharply individual portrayal of life as the audience know it.

The supply of programmes of the right kind from abroad is vital, but has its sharp limitations. The Centre for Educational Television Overseas has gone far towards surmounting some of them by its brilliant development of the "Programme Kit"—a package of film sequences, of still pictures, of simple animated diagrams, of models and apparatus. These are accompanied by handbooks, by a script, and by instructions to the "television teacher" overseas (who will act as the "live" narrator) which enable him to follow a rigidly determined plan, or to adapt, add, modify, and change as local resources, local circumstances, and his own teaching skills may suggest.

The range of the "kit" remains limited. The fundamental help that new television services require is advice, and then such help with training as will enable them to stand firmly on their own feet. There can be few national investments that would pay better dividends in friendship, in a continuing and cordial link with the great and growing organs of opinion and of education overseas, in cultural sympathy expressed through a common language than the provision of adequate help at this juncture, and most of all in the educational field. It is forthcoming now from Russia, from Japan, from the United States, from Australia, from West Germany, from Britain—but Britain is no longer in the lead. Syria uses British equipment, but sends the engineers and technicians who will use it to be trained in France, because France offers a far more generous supply of bursaries.

The BBC has an incomparable reputation as a world training centre. In radio it has enabled Britain to out-distance every competitor by far. In television its plans have been interminably delayed by the financial hesitations of the Ministry of Overseas Development. New agencies, working closely with it, are supplementing the work that it does. In Glasgow the Thomson Foundation caters for the needs of overseas engineers, producers, and programme planners. The demand for places is far greater than it can supply. In London there has grown up an institution uniquely equipped to serve educational needs, the Centre for Educational Television Overseas. It is a pioneering venture established through the initiation of the Nuffield Foundation, supported financially for an experimental period of five years by business enterprises, by Independent Television companies and by the British Government. It works in close partnership with the Television School Broadcasting Department of the BBC. CETO faces a doubtful future at precisely the time when it has established and consolidated a world-wide reputation. The training needs of educational television are highly specialized. Work in the developing countries imposes its own special conditions. The business of training can be effectively carried out only by people primarily concerned with education, equipped with an intimate knowledge of conditions overseas, and thinking in terms of the equipment and resources that are likely to be available to its students. It calls for the organization of seminars and courses abroad as well as in England, for the creation of a world-wide network of contacts, and above all for the establishment of confidence. Britain has through CETO and the BBC the opportunity of creating a world centre (which might ideally be allied with the work of one of the universities) unique in kind, steadily growing in its usefulness, and capable of establishing a fruitful relationship with the continental training centres that are already envisaged at Addis Ababa and elsewhere. It is an opportunity that will not recur.

EPILOGUE: SOME COSTS AND CHOICES

THE present expenditure of the United Kingdom on broadcasting is of the order of £400 million a year. The operating expenses of the BBC and the commercial programme companies account for some £150 million of this total. The rest goes on the purchase of receiving sets. If we are to spend even more it is a matter of national concern that we should receive value for money.

It seems likely that we shall place our largest investment in the development which offers least promise of any social dividend. There is no popular "demand" for colour television, and the BBC will have to work hard to arouse a public interest in its dubious attractions. The experience of other countries is by no means encouraging. In Japan Nippon Hoso Kyokai has recently completed a national colour transmission network at great expense. After five years of effort and publicity there are still only 100,000 private receivers distributed among the 19,000,000 Japanese subscribers to television. For many years sets will be so dear that they can be no more than a middle-class luxury. Colour will contribute nothing to the effectiveness of the great majority of educational programmes; and it is doubtful whether it will be possible to offer a news service in colour to the home viewer, at any rate in the early years, since colour cameras are expensive, cumbrous, and delicate for "on-the-spot" use, and since the processing of colour film is costly. The pressures of the electronics industry, the desire of the BBC engineering service to show what it can do, and the national pursuit of prestige will no doubt enable the country to see the Black and White Minstrels in pinks and blues; as in America the cost of show-business television will rocket upwards. A vigilant public opinion will be needed to prevent colour from absorbing resources that are urgently needed for other and more socially useful purposes.

The demand for a second commercial television channel is at present in abeyance. Since there is not enough material of tolerable quality to keep even the existing three channels supplied with entertainment programmes it is fortunate that a fourth offers little prospect of profit to the speculator. If the "Open University" succeeds it will need more evening time than can be provided on the present channels. The plans of the present Government envisage a possible long-term need for a specifically educational channel. The capital cost of establishing it would, however, be of the order of £35 million, and government expenditure on that scale seems highly unlikely until we have surmounted our economic problems. In the meanwhile, the unused time on the second BBC channel, which stands idle until 7.30 each evening, offers the opportunity of doubling the service for schools and technical colleges and of providing television support for the early, experimental, stages of the "Open University" project without embarking on any major capital investment.

As for radio, a dual-purpose network of VHF transmitters capable of serving either local or national needs would cost little more than £500,000, a trivial amount in relation to its educational potentialities. The proposed experiment with nine local radio stations can be mounted with an initial expenditure of perhaps £350,000 and an annual running cost of £500,000.

The 1966 White Paper holds open the prospect that these new developments will have priority over any extension of the commercial operation, and they will be planned as integral parts of our total system of public service broadcasting.

In the last resort the claims of public service broadcasting rest not on theory, but on its solid achievements. In range, in quality, and in enterprise the services of the BBC, of its Japanese counterpart, NHK, of Radiotelevisione Italiana, and, on a smaller scale, those of the Scandinavian broadcasting organizations, are the best in the world. They are all in the hands of public corporations of one kind or another. Their closest rivals are government-sponsored monopolies, as in France. Wherever commercial broadcasting has been allowed to gain a dominant position the quotations from John Stuart Mill and the lip-service to consumer choice have been followed by a remorseless narrowing of programme categories, and a weakening of the educational impulse throughout the whole of the nation's broadcasting output. We still have time to prevent that from happening here. We can best do so by helping the BBC to regain its old commanding position as the national instrument of broadcasting and the authority that goes with single-mindedness.

Lord Reith, whose incomparable legacy we could only too easily fritter away, believed that public service broadcasting must rest on two foundations: a sense of moral obligation and assured finance, and that the one could hardly persist without the other. The pusillanimous way in which successive governments have denied to the BBC the modest financial resources called for by extensions of broadcasting which those same governments have sanctioned has kept the Corporation living from hand to mouth and watching the political signs of the times when it should have been thinking boldly for the future. The £6 licence fee which it requires would still be lower than that of any Western European country except Holland, and would enable it to meet its commitments without having to think of its publications and its exports as possible sources of revenue, its experiments and investigations as a financial burden.

A £6 licence fee would not, however, provide for the extensions of educational broadcasting which are urgently needed. The Pilkington Committee had before it a proposal from the Independent Television Authority that the fourth national television channel should be devoted to a specialized educational service under the control of a new public authority, and financed from public funds. The Committee rejected this proposal because it held that education was a necessary function of all broadcasting services, and that nothing must be done to weaken the responsibility of the existing organizations for providing both educative and educational programmes. It was, furthermore, reluctant to see any segregation of such programmes on a separate channel which would appeal only to a limited audience. The growing needs of the educational system at every level and the corresponding change in the character of educational broadcasting make it imperative to revise these findings and to draw a sharper line between the two kinds of programme. All those programmes which are designed to contribute to general enlightenment without having any specific vocational aim or academic examination in view must indeed constitute part of the general programme output if they are to serve their social purpose. They are properly financed from the general revenue of the broadcasting organizations concerned. Programmes for schools, and programmes of higher education defined as the provision of systematic courses above the advanced level of the General Certificate of Education, are another matter. A programme constituting part of a second-year course in Russian, or aimed at structural engineers in need of professional refreshment, has no missionary value for the general public. If it is placed at a time convenient for its target audience, it must displace a programme of wider interest. As the demand for such programmes increases, the need for a specialized educational channel will grow. Programmes for schools and colleges can be placed in the day-time, when there is less competition for air-time, but might just as readily be transmitted on a special channel. All pro-grammes of specialized education, whether for schools or for adults, present a financial problem as their number in-creases. It is very doubtful whether they can properly be financed out of general licence revenue on a scale commensur-ate with educational needs, and certain that licence fees will not be raised in this country to a level that would make a major expansion possible. In any event, the time has passed when it was appropriate for the Board of Management or the Board of Governors of the BBC to weigh the claims of specifically educational broadcasting against those of informa-tion and entertainment. In so far as broadcasting now makes a direct and central contribution to the work of the national system of education, the only valid cost-accounting must be carried out in relation to other forms of educational expendi-ture, not in relation to other forms of broadcasting. The principle has already been accepted in relation to broadcasting support for the Open University. The BBC will be paid for any services that it may render by the Department of Educa-tion. It is difficult to resist the conclusion that the school broadcasting service should now be financed in the same way, together with any extensions into the field of in-dustrial training or of higher education that may be agreed with the Department of Education and Science.

The Department as paymaster would clearly have a larger say in the formation of policy than at present. The experience of the Overseas Services of the BBC shows that it is possible to reconcile the functions of a government department or departments acting as a prescribing body with a full measure of professional freedom. A closer integration with the work of the Department and its inspectorate, and an assurance that their whole weight would be thrown behind the effort that the Corporation has made in the past to ensure that the programmes were well used, would be of far more value than a nominal independence at this stage in the progress of the medium. In France, in Sweden, and in Italy that integration has already been achieved. In Britain, the establishment of a Schools Council through which the Department shares with the teaching profession the task of organizing a more rapid and more effective curricular response to change has provided a model which might be of significance for the remodelling of the present School Broadcasting Council. A unified national service, bringing within its scope the school programmes of the Independent Television Authority and the companies would be the logical sequel of a reorganization. The present dualism will inevitably lead to wasteful duplication as the output increases, and some allocation of functions between the BBC and the ITA would be a modest price to pay for a greater educational efficiency.

It may be argued that an educational service so conceived will in time be large enough to stand firmly on its own feet, and will outgrow its dependence on the Corporation which first called educational broadcasting into existence and has fostered its growth to maturity. The educational service of the future must indeed achieve an even larger measure of autonomy than the BBC service now enjoys and an undisputed control of resources adequate to its tasks. It will need the status of a Directorate of the BBC, with its own representative on the Board of Management. It will derive strength, as it always has done, from its association with a broadcasting organization that touches the national life at many points. Perhaps in the last resort the best argument for entrusting the BBC with large new educational responsibilities lies in the strength that they would bring to the BBC itself by identifying it fully and at every point with the most significant of all social purposes.

The use of broadcasting for strictly educational purposes must increasingly be thought of as an important part of the total educational strategy of every nation in the world. It makes possible a far more efficient use of the available force of teachers, and is the most rapid way of diffusing a knowledge of new approaches among them. It calls for a concentration on the process of educational communication which can go far by practice and example to raise the standard of teaching. It can offer new avenues to education for those whose opportunities have been limited by social or geographical circumstance. It can develop the abilities of those older men and women who where born too soon to profit from the wider range of educational facilities that now exists. It can minister to the needs of an age that makes more and more demands for professional and technological efficiency, and at the same time offers more and more leisure. It can best do so in a community that has determined to use the immense powers of general broadcasting as the most powerful instrument of the educative society.

BIBLIOGRAPHY

THE books marked * contain useful specialized bibliographies.

PERIODICALS AND WORKS OF REFERENCE

Annual Reports and Accounts of the British Broadcasting Corporation.
1927 to date. 1964–65 (Cmnd 2823).

Annual Reports and Accounts of the Independent Television Authority.
1958 to date. 1964–65.

* *BBC Handbook* (annual), BBC, 1966.

COLONIAL OFFICE, *Sound and Television Broadcasting in the Overseas
Territories*, handbook, Colonial Office, 1949–65, annually.

* INDEPENDENT TELEVISION AUTHORITY, ITV, 1966, *A Guide to
Independent Television*, London, 1966 (annual).

UNESCO, *World Communications. Press, Radio, Television, Film*,
Paris, 1964.

Much of the best writing on radio is contained in the files of—
The BBC Quarterly, a journal intended for those engaged in the art
and science of broadcasting. Spring, 1946–Autumn, 1954.

Two other periodicals are indispensable for the study of overseas
developments—

EBU Review. Part B—General and Legal. Published every two
months by the Administrative Office of the European Broadcasting
Union, 1 rue de Varembé, Geneva, Switzerland. Annual Sub-
scription: £1 15s.

CETO News. July, 1963 to date. Published quarterly by the Centre
for Educational Television Overseas, The Studio, Nuffield Lodge,
Regent's Park, London, N.W.1.

2. GOVERNMENT PUBLICATIONS (IN CHRONOLOGICAL ORDER OF
PUBLICATION)

Broadcasting Committee Report, 1923 (The Sykes Committee Report),
Cmnd 1951.

Report of the Broadcasting Committee, 1925 (The Crawford Report),
Cmnd 2599.

Report of the Television Committee, 1935 (The Selsdon Report),
Cmnd 4793.

Report of the Broadcasting Committee, 1935 (The Ullswater Report), Cmnd 5091.

Report of the Television Committee, 1943 (The Hankey Report). *Broadcasting Policy*, 1946, Cmnd 6852.

Report of the Broadcasting Committee, 1949 (The Beveridge Report), Cmnd 8116. Report of a committee appointed in 1949 under the chairmanship of Lord Beveridge to consider the constitution, control, finance, and other general aspects of the sound and television broadcasting services of the United Kingdom.

POSTMASTER GENERAL, *Broadcasting: Memorandum on Television Policy, 1953*, Cmnd 9005.

Television Act, 1954, to make provision for television broadcasting services in addition to those provided by the BBC, and to set up a special authority for that purpose.

Report of the Committee on Broadcasting, 1960 (The Pilkington Report), Cmnd 1753. Report of a committee under the chairmanship of Sir Harry Pilkington to consider the future of the broadcasting services in the United Kingdom.

POSTMASTER GENERAL, *Broadcasting: Memorandum on the Report of the Committee on Broadcasting, 1960*, Cmnd 1770.

POSTMASTER GENERAL, *Broadcasting: Further Memorandum on the Report of the Committee on Broadcasting, 1960*, Cmnd 1893.

The Future of Sound Radio and Television, a short version of the Report of the Pilkington Committee, 1962.

POSTMASTER GENERAL, *Broadcasting*, copy of the licence and agreement dated 19th December, 1963, between H.M. Postmaster General and the British Broadcasting Corporation, 1963, Cmnd 2236. (Reprinted in *BBC Annual*, 1966.)

POSTMASTER GENERAL, *Broadcasting*, copy of Royal Charter for the continuance of the British Broadcasting Corporation, 1964, Cmnd 2385. (Reprinted in *BBC Annual*, 1966.)

Television Act, 1964, an act to consolidate the Television Acts, 1954 and 1963, 1964.

3. CRITICAL AND DESCRIPTIVE

BEADLE, SIR GERALD, *Television: A Critical Review* (London, Allen & Unwin, 1963).

R

COASE, R. H., *British Broadcasting: A Study in Monopoly* (London, Longmans, 1950).

CROZIER, M., *Broadcasting: Sound and Television* (London, O.U.P., 1958).

JENKINS, C., *Power Behind the Screen. Ownership Control and Motivation in British Commercial Television* (London, McGibbon & Kee, 1961).

MATHESON, H., *Broadcasting* (London, Thornton Butterworth (Home University Library)), 1933.

PAULU, B., *British Broadcasting: Radio and Television in the U.K.* (London, O.U.P., 1957).

PAULU, B., *British Broadcasting in Transition* (London, Macmillan, 1961).

SIEPMANN, C. A., *Radio, Television and Society* (New York, O.U.P., 1950).

SIMON OF WYTHENSHAWE, E. D. 1ST BARON, *The BBC from Within*, (London, Gollancz, 1953).

THOMAS, HOWARD, *The Truth about Television* (London, Weidenfeld & Nicholson, 1962).

4. HISTORICAL AND AUTOBIOGRAPHICAL

ARCHER, G. L., *History of Radio to 1926* (New York, 1938).

BRIGGS, ASA, *The History of Broadcasting in the U.K.*, * Vol. I, *The Birth of Broadcasting* (London, O.U.P., 1961); * Vol. II, *The Golden Age of Wireless* (London, O.U.P., 1965).

BURROWS, A. R., *The Story of Broadcasting* (London, Cassell, 1924).

ECKERSLEY, P. P., *The Power Behind the Microphone* (London, Cape, 1941).

ECKERSLEY, R., *The B.B.C and All That* (London, Low, Marston, 1946).

FIELDEN, L., *The Natural Bent* (London, André Deutsch, 1960).

GIELGUD, VAL, *Years of the Locust* (London, Nicholson & Watson, 1947).

GIELGUD, VAL, *Years in a Mirror* (London, Bodley Head, 1964).

GORHAM, M., *Sound and Fury* (London, Marshall, 1948).

GORHAM, M., *Broadcasting and Television since 1900* (London, Dakers, 1952).

GRISEWOOD, F., *The World Goes By* (London, Secker & Warburg, 1952).

HALL, H., *Here's to the Next Time* (London, Odhams, 1956).

HIBBERD, S., *This—is London* (London, Macdonald & Evans, 1950).

LAMBERT, R. S., *Ariel and All His Quality* (London, Gollancz, 1940).

LEWIS, C. A. *Broadcasting from Within* (London, Newnes, 1926).

MASCHWITZ, E., *No Chip on My Shoulder* (London, Jenkins, 1957).

MOSELY, S. A., *Broadcasting in My Time* (London, Rich & Cowan, 1935).

REITH, J. C. W., 1ST BARON, *Broadcast Over Britain* (London, Hodder & Stoughton, 1924).

REITH, J. C. W., 1ST BARON, *Into the Wind* (London, Hodder & Stoughton, 1949)

ROSS, GORDON, *Television Jubilee: The Story of 25 Years of British Television* (London, W. H. Allen, 1961).

WILSON, H. H., *Pressure Group: The Campaign for Commercial Television* (London, Secker, 1961).

5. CULTURE AND THE MASS MEDIA

ANNAN, N., *Romanes Lecture: The Disintegration of an Old Culture* (O.U.P., 1965).

BELSON, W. A., *The Effects of Television upon the Interests and the Initiative of Adult Viewers in Greater London* (BBC, 1956).

BELSON, W. A., "The Effects of Television on Family Life", *Discovery*, vol. 21, no. 10.

BROWN, J. A. C., *Techniques of Persuasion* (Harmondsworth, Pelican Books, 1963).

Communication in the Modern World. British Association-Granada T.V. Lectures (1959 and annually to date).

DEXTER, L. A. and WHITE, D. M., *People, Society, and Mass Communications* (Glencoe, The Free Press, 1964).

ELIOT, T. S., *Notes Towards a Definition of Culture* (London, Faber & Faber, 1948).

Facts and Figures about Viewing and Listening (BBC, 1961).

GREENE, SIR HUGH, *The Conscience of the Programme Director*, 14 pp. (BBC, 1965).

GROOMBRIDGE, B., *Popular Culture and Personal Responsibility*, Report of a Conference (London, National Union of Teachers, 1960).

HALEY, SIR WILLIAM, *The Responsibilities of Broadcasting*, Lewis Fry Memorial Lecture, 32 pp. (BBC, 1948).

HOGGART, R., "Mass Communication in Britain" in *The Modern Age*, ed. Ford, B. (Harmondsworth, Pelican Books, 1961).

HOGGART, R., *The Nature and Context of Mass Communications* Harvey Memorial Lecture, 1960.

HOGGART, R., *The Uses of Literacy* (Harmondsworth, Penguin Books, 1958).

JACOB, SIR IAN, *The B.B.C.: A National and an International Force*, 23 pp. (BBC, 1957).

KLAPPER, J. T. (Ed.), *The Effects of Mass Communication* (Glencoe, The Free Press, 1960).

LAZARSFELD, P. F. and FIELD, H., *The People Look at Radio* (University of North Carolina Press, 1946).

MACDONALD, DWIGHT, *Against the American Grain* (London, Gollancz, 1963).

MCLUHAN, MARSHALL, *Understanding Media* (New York, McGraw-Hill, 1964).

ROSENBERG, B. and WHITE, D. M. (Ed.), *Mass Culture. The Popular Arts in America* (Glencoe, The Free Press, 1957).

SCHRAMM, W. (Ed.), *Mass Communications* (Urbana, University of Illinois Press, 1960).

SELDES, G., *The Public Arts* (New York, Simon & Schuster, 1958).

SELDES, G. *The Great Audience* (New York, Viking Press, 1956).

SKORNIA, H., *Television and Society: An Inquest and Agenda for Improvement* (New York, McGraw-Hill, 1956).

WHITLEY, O., *Broadcasting and the National Culture*, 32 pp. (BBC, 1965).

WILLIAMS, R., *Britain in the Sixties: Communications* (Harmondsworth, Penguin Special, 1962).

WILLIAMS, R., *Culture and Society, 1780–1950* (Harmondsworth, Penguin Books, 1961).

WILLIAMS, R., *Communication and Community*, Harvey Memorial Lecture, 1961.

ZWEIG, F., *The Worker in an Affluent Society* (London, Allen & Unwin, 1961).

6. PROBLEMS OF PERCEPTION AND COMMUNICATION

ABERCROMBIE, M. L. JOHNSON, *The Anatomy of Judgement. An Investigation into the Processes of Perception and Meaning* (London, Hutchinson, 1960).

CHERRY, COLIN, *On Human Communication* (New York, John Wiley & Sons, 1957).

GIBSON, J. J., *The Perception of the Visual World* (Cambridge, Mass., The Riverside Press, 1955).

GOMBRICH, E. H., *Art and Illusion* (London, Phaidon Press, 1960).

PRICE, H. H., *Thinking and Experience* (London, Hutchinson, 1953).

TRENAMAN, J., *An Investigation by Statistical Methods, of the Effective Communication of Educative Material, and an Assessment of the Factors making for such Communication, with Special Reference to Broadcasting* (Oxford Ph.D. thesis, 1961). Trenaman's work is the most substantial and important study yet undertaken in Great Britain. A shortened version of the thesis will be published in 1967 by Longmans, under the title *Communication and Comprehension*.

VERNON, M. D., *The Psychology of Perception* (Harmondsworth, Penguin Books, 1962).

7. TELEVISION AND CHILDREN

Children and Television Programmes. The Report of a Joint Committee set up by the BBC and the ITA (London, BBC/ITA, 1960).

Children's Viewing of Children's Television Programmes (London, Rediffusion, 1963).

Parents, Children and Television. An Opinion Survey (London, ITA, 1958).

HALLORAN, J. D., *Attitude Formation and Change* (Leicester, University Press).

HALLORAN, J. D., *Problems of Television Research: A Progress Report of the Television Research Committee* (Leicester, University Press, 1966).

HALLORAN, J. D., *The Effects of Mass Communication with Special Reference to Television* (Leicester, University Press, 1965).

HIMMELWEIT, H. T., OPPENHEIM, A. N. and VINCE, P., *Television and the Child. An Empirical Study of the Effect of Television on the Young* (London, O.U.P., 1958).

MASHEDER, M., HOLME, A. and HIGGINS, A., *Family Viewing* (London, Council for Children's Welfare, 1960).

SCHRAMM, W., *The Effects of Television on Children, Annotated Bibliography* (Paris, UNESCO).

SCHRAMM, W., LYLE, J. and PARKER, E. B., *Television in the Lives of Our Children* (London, O.U.P., 1961).

Television and Juvenile Delinquency. Report of the Committee on the Judiciary, Report No. 1466 (US Government Printing Office, 1956).

Under Observation, an inquiry into a new technique for assessing the response of children to television conducted jointly by the University of Cambridge and ABC Television (London, ABC Television, 1963).

What Children Watch, a survey of children's television viewing (London, Granada TV Network, 1961).

SEE ALSO—

The Influence of the Cinema on Children and Adolescents. An Annotated International Bibliography (491 abstracts) (Paris, UNESCO, 1961).

8. RELIGIOUS BROADCASTING

BACHMAN, J. W., *The Church in the World of Radio-Television* (New York, Association Press, 1960).

GRISEWOOD, H. J. G., *Broadcasting and Society: Comments from a Christian Standpoint* (London, S.C.M. Press, 1949).

HOUSE, F., "Some Aspects of Christian Broadcasting", *BBC Quarterly*, Summer, 1950.

LAMB, K., *Religious Broadcasting*, 14 pp. (BBC, 1965).

McKAY, ROY, *Take Care of the Sense: Reflections on Religious Broadcasting* (London, S.C.M. Press, 1964).

MORRIS, SIR PHILIP, *Christianity and the World of Today*.

Religion in Television, an account of the consultation arranged by the Independent Television Authority (London, ITA, 1963).

Religious Programmes on Independent Television (London, ITA, 1962).

Television and Religion, a report prepared by Social Surveys Ltd. on behalf of ABC Television Ltd. (London, University of London Press, 1964).

TIMMINS, LESLIE, *"Vision On": Christian Communication through the Mass Media* (London, Epworth Press, 1965).

WELCH, J., "Religion and the Radio", *BBC Quarterly*, October, 1940.

9. SOME OTHER SPECIAL ASPECTS OF BROADCASTING

BBC Lunch-time Lectures—First Series (November, 1962–April, 1963)
The Future of BBC Television, by LEONARD MIALL.
BBC News and Current Affairs, by DONALD EDWARDS.
International Television, by MARTIN PULLING.
Reflections on the Impact of Broadcasting, by ROBERT SILVEY.
The Revolution Overseas, by E. TANGYE LEAN.
The BBC's Music Policy, by WILLIAM GLOCK.

BBC Lunch-time Lectures—Second Series (October, 1963–March, 1964)
Broadcasting to Europe, by JAMES MONAHAN.
Broadcasting and Education, by JOHN SCUPHAM.
The Prospect Before Us, by STUART HOOD.
The National Theatre of the Air, by MARTIN ESSLIN.
The Challenge of Circumstances, by W. PROCTOR WILSON.
Sound Radio in the Television Age, by FRANK GILLARD.

BBC Lunch-time Lectures—Third Series (October, 1964–March, 1965)
The Work of a BBC Foreign Correspondent, by JOHN CRAWLEY.
Broadcasting to the USSR and Eastern Europe, by MAURICE LATEY.
Television and the Arts, by HUW WELDON.
The Role of the Regions in British Broadcasting, by HYWEL DAVIES.
Religious Broadcasting, by KENNETH LAMB.
Political Broadcasting, by DONALD EDWARDS.

GIELGUD, VAL, *British Radio Drama, 1922–1956* (London, Harrap, 1957).

McWHINNIE, D., *The Art of Radio* (London, Faber & Faber, 1959).

SWALLOW, N., *Factual Television* (London, Focal Press, 1966).

TRENAMAN, J. and McQUAIL, D., *Television and the Political Image, A Study of the Impact of Television on the 1959 General Election* (London, Methuen, 1961).

FOR LOCAL RADIO SEE—

Local Radio in the Public Interest (BBC, 1966).

POWELL R., *Possibilities for Local Radio* (Birmingham, The Centre for Contemporary Cultural Studies, 1965).

10. EDUCATIONAL BROADCASTING

There is a full bibliography dealing with school broadcasting—
BBC Radio and Television Broadcasts to Schools. Selective Bibiography of Titles, (1) Radio and television broadcasts to schools, (2) General broadcasting, issued by the School Broadcasting Council for the United Kingdom, 3 Portland Place, London, W.1, 1966.

The greatest body of information on all aspects of school broadcasting is contained in—
Proceedings of the First International Conference of Broadcasting Organizations on Sound and Television School Broadcasting (Rome, Radiotelevisione Italiana, 1960).

Proceedings of the Second International Conference of Broadcasting Organizations on Sound and Television School Broadcasting, 881 pp. (Tokyo, Nippon Hoso Kyokai, 1963).

SEE ALSO—

Annual Programme of Radio and Television Broadcasts to Schools and Colleges, 1966–67 (BBC, 1966).

Audio-Visual Aids in Higher Scientific Education. Report of the Brynmor James Committee (London, HMSO, 1965).

BAILEY, K. V., *The Listening Schools* (BBC, 1957).

CASSIRER, H. R., *Television Teaching Today* (Paris, UNESCO, 1960).

Closed Circuit Television in Education in Great Britain (London, National Committee for Audio-Visual Aids in Education, 1965).

Correspondence Teaching and Television. A Report of a Small Pilot Experiment (Cambridge, National Extension College, 1966).

Current Developments in Educational Television (New York, National Educational Television and Radio Centre, 1962).

DIEUZEIDE, H., *Teaching through Television: A Report on Teaching Science by Use of Television in Schools* (Organization for European Economic Co-operation, 1960).

Educational Television. Some Suggestions for a Fourth Service (London, ITA, 1961).

Educational Television and Radio in Britain. Papers prepared for a national conference organized by the BBC and the University of Sussex (BBC, 1966).

GAGE, N. L. (Ed.), *Handbook of Research on Teaching* (Chicago, Rand McNally, 1965).

HICKEL, R., *Modern Language Teaching by Television* (Strasbourg, Council of Europe, 1965).

MACLENNAN, D. W. and REED, J. C., *Abstracts of Research on Instructional Television and Film* (Stanford, Institute for Communication Research, Stanford University, 1964).

MILIARET, G., *The Psychology of the Use of Audio-Visual Aids in Primary Education* (London, Harrap, 1966).

OLDMAN, H., *Educational Television: Impressions Following a Visit to the U.S.A.* (Leeds University, Institute of Education, 1964).

Outlook, 1966–67, annual programme of educational courses for adults (BBC, 1966).

PALMER, R., *School Broadcasting in Britain* (BBC, 1947).

SCHRAMM, W., LYLE, J., and POOL, I. DE S. *The People Look at Educational Television* (Stanford University Press, 1963).

Survey of British Research in Audio Visual Aids: Bibliography and Abstracts. (London, National Committee for Audio-Visual Aids in Education, 1965).

Teaching by Television. Report from the Ford Foundation and the Fund for the Advancement of Education (New York, Ford Foundation, 1961).

A University of the Air (White Paper) (London, HMSO, Cmnd 2922, 1966).

University Intercommunication. A report by the Universities Television Research Unit (Pergamon Press, 1967).

WALLER, JUDITH and GROSS, RONALD, *Learning by Television* (New York, The Fund for the Advancement of Education, Ford Foundation, 1966).

WEDELL, E. A. O. G., *The Use of Television in Education* (London, Association of Technical Institutions, 1963).

WILTSHIRE, H. and BAYLISS, F., *Teaching through Television (an Account of an Experiment)* (London, National Institute of Adult Education, 1965).

World Year Book of Education, 1960, Communication Media and the School (London, Evans Bros. Ltd.).

World Year Book of Education, 1965, The Education Explosion (London, Evans Bros. Ltd.).

For the training of discrimination in schools see—

HALL, S. and WHANNEL, P., *The Popular Arts* (London, Hutchinson, 1964.

HANCOCK, A., *The Small Screen* (London, Heinemann, 1965).

HIGGINS, A. P., *Talking About Television* (London, British Film Institute, 1966).

TUCKER, N., *Understanding the Mass Media* (Cambridge University Press, 1965).

11. BROADCASTING IN THE DEVELOPING COUNTRIES

CETO News.

DUMAZEDIER, J., *Television and Rural Adult Education* (Paris, UNESCO, 1956).

Educational Television in Developing Countries. A Report of an On-the-spot Survey (Australian Broadcasting Commission/Nippon Hoso Kyokai, 1965).

Film Centre, London, The Use of Mobile Cinema and Radio Vans in Fundamental Education (Paris, UNESCO, 1949).

LEWIS, R. and ROVAN, J., *Television and Teleclubs in Rural Communities* (Paris, UNESCO, 1955).

MATHUR, J. C. and NEVRATH, P., *An Indian Experiment in Farm Radio Forums* (Paris, UNESCO, 1959).

* SCHRAMM, W., *Mass Media and National Development* (Stanford University Press, Stanford, California, 1964; UNESCO, Paris).

UNESCO, *Adult Education Groups and Audio-Visual Techniques* (Paris, 1958).

UNESCO, *Developing Information Media in Africa* (Paris, 1962).

UNESCO, *Developing Mass Media in Asia* (Paris, 1960).

UNESCO, *Illiteracy at Mid-century* (Paris, 1957).

UNESCO, *Mass Media in the Developing Countries* (Paris, 1961).

UNESCO, *Rural Television in Japan* (Paris, 1960).

UNESCO, *Social Education through Television* (Paris, 1963).

UNESCO, *Space Communication and the Mass Media* (Paris, 1963).

UNESCO, *World Illiteracy at Mid-century* (Paris, 1964).

WILLIAMS, J. G., *Radio in Fundamental Education* (Paris, UNESCO, 1950).

See also the *Proceedings of the Rome and Tokyo Conferences on School Broadcasting*.

INDEX